DEAR DA-LÊ

# *Dear Da-Lê*

## A FATHER'S MEMOIR
## OF THE VIETNAM WAR AND
## THE IRANIAN REVOLUTION

# ANH DUONG
### Foreword by ASHLEY DA-LÊ DUONG

Douglas & McIntyre

DOUGLAS AND MCINTYRE (2013) LTD.
P.O. Box 219, Madeira Park, BC, V0N 2H0
www.douglas-mcintyre.com

PHOTOS OPPOSITE TABLE OF CONTENTS courtesy of the author
EDITED by Ariel Brewster and Diana Duong
COVER DESIGN by Naomi MacDougall | DSGN Dept.
COVER ILLUSTRATION by Diana Nguyen
TEXT DESIGN by Libris Simas Ferraz / Onça Publishing
MAP by Peter Hermes Furian - stock.adobe.com
PRINTED AND BOUND in Canada
PRINTED on FSC-certified, 100% recycled paper

DOUGLAS AND MCINTYRE acknowledges the support of the Canada Council for the Arts, the Government of Canada, and the Province of British Columbia through the BC Arts Council.

LIBRARY AND ARCHIVES CANADA CATALOGUING IN PUBLICATION
Title: Dear Da-Lê : a father's memoir of the Vietnam War and the Iranian Revolution /
    Anh Duong ; foreword by Ashley Da-Lê Duong.
Names: Duong, Anh (Anh Ngoc), author.
Identifiers: Canadiana (print) 2024040436X | Canadiana (ebook) 20240404416 |
    ISBN 9781771624282 (softcover) | ISBN 9781771624299 (EPUB)
Subjects: LCSH: Duong, Anh (Anh Ngoc) | LCSH: Vietnamese—Canada—Biography. |
    LCSH: Vietnam War, 1961-1975—Personal narratives, Vietnamese. |
    LCSH: Iran—History—Revolution, 1979—Personal narratives, Vietnamese. |
    LCSH: Refugees—Iran—Biography. | CSH: Vietnamese Canadians—Biography. |
    LCGFT: Autobiographies.
Classification: LCC DS559.5 .D86 2024 | DDC 959.704/3092—dc23

*Dear Da-Lê* is based on the author's real-life experiences during the Vietnam War and the Iranian Revolution and his long journey to the West. Since this subject matter is still sensitive in both Vietnam and Iran and in their diasporas, aspects of storylines and scenes have been modified, some characters are composites of many people and their names have been changed to protect their identities.

The author at ten years old with his parents and siblings, in 1963.

The author at eleven years old, in 1964.

The author at nineteen years old, in 1972.

The author's identification card as a university student in Iran, in 1975.

# Table of Contents

# PART 2 DIVISION 73

# PART 3 RUNAWAY 155

# PART 4 HOME                                                                   223

# LAST LETTER, HOPE                                                             294

# PRE-1975 VIETNAM MAP

CHINA

Ha Giang
Cao Bang
Lao Cai
Bac Kan

CHINA

**NORTH VIETNAM**

Dien Bien Phu
Son La

Cai Bau

**HANOI**
Haiphong

LAOS

Ninh Binh
Thanh Hoa

Bach Long Vi

Gulf of Tonkin

Hainan

Nam Ngum Reservoir

Vinh

**VIENTIANE**

Ha Tinh

Song Ca

Sirikit Reservoir

Dong Hoi

17th parallel

EAST SEA

Dong Ha, Quang Tri
Hue

Ubon Rat Reservoir

Da Lê
Da Nang

Paracel Islands

THAILAND

Cu Lao Cham

Tam Ky
Cu Lao Re

Mekong

**SOUTH VIETNAM**

Pleiku

**BANGKOK**

Quy Nhon

Tuy Hoa

CAMBODIA

Buon Ma Thuot

Tonle Sap

Nha Trang

Ho Dau Tieng

Da Lat
Cam Ranh

**PHNOM PENH**

Ho Tri An

Phan Rang-Thap Cham

Gulf of Thailand

Bien Hoa
Phan Thiet

**SAIGON**

Cu Lao Thu

Phu Quoc

Rach Gia

Vung Tau

Can Tho

Ca Mau
Bac Lieu

Con Dao

EAST SEA

0   50   100 km
0      50      100 mi

# Foreword

BY ASHLEY DA-LÊ DUONG

In the spring of 2012, I stood on my balcony in Montreal and half-listened as my father warned me that student protests could turn dangerous. His voice, thin through my cellphone, was drowned out by the clanging of pots and pans as neighbours and marchers protested tuition hikes. Having just sauntered in the sun for a few hours, blocking the streets with my undergraduate friends, I told him that he wouldn't understand—that reality was different from the news I imagined he was watching from his suburban neighbourhood in another city in Canada.

Not long afterward, unexpectedly, he emailed me a long Word document. He wrote about how he, in fact, did understand revolutions and student protests. He described some of his experiences in Vietnam during the war. I was surprised that he was writing to me since I know him to be a laconic man, prone to communicating through grunts. However, as I read further, I was even more confused. He wrote about escaping to Iran. The thing is, before this, my father had never mentioned to me that he had lived in Iran, let alone during the Islamic Revolution.

In the summer of 2019, I travelled to Vietnam to film a documentary in Dạ Lê, my dad's childhood village. I often wondered why my father named me Da-Lê, after a place he worked so hard to leave and that he's been so reluctant to return to. Dạ Lê is still where most of my paternal family lives, in those few rows of houses between a dusty highway and rice paddies.

On my first day in the village, I went with my grandmother to the Dạ Lê market. I was delighted by the mounds of fruit and chirping chicks that you could buy by the kilo. I took a photo of the big banyan tree in the centre of the small market, intrigued by the incense sticks tucked in its bark. I met a lot of friendly market vendor women who instantly recognized that I was my father's daughter. That evening, I video chatted with my parents. They asked me how my trip to Malaysia was going. I had not told them that I was working on a film in Dạ Lê, interviewing our relatives. I have always felt some tensions in my family about visiting the village, and Vietnam as a whole, that I didn't understand. Unwittingly, I had adopted the attitude of my parents—that many things were better left unsaid. I responded tersely and assured them that the vacation was going well.

While I was in Vietnam, my dad emailed me a draft of his manuscript based on his original letters. I had surreptitiously travelled to the other side of the world to learn about my family, and here my father was, trying to hand me these stories, all typed out in English from his home in Calgary. Reading my father's draft, I realized that the market I had just visited was where my grandmother used to make a living to support her large family. The big banyan tree in its centre was where my father witnessed the cruelties of war, and perhaps that was why there were many incense sticks in its trunk. However, this is also a place where life goes on—where my aunts and uncles still buy their groceries daily.

I called my father from my grandparents' backyard, outside my father's childhood house. Unlike when I spoke to him on my balcony many years ago, this time only cicadas and swallows competed with his voice. When I asked him why he decided to write his story in the form of a series of letters addressed to me, he said:

"It's to connect to you, but it's also to connect to me. The war was several decades ago. What effect is still inside me? I wrote to you to get that out."

As a filmmaker, I was used to being the one in control of the narrative. So it was uncomfortable to be on the other side—to be turned into a narrative device.

I scoffed. "My character feels flat."

To this, he had a straightforward response: "That's why you need to read it through and work with me."

As I looked out over the rice paddies in Dạ Lê, I thought about how my dad and I are on parallel quests. We are both crafting stories in order to help us find our bearings in the world. Fortunately, we can be each other's narrative devices.

# PART 1

# *Roots*

Houston, Spring 2015

Dear Da-Lê,

We are a father and a daughter, but communication between us is challenging. You are not fluent in Vietnamese, while English is not my native tongue. The difficulty is not only about the languages, but also the narrative itself. The journey of my youth is long, complicated and hard to relate in words.

This communication will trigger the wounds I have kept buried for years. That is why I prefer to write; it gives me time to retrieve and relive my many suppressed and forgotten memories. I have also needed time to distance myself from the events—to heal the pain of hiding my past and to keep my emotions in check. My long-held burden of silence needs to be released slowly.

Like any refugee or newcomer to Canada, I have had to work twice as hard as my colleagues to be on the same level as theirs. At home, I always needed to catch up on my work, so I had no time left for you and your brother. Whenever you asked about the war, I said I would tell you later. Once I opened my eyes, many decades had passed, and you two had left home. You have grown up, and your mom and I have become empty nesters and moved to the US for a time as expats.

Several years back, when we talked about you going to rallies and protesting at McGill, you told me I had become a have-it-all person with a good job, living in a big house with a lovely family, but knew nothing about the students' living conditions.

Yes, I know nothing about student living conditions in Canada. I know best what a student's life is like in a war zone in Vietnam, or what a student's uprising during the Iranian Revolution looks like. I bet you don't know all about those—because I haven't told you. Like many, I did some things in my youth that I don't want anyone to know about. I've been waiting for the right time to tell you of those years.

On the date of our conversation, I wanted to remind you to be careful and to tell you not to let anyone take advantage of you. But you wanted more of an explanation.

When you were a little girl, about six, we visited the Head-Smashed-In Buffalo Jump World Heritage Site in Fort MacLeod, Alberta, over an hour's drive from our house. You may not even remember. You were excited to see the high cliffs until you saw many piles of bones at the base and heard a park warden say that the buffaloes had jumped to death. You asked him why, and the warden said the beasts had followed the crowd, which, in turn, had been controlled by a human. The event reminded me of how leaders, only looking out for their own interests, had taken advantage of the Vietnamese people's love of their country for their own gains.

2

You did what you believed in, just like I don't regret my involvement in my anti-war rallies. I still have a strong feeling in me each time I think of Lam, my best friend at the time, getting shot during one of those rallies. He survived the injury and will visit Montreal next summer. You can meet and interview him if you want to know more.

We did what we thought was right at the time, without knowing that whatever we had done at the time would not affect the war's outcome. Someone had decided to end the war long before that. Even if millions of Vietnamese died, they wouldn't lose any sleep over it, as long as they got what satisfied their ego or their country's interest. But I still cherish everything I did in my youth because it has become a part of who I am.

Like you, I left home as a teenager. Once I was no longer there, I dearly missed my brief childhood in the village of Dạ Lê, during a rare short period of peace between French colonization and the Vietnam War. Even though I ran away from the village, I could not get the war out of me. My mind never actually leaves home; Dạ Lê is still part of who I am—forever.

Do you see a paradox? On the one hand, I have already let you remind me where I was from, since I gave you the name of my birthplace. On the other hand, I have kept quiet about my youth. Even though I never told you, you and your brother always reminded me of my village and the war. Sometimes, I acted like I was still living in Dạ Lê. Like when I saw a police car approaching, I became nervous. You asked me, "Why are your hands shaking at the wheel?" And I shouted back, "Keep quiet." Or when you made some noise, I scolded you. You cried and ran away, hiding. I can't tolerate raucous noise, especially at home or while driving. Another time, when you got a new camera as the first prize in an essay-writing competition in your junior year of high school, you asked me to load a new roll of film, and I took too long. You wanted it back, and I threw it at you. The camera broke. I don't know why I did that. I got angry or upset without reason. I still feel guilty and regretful about the incident.

My youth was not easy, but it is not an excuse for those behaviours. I understand that you and your brother have had a hard time growing up with not only one, but two parents with emotional baggage from the war. You often wondered why your parents were so challenging to live with. We exploded without any warning, and our moods kept changing unpredictably. We didn't tell you about the illness—what we would now call PTSD—since we didn't know we had it. Even if we knew, we wouldn't admit we had the illness. We just lived by ignoring it.

Da-Lê, I found it hard to look back. Do you remember the time when you were about age ten, and you were watching television, and you asked me, "Ba, do you want to see your hometown?" I shook my head and walked out of the living room. The TV was showing a scene of a fighting helicopter flying over a rice paddy. You thought it would be good for me to see my homeland, but you were wrong. It left me chilled and shivering.

After leaving Vietnam, I avoided watching movies about any kind of fighting or reading books about the Vietnam War. That is the part I wanted to forget or keep to myself as long as I could—until now.

Even though we didn't talk about the war at home, it still followed your brother to school. One day, his preschool teacher asked us to see her after school. While I was at work, you accompanied your mom to talk to his teacher. The conversation went something like this:

"Your son told me you and your husband are Vietnamese refugees."

"Yes, we are."

"Your son made a hand signal and pretended to shoot at his classmate, saying, 'Bang, bang.'"

The teacher looked at your mom's face and then raised her voice. "The school won't tolerate that behaviour. You should not teach that kind of violence to your kid."

"I never taught him that behaviour."

"How about your husband?"

That was one of the reasons I hid my past, not telling you two. But I made the mistake of letting your brother watch cowboy movies at home with me and brought him to the Stampede grounds with many real-life cowboys.

That was a hard time for our diaspora community. We were new to Western culture and started to build our lives from nothing. We worked hard but made many mistakes at the same time. Some ran into the law with their businesses, while their kids got in trouble with the police, in schoolyards or in back alleys. They gave our young community a bad name. That made some members hide their identities, change their names or avoid associating with their diaspora group.

Da-Lê, your mom and I did make several mistakes in parenting. One of these was building a wall around our past. We expected you and your brother would choose an easy path like many members of the Vietnamese diaspora and children of refugees. Just follow, don't ask. Doing that would make it easier to keep safe and have less conflict with others around. We didn't know how to react if you questioned or challenged our authority. Looking back, we should not have been overly selfish, protecting ourselves while ignoring your needs.

At home, you are Da-Lê, but at school, you are Ashley. We gave you an English name, encouraged you to master the English language and postponed any Vietnamese learning. You have questioned us—did we do it to erase our culture? No. We did that with the hope that you would have a better opportunity to succeed in this new land and your classmates would tease you less. One consequence of this encouragement was making you feel uncomfortable among our extended family. You were afraid people would make fun of you speaking the language. The same word in Vietnamese has many meanings depending on which tone we use—up to six for each word. That is a lot, and it increases misunderstandings. At every family reunion, you flinched and frowned all the time.

You have been offended when people laugh. But the Vietnamese laugh at everything; they aren't laughing at you speaking the language. They are fond of your willingness to try. You resent people around you even if they show their love. You frown whenever your grandma tells you to eat more or asks when you will get married. You don't like it when she compliments your good health, saying, *trông con mập ra*—"you look fatter"—or your beauty: *da trắng trẻo* (complimenting

6

your pale skin). You get upset whenever someone tells you that you are just *con gái*, and not to do boy things like climbing trees or playing soccer. You raise your voice: "*Con gái, con gái*. So what if I'm a girl? If a boy can do it, I can, too." At home, you feel you are an illegitimate child of Vietnamese culture.

You question how we express love and you wonder if our language even has a vocabulary of love or praise. If there is, why haven't you heard us say "I love you" or "I am proud of you" to you or your brother? Actually, we used to say those things a lot. We used them only when both of you were still babies. Once you started to recognize those expressions, we stopped saying them. We were brought up under the premise of "*thương cho roi cho vọt, ghét cho ngọt cho bùi,*" which means "whipping for love and sweetening for hate." So, we don't know how to express how much we care, except through food and concern for your well-being. We believe we might spoil you if we pamper you with love and compliments.

Da-Lê, you want to know about the village of Dạ Lê, the Vietnam War and how I came here. Those are not only significant parts of my past, but it's also your own roots and part of your identity. I understand you feel you have two distinct versions of yourself, but none is complete or belongs to you. You want to rediscover who you are, but you can't look at the history books, since the conquerors and the mighty have written them from their points of view. The North—the conquerors—write the war stories you read, and the mighty Americans produce the war movies you watch. Your identity is not in either one. You are not a refugee, but your parents are. You come from

the losers, or what's referred to as *Nguy*—anyone associated
with the previous South Vietnam government—and that is what
the history books have labelled you. But you are not a loser,
even if no one is writing about your identity.

I'm no historian, but I can transport you back in time
to experience those eras through the eyes of a young boy who
comes of age in a war zone.

Love, Ba

## CHAPTER 1

# Dạ Lê, 1964

Dạ Lê (pronounced "Ya-lay") is a typical settlement in central Vietnam, surrounded by rows of bamboo. The full name is Dạ Lê Thượng, or Upper Dạ Lê, to distinguish it from its sister village of Lower Dạ Lê. The lower village is well known for the production of *nón lá*, the conical hat, one of the national symbols of Vietnam. The upper village is six kilometres south of the old imperial city, Huế, at the midpoint between Saigon and Hanoi. Everyone knew everyone else by name, and the people lived mainly on agriculture: planting wet rice in the lowlands and cultivating cassava and sweet potato in the highlands. Some were fishermen, herb pickers and woodcutters. There was no tap water or electricity. The place had endured all—poverty, severe weather, bad soil, annual flood, drought and, worst of all, war.

The war had always been here, even before I was born in 1953, the last year of Vietnam under French colonization. Like any village in the northern part of Vietnam, Dạ Lê was surrounded by a thick row of bamboo trees and constructed as a mini-nation within a nation; it provided a resistance front against any invaders, including colonial rulers or even the imperial court in Huế. This village structure may explain why Vietnam was under Chinese rule for over a thousand years, but has resisted assimilation into Chinese culture. As in recent times, many hamlets still enjoyed pre-colonial life, even though the whole country was under French domination. As the elders said, *"Phép vua thua lệ làng"*— even the monarch's law loses to a village's norms. For example, the king used to collect taxes or recruit soldiers through the village chief instead of directly from each individual.

My first taste of war was when I was a newborn—just three days old, my mother told me. She and I fled a burning house in the last raid of the village by the French. Because of that incident, I know the exact day I was born. Of course, I was too young to witness the event, but my mạ kept telling me about it year after year. Now, I can see things, hear the sounds and feel the tension even though I had no idea then.

When I close my eyes and touch my left temple, I can reimagine it.

---

*... Swaying in the air, looking up at the hazy sky, I hear crackling in the distance: the sound of my village burning in the valley below. Mom is crying out several feet below me on the ground:*

*"My son! Where is he? Help!"*

*First, there is no answer. Then, the sound of people rushing towards her.*

*"Where is my baby? Help!"*

*"Your baby?" An elder with a battered conical hat asks in surprise. "You're bleeding! Let me bandage your head and foot."*

*My mom pushes the elder away from her and waves her left hand. "No. You go. Please, find my baby," Mom says.*

*The rustling continues as people search. Every bush is examined, and every big rock is looked behind.*

*"I don't see any baby," replies another old woman.*

*"Cu tý!" shouts the young mother. "Cu tý!"*

*Cu tý is a term of endearment for a baby. Literally, it means "tiny dick." At first, it was a Vietnamese superstition to call a newborn the worst name possible so that the Otherworld would leave the infant alone. Now, it has become a popular young boy nickname.*

*Mom keeps crying and looking.*

*Earlier in the day ...*

*A bomb explodes. Several gun fights follow. The explosion is intense and close enough to shake our house like an earthquake, and the broken concrete tiles keep falling from the roof. Mom jumps out of bed and runs barefoot on the floor full of debris to my bamboo crib. She bends down, using her slim body to cover me. I am awake, gazing at her face in the dim light.*

*"Thanks, Bà mụ," she whispers. Bà mụ, meaning "midwife," is a deity from Vietnamese mythology who teaches babies various prosperous traits and skills. She is not only the protector of newborns but also the guardian goddess of the local midwives. If childbirth happens safely, that is because of her. She is also responsible for the baby's learning skills, such as sucking, gazing and smiling. If an infant falls but isn't hurt, that is also because of Bà mụ.*

*Mom grabs me from my crib, swaddles me in a blanket and runs out of the house. The air is hot and full of smoke. Explosions from the air trapped in the bamboo rooftops mix with the cracks of gunfire. The bewildered voices of mothers calling for their children mingle with other desperate cries for help. In the distance, you can hear the shouts of French soldiers telling people to flee.*

*She follows her neighbours up into the hills. Many use bamboo carrying poles with two baskets to transport their children, clothes and livestock on their shoulders. The kids sit in one of the baskets, holding onto the rattan fibres hanging from each end of the pole, while the other basket carries the animals. The children and the piglets cry, side by side. Because I'm so tiny, my mom holds me tight to her chest, as if someone is trying to take me away. Her cheeks turn red and her sweat drips on my face. The thumping sounds from her chest are right in my left ear. The sounds of that first sweet lullaby and her up-and-down steps keep me calm in her arms. I fall asleep.*

*I only wake up when Mom trips and falls. To protect me, she heaves me up. Because of the toss, I bounce off the ground, fly into the air and then land on a tall rose myrtle bush by the roadside.*

*I feel the comfort of being tied up in a blanket. I look up at the empty sky; it fills the warmth of the hot, burning air. Below, many people are busy looking for me. Some look inside the bushes and others slide down the wild grass along the rocky road. Finally, a tall man spots me, caught in the high chaparral, and brings me to my mom. My left eye is full of blood, and it's dripping onto her hand.*

*"Oh! He is injured," she screams.*

*"Just a small cut outside his left eye. Put slight pressure on it," the same elder says to Mom.*

*Mom holds me for a few minutes and then lets me lie on the ground. She uses her right hand to examine my body while keeping her left thumb on the wound. The world around her stands still. She feels my face and head, chest and stomach, and hands and legs. She starts to breathe again when she realizes I am alright. She looks up when the same man returns with charcoal powder on his left palm. He asks her whether he has her permission to put it on the cut. This substance will stop the bleeding and prevent any infection. She nods her head in agreement. After the wound has been fixed, she cleans the blood off my face.*

*"How could he have been up there in the bushes?" Mom asks.*

*"Bà Mụ put him there when you fell," the elder explains.*

*So Bà Mụ has done her job, but not a perfect one.*

*After half an hour on the run, my mạ emerges from a small trail of sharp rocks onto a wide road, still clutching me. We arrive at the only primary school in the village. A few hundred people are already there, jammed into five classrooms. The evacuees are mainly older men, women and children. Young men like my ba have long ago disappeared over the rice fields to join the Việt Minh. After the Việt Minh claimed responsibility for blowing up the armoured train, the French raided our village.*

*Mom crouches with me in her right arm in the corner of one room. Having just given birth and lacking food, she cannot produce any milk to nurse me. I am cold and hungry. My patience has run out. I cry without stopping. Several other mothers with newborns have to take turns feeding me with their milk to keep my mouth shut. One of them tells my mom that she breastfeeds me because maybe I'll be her son-in-law one day. So, the family joke is that I got engaged at three days old.*

*A few days later, a group of French soldiers arrives. "Rentrez chez vous," one of them says. He tells the refugees to go home.*

*But when my mom returns home, she discovers that the colonists have burned down several houses, including where I was born. The fire consumed everything, including clothes, legal papers and my bamboo crib. The fire also destroyed the barn. Most of the water buffaloes got away, but one was trapped and burned alive inside.*

———————————————

Each time she recounted the story, Mạ ended it by looking at my face: "You still carry that old scar."

Yes, I have a black mark, one inch long, just outside my left eye. It is my first tattoo, and it always reminds me of war and of Dạ Lê.

CHAPTER 2

# First Lesson

That self-determining war against French colonialism affected my parents and grandparents, but not me directly. During my upbringing, the French had already left Indochina. Vietnam had become an independent country and Dạ Lê was a peaceful place. We were happy even though we were poor.

My earliest recollections of my childhood are from when I was about six. I felt lonely; no older male was around to play with. The whole hamlet consisted primarily of children, women and older people. I thought that was normal. My mother told me that my father was a soldier fighting some bad guys and that he must live in barracks in a land far, far away. That was a simple answer she could give to a child. Dad's story was more than that: He was one of the young villagers who had fought the French even before I was born.

Once the French had left in 1954, the world powers temporarily divided Vietnam in half at the 17th parallel. The Democratic Republic of Vietnam in the North adopted the communist ideology under Hồ Chí Minh, and the Republic of Vietnam in the South followed a capitalist ideology, first headed by former emperor Bảo Đại, and later by Ngô Đình Diệm, as its president. The North had the support of the Soviet

Union and China, while the South had America's support. The accords allowed the population to move freely between the North and South zones for three hundred days and called for elections within two years to reunify the country.

During this period of free movement, nearly one million Northerners moved south, either on foot or aboard US Navy vessels as part of Operation Passage to Freedom, and about forty thousand civilians and one hundred thousand Việt Minh fighters moved in the opposite direction, on foot. Dạ Lê was part of South Vietnam, about ninety kilometres south of the 17th parallel—the dividing line between the North and the South. My father and over a few dozen young Việt Minh fighters from the village began to head north, a movement or migration called *đi tập kết*. But at the halfway point, he learned he was exempt from the march since he was the family's sole provider. Besides caring for an elderly mother and a younger brother, he was also responsible for his one-year-old child—me—and my mom. She was heavily pregnant with her second child, Lanh, and could deliver at any moment.

As it turned out, the reunion of my parents was short-lived. A few years after his return, he received a draft notice from the South Vietnam government telling him he must enlist in its army. The enlistment could not be deferred if at least one adult son was still left at home. His younger brother had recently come of age, so he couldn't escape it. The penalty for draft evasion was jail. My mom begged him to run away, suggesting he could go into hiding in Rào—a hamlet on the other side of the rice paddy, where the government had no control—and wait there until the draft was over. My father said he was tired of running, and that he didn't want to go anywhere. It was a time of peace, he argued, and there would be no more fighting—so he wasn't worried. She disagreed. She felt that if he joined the army, he would go away for a long time. She was angry and wouldn't talk to him until he left home.

Along with all remaining young men in the village, my father joined the Saigon army.

During my early childhood, Ba was rarely home; he came and went like a ghost. If he was home, he spent the time sleeping. He didn't have any time left for me. So I created some toys from the garden plants, like a banana leaf gun or a coconut leaf windmill. My favourite was a slingshot. I played alone with it in the garden day after day, looking for a target to practise my shooting skills.

A beehive on the jackfruit tree behind my house kept coming to mind. Ma said that all the bees we saw were female workers who would attack and sting anyone approaching close to their nest, and she had warned me not to go near it. But the vision of using the nest for target practice was so strong that I forgot all about what Ma had said and shot the hive. I went to war with the bees.

The first shot hit the bottom of the nest. A small group of bees flew out in all directions, and I ran away before they could catch me.

The next day, I went back. Everything was back to normal. I hardly saw the damage I had caused. I made my second attempt to remove the colony from the branch. I slightly missed the target; only a tiny part fell on the ground. I escaped. After the third shot, I stopped and started to observe. Each day, the working bees flew away, looking for flowers to get nectar and pollen to make honey, and for food to feed their queen, young bee larvae and drones. I never saw the drones. Ma said they stayed inside the nest and did nothing except eat and surround the queen. They were born into a higher position in the hierarchy—unlike the worker bees, who not only worked hard but also, at the same time, defended their home against the outsiders. I also noticed another bee-hive which was much smaller, in the corner of the garden and closer to my house. I had been too focused on the game of destruction and hadn't noticed the smaller colony before.

The worker bees from the small pack came and went. They always followed the same narrow path; they could not fly in from any direction except under the eaves of my house. The other nest's giant swarm had expanded its airspace, including the rice field and the garden, to landlock the weaker group. However, the smaller group kept its ground and would survive for many years to come.

When I asked my mom about the bees, she thought I was being nice to those insects and awarded me a big piece of brown sugar. She said we were Buddhists; we lived with all kinds of things, killing none.

After a few weeks, it became tiresome to watch the bees and I started looking for someone to play with. One day, I found Thai, who was much older than me, playing cards with his friends at the back of the ancestral family chapel. I asked him whether I could join.

"Do you know how to play?" Thai asked me.

"Yes, I do," I answered, shrugging my shoulders.

"You know this game?" he asked, surprised.

"It's a game of *cắt tê*."

"Good." Thai showed me one of his cards and asked, "What is this card called?"

"King of diamonds," I proudly answered.

"Okay, how do you play the card game of *cắt tê*?"

"I can't tell you. Just let me play. I will show you whether I know or not," I insisted.

"You don't know the game," Thai said, waving me out of the room. "Go play with some little kids."

"I know the game well. Let me play," I said, trying to convince the gang.

"We play with money."

"With money?" I was surprised. "But I don't have any."

"Go away. Come back when you have a *đồng* or two," Thai ordered.

17

"This is a *đồng*," Thai said, showing me a grey paper bill that I'd never seen before.

"Is it better than a fifty-*xu*?" I asked. A fifty-cent coin was all I knew about money. My mother used to give me that coin, an aluminum one with a bamboo bush on one side, to pay for a haircut or a *bánh mì* from the street vendors.

Thai opened his eyes widely and said, "Of course it is." Then he asked, "Do you have a fifty-*xu* coin?"

"No, I don't."

The big boy then repeated his condition for play: "Come back when you have a *đồng* or two."

I went home, kicking some rocks on the way. *How dare he tell me I don't know the game without letting me show him?*

My father was sleeping on my bamboo bed. He was snoring so loudly that I could hear it from outside. Each time he came home, he gave Mom a pile of money. I envied her and resented him. I looked at his army jacket hung on the mosquito pole at the headboard—its upper pocket was opened. The idea of borrowing money from him came to my mind. I would return it after playing. Without any hesitation, I put up a chair to reach the height. I picked out a piece of paper money that had a different colour than the money Thai had shown me. It was a purplish red, not grey. I held the piece of paper tightly and walked silently out the door.

I returned to the game site where Thai and his gang were still playing cards.

"I have money," I said, showing them the piece of paper money.

Thai looked up at my hand and then winked at his friends. "It is a bill of five *đồng*. I'll exchange it for ten coins of fifty-*xu* so that you can play," he told me.

I agreed and received the coins from him. I joined in playing. After a short time, I lost it all.

Without looking up, I went home. I had nothing left and felt ashamed and sick to my stomach. My hands were shaking. Why did I do that? Stole money and gambled. Those were two of the sins that Mom had told me to stay away from. But I couldn't. I felt the sky was falling, and everything was closing in on me. About halfway home, I was thinking about running away. Where should I go? Aunt Lâu's house? But it was an easy target; Dad would find it out. If I ran away, I had to get out of the village; otherwise, people could identify me in no time. And I reached home before I knew it. From a distance, I saw my neighbours gathering around the house.

I ran home to see what was going on. I sneaked in through the back door. Mother's face turned pale when she saw me. "Run," she told me while she pushed me out of the house. But it was too late. My dad grabbed my right hand and held it tightly, pulling me in.

"Lie down," he ordered me and pointed to the dirt floor. I followed his order. From the floor, I saw him holding a rattan whip.

"Did you steal money from my pocket?" he shouted while his face wrinkled. He looked ugly and old.

"Yes, I did."

"Where is the money?"

"Ah!" I shouted in pain. He hit my buttocks after each question. "I lost it."

"Where did you lose it?"

"Ah! In a card game."

"What? You gambled?" he asked, surprised.

"Ah! Yes, sir."

"You lost all of one hundred *đồng*?"

"Ah! Just five *đồng*, Ba," I argued.

"You took a one-hundred-*đồng* bill, not five," he said slowly, emphasizing each word as if they presented something unbelievable.

"Ah!" I felt something heavy on top of me. Mom had just jumped in and used her body to cover me.

"It's enough!" she said.

They started to argue and yelled at each other. I ran out of the house.

"I won't let him eat in this house for a month," he told her.

When I was at a safe distance, I saw my mother standing on the roadside and facing in my direction. She knew my father would yell, but he never hit her.

Thai had cheated me. He knew I couldn't read and count anything beyond ten and had no idea of the difference between a one-*đồng* bill and a hundred-*đồng* one. He had tricked me into my first gambling experience. How could I forget such a memorable day and such a valuable life lesson?

CHAPTER 3

# First School

After that gambling incident, Mạ was eager to get me an education. I liked going to school. With many mouths to feed on the salary of a low-rank soldier, she had no extra money to pay for school materials and fees. She needed to work, and she had worked ever since I could remember.

Each day, she bought goods from the village market—wood charcoal, *trái sim* (a kind of wild blueberry), green tea leaves and several herbs—depending on the season and availability. She then resold those in the suburbs of Huế—six kilometres away—for a small profit. She was diminutive, about four-and-a-half feet tall and under eighty pounds. Still, she could carry those goods on a bamboo pole across her shoulders, forty pounds on each side. With the weight of her body and so much family responsibility on her shoulders, she kept moving all day to look for customers, walking over thirty kilometres barefoot.

My mother's full name is Nguyễn thị Bảy. *Bảy* means seven, and she was the seventh and the last born in the family, while thị is the most common middle name for Vietnamese females. Since she was the youngest child, she grew up playing and getting to attend school. Now she had to work. Mạ left home in the early morning under the still-dark sky and returned late at night under the light of a kerosene lamp. The villagers called it *dèn Huê-kỳ*, or an American lamp, since Standard Oil had introduced it to Vietnam in the late nineteenth century. The company had given the *dèn* for free to people who bought its gas. It had become a house lamp of choice in every village where electricity was unavailable.

"Cu tý," she called out each morning, when I was still deep asleep.

"Yes, Mạ?" I said, still sleeping.

"Wake up."

"It's still dark, Mạ," I complained. "Give me five minutes." Grumbling, I crawled through the opening of the mosquito net and got out of the pallet. Like a robot, I walked in the dim light of the oil lamp towards the front door.

She believed it was my duty to bid her farewell at the front gate each morning to give her luck. I was not only to send her off, but to be cheerful about it, too. If I didn't greet her with a smiling face, she'd blame me for her bad day. It was me and nobody else she wanted to see first thing in the morning. She needed a good luck charm: my face. Day after day, she made me believe in that ritual. I didn't want her to have a bad day, let alone be blamed for it. But I hated the routine. Why me? At seven years of age, waking up early with a happy face was no easy task. Everyone knew that if I didn't like something, my face would show it, like the Vietnamese expression about a monkey eating chilli peppers. So I splashed my face with cold water and put on a good act. While waiting for Mạ to disappear behind the corner, my neighbour asked me each morning when I returned home to my bed, "Are you sick? You look too thin."

I just smiled. Because of my laziness, I preferred playing rather than cooking each day. My two younger siblings and I ate what was left from the meal the night before.

In the evening, my mother went straight to the village market to buy goods for the next day's trip and some groceries for us at home. The market stayed open late at night under the oil lamps so the villagers could bring their products, pickers' herbs and catches of the day for trading. Because of that, people called it Chợ Hôm, or the night market.

With her savings from the street vendor sales, Mạ had gotten me into a one-room school to learn how to read and write. Chú Han was my first teacher. Best of all, I had a school friend, La; we were both the same age and we were both the oldest sons of government soldiers.

————————

La had become my best friend. But I hadn't seen him in school in the last couple of days, which prompted me to look for him to find out what was happening. From afar, I could see a makeshift tent in front of his house.

A village custom was to make a temporary tent for a special occasion such as a wedding or a funeral. For a wedding, people needed more room; the village's houses were tiny for such a gathering. It was taboo to hold a funeral inside one's own residence if the deceased person had died away from home. So, during wartime, a makeshift tent beside a house meant a funeral.

I started walking faster to the tent in front of La's house. "What has happened to him?" I asked myself, feeling anxious in my stomach while my eyes kept blinking.

"Look out!" someone shouted.

I looked up. A giant water buffalo was striding toward me, just a few feet away. Face to face, I could see a botfly landing above the beast's left eye. Without thinking, I jumped off the road and into the canal while the buffalo boys laughed at me. Once in the water, my eyes kept tracking the animal to see whether it followed me. The beast walked away. I took a deep breath to calm myself down and climbed up the bank, clutching my damaged notebooks.

Without bothering about my wet clothes, I went to the tent. Inside, La's mother, O Chinh, and several women sat on the ground, crying, while several men stood by. Most of the family members—men, women and children—donned long white dresses, the makeshift type made of cheap cloth, worn by the dead's loved ones and burned after the funeral. I had never seen anyone crying as hard as O Chinh. She tried to grab something in front of her, but the other women held her back. I looked for La but couldn't find him anywhere. My heart was heavy.

I got closer to O Chinh. A South Vietnamese flag of three red stripes on a bright yellow background was on top of the coffin. My thudding heartbeat eased once I realized the body in the coffin was not La's but that of his father, a soldier. Like my dad, La's father was a sergeant in the South Vietnamese government army, but his dad had been shot down on a battlefield in the South.

La's father, Chú Chinh, was laid inside the coffin in front of a simple altar—an incense bowl between two wooden candleholders. Behind those was a picture of him in military uniform, smiling. I approached the altar, picked up three incense sticks, and burned its ends to the candle flame. I bowed three times in front of the coffin, then placed the burning incense sticks in the bowl. I thought of my father. He and Chú Chinh were childhood friends. *One down. Oh no.* I cut off the thought, instantly.

I hustled to the back of the tent, where La was sitting with his younger sibling in the corner. They were also in a white mourning dress with a headband made of the same cloth. My friend, like me, was the oldest son in the family. La was carrying his one-year-old brother in his right arm. They were both crying while looking at the coffin and their mother. I gently put my arm around La's left shoulder, squeezed it and felt a tear on my hand. La looked up at me with his wet eyes.

A month later, La left the village. After receiving some monetary benefit from the South Vietnam government for his father's death on the battlefield, his family moved somewhere to start a new life. He went without saying goodbye to me. I didn't believe it at first. Now and then, I walked by his old house, hoping to find some news about him. But that was no use. The place was closed, and no one was at home. His neighbours had no idea where the family went.

## CHAPTER 4

# New Strangers

One spring afternoon in 1963, when I was ten years old, I was walking along Route 1 on my way home from school. Suddenly, I felt something was wrong. I looked over my left shoulder. A civilian truck loomed over me like an animal that wanted to pounce on prey. Without thinking, I jumped into a ditch on my right to escape the danger. No honking. No warning. Just the sound of its growling engine.

I was lucky. The ditch was dry and shallow, and no damage had been done. I looked up through the high grass. A foreigner with white skin like limestone was sitting on the passenger side, laughing, and waving at me. I waved back even though I was angry and humiliated. He threw something green in front of me to reward me for my suffering, but I looked away from the package as if it did not exist. But I still wondered what it was.

Once the truck passed, I picked up the green pack with "Salem" written in white. It smelt of fresh mint. I hid the cigarettes inside my shirt close to my tummy, where the elastic waistband of my shorts held it tight. I felt an uncomfortable coolness in my belly as I walked home and kept thinking about it and my mother. *Oh! What will I do? Will I throw those cigarettes away or keep them? Better not to waste them; I'll hide them from Mom for now.*

Once I got home, I hid that pack of cigarettes in the banana bushes behind the house, away from Mom's sight. The next day, I brought it with me when I met the buffalo boys who looked after their family beasts on the rice field. I saw their leader, Old Dog, on the dirt bank next to a grass field where a half dozen teenagers practised their ball-shooting skills. Close by, several herds of buffalo bathed in the waterhole. The beasts liked to immerse in water, especially in the mud, to cool themselves in the evening. Even though my family had no herd for me to look after, that didn't stop me from joining the gang.

The buffalo boys had just gotten a soccer ball made of leather that I dreamed of putting my feet on. It was a gift from O Lai, who lived in Huế. Her ancestor's graves were in the village, close to the Buddhist temple. A couple of months earlier, water buffaloes had damaged the tombs. She'd hired some villagers to repair the graves. To prevent any such incidents in the future, she'd asked the boys to keep an eye on the tombs for her. She awarded them a new ball. I wanted to join them in playing soccer, but Old Dog ignored my request. He said I was too small and weak. And worst of all, I had no animals to look after except my younger siblings, who followed me everywhere I went. They needed my protection; I had to keep them away from the beasts and any bully kids. Because of that, I resented my siblings and wished I didn't have them. I thought the gang would never consider me one of them, but I still wanted to befriend its leader so I could play soccer and join them in other activities. I wanted to convince Old Dog I could be helpful to the group.

"I have a gift for you," I said, smiling.

"What?" the leader asked, with a sharp voice.

I gave him the pack of cigarettes I hid under my belt. Old Dog opened his eyes big and stared at the gift. He snatched it from my hand and then put it up to his nose, smelling.

"Great! Cu tý," he said while patting my shoulder. He picked out a cigarette.

"Do you have a light?" he asked, while nodding his head.

I gave him a matchbox I had borrowed from home.

"The smell is so fresh, Cu tý. Do you smoke?"

I was going to say that I never smoked, but I changed my mind.

"I just did," I lied.

"Here. Smoke another," Old Dog said. He looked at me and gave me a cigarette. Once I put the lit cigarette into my mouth, I started to cough hard.

"So, you don't smoke?" said Old Dog. Smiling, he added, "Now you learn."

I was still coughing.

"Come on," Old Dog said to me, standing up. "You can play goalie."

Nobody ever wanted to be a goalie, but it was still good to be playing.

Both of us joined the other boys.

That was when I started smoking.

---

Since the group had received the ball, Old Dog kept it and decided when to play and who to play with. He was born a twin and a year older than me. His supposedly younger brother, Chó Em—Young Dog— came out, in fact, a few minutes ahead of, and even an inch taller than, him. But in the case of multiple births, the custom considers whoever comes out last to be the highest rank, like the captain of a sinking ship. Old Dog protected his twin brother as a big brother, and in return,

Chó Em got orders from him. That made the duo stronger; they took over the gang's leadership. Old Dog's ranking had also been enhanced since he caught a white water snake, a natural white, that nobody in the village had ever seen. The colour of a water snake in the wild was brown or sometimes greyish. The news of that white reptile spread fast. In the old Vietnamese belief systems, snake worship was prevalent; it connected with the rivers and water of agricultural populations and represented two opposite characteristics—good and bad omens.

People came in the thousands, not only from the village or the nearby city of Huế, but some even travelled hundreds of kilometres. Some arrived with curiosity, but most hoped for healing. They believed the snake could make a paralyzed person walk and the deaf hear again. That was a good thing. But what would be the bad one?

Since the gang had accepted me as one of them, I could come to Old Dog's house anytime to witness the snake worship.

A long line of people was always there, waiting at the front door of a thatched house that smelled like rotten wood, and its dirt floor was the colour of dark chocolate. Once inside, one by one, people put a small tray of local fruit or an envelope containing cash on a big table between two big burning candles. At the centre of that table was a clear glass vase with a closed plastic cap, and inside it was a white snake the same circumference as my toe. The snake looked out with curiosity when people took turns kneeling in front of it to pray. I didn't know whether I would be more thrilled to see the snake or to witness so many strange people. But I was sure I was most excited about having fruit to eat.

Old Dog brought out those same fruits for the boys when we met for a soccer game. One day a banana, another day an orange or a pomegranate. After many days at Old Dog's house, I still hadn't seen anything out of the ordinary. But one thing I knew for sure: The welfare of Old Dog's father, who sat on a bamboo pallet in the back room looking out the window through a thin curtain, had not changed. The elder's left leg was paralyzed, and he used homemade crutches to move around. His movement had not improved even with the "deity" reptile in the house for the past month.

One day, the snake changed its colour from white to greyish. People stopped coming. Nobody knew what had happened to the snake after that. It just disappeared.

---

I became Old Dog's right-hand boy after I had helped him build a bamboo machine gun. We made a gun that could continuously fire multiple shots from a piece of bamboo. Making a single-shot gun was easy, but the firing was too slow. A bamboo machine gun was far superior in battle and thus in high demand. Old Dog had seen a bamboo machine gun in action and wished to own one. He wanted to use it in the friendly war with the boys in the neighbouring hamlet. Every group member knew how to make a single-shot gun based on the principles of a hand-powered bicycle air pump. A bamboo tube works like an air cylinder, and a long chopstick acts like a piston rod. For bullets we used *trái bời lời*, or *Litsea glutinosa* seeds, from a type of rainforest laurel tree. They contained lemon essential oil on the skin, helping seal the compressed air. The oil also stained the target, whether it was an enemy's face or body. In the battle, we covered our faces with the outer stem of a banana tree, held it in place with a rubber band and cut two holes for the eyes. We pushed the chopstick piston forward to press the back seed to compress the air for firing. The back seed then became the front seal for the next shot.

Every kid in the group wanted to know how to make a bamboo machine gun, and I was the only one who had learned and could make one that worked.

But it was just a kid's toy. We weren't kids anymore. Tonight, Old Dog and I would set our eyes on a real one, which might change our future and end our childhood.

That evening, we were on our way to O Lan's house to attend a music play. After a soccer game in the afternoon, Old Dog told me about live music. When I heard the name O Lan or Miss Orchid, I got excited and asked him to take me there. O Lan was about eighteen, with long and charming black hair and gentle brown eyes. And most of all, she smelt of orchid fragrance, like her name. I loved standing next to her so I could sniff at her scent and feel comfort. Her figure was slim, but whatever she lacked in weight, she made up for with balance and strength. She could carry a pair of water buckets while crossing a single-beam bridge. I had hated her at first, and that was when Anh Hai met her.

A month before the 1963 Lunar New Year, Anh Hai returned to Dạ Le after four years of studying at the Vũng Tàu cadet school, a military academy. He was the only son of my mother's deceased brother, a fallen soldier during the colonial time. I was so happy and excited to see him and have him as a big brother. Nothing was better than that. Anh Hai was the first person who opened my eyes to the outside world and took me outside that thick bamboo fence. He made me ride a bus and see movies in town.

But the good time didn't last long. After two weeks in the village, Anh Hai met O Lan, and I became a go-between the two, some sort of Cupid without bows and arrows.

I remember the time that I entered a dock, under a big red flowering tree behind my house, with a blue handkerchief in my right hand. The entrance, which had five stone steps to assess the water, was one of the playgrounds for the village kids. The buffalo boys and I never entered the water through those steps; we preferred to climb up the tree and jump down from one of its branches. The village kids stood on the bank, watching and cheering our acrobatic show. But not that day. Anh Hai had called me home and asked me to deliver his borrowed handkerchief to O Lan. She was with several teenage village girls doing laundry at the lowest step. They were still laughing and talking when I returned with a piece of cloth in my right hand. Everyone stopped working and looked at me and then at O Lan. Her face turned red, especially her cheeks. Without speaking, she walked up the steps and took the piece of cloth from me before I could relay the message: "Anh Hai asked me to bring this handkerchief to you. Please, wash it for him." The other girls had a good laugh, but I hated it. I hated him and her, but I couldn't afford to disobey Anh Hai. I still hoped he would tire of her and be back playing with me again. But my mind started to change after I got to know her better.

When we arrived at her house, there were many strangers there. They were primarily young men that I had not met before. They played guitar and sang revolutionary songs when darkness fell. I didn't believe it when the Old Dog told me they were Việt Cộng (VC). I smiled at my naiveté a year back, when I had seen an illustration of VCs in a magazine: a propaganda cartoon of skinny men with two huge front teeth. They were so malnourished that several could swing on a papaya leaf, and I believed that Việt Cộng should look like those skinny cartoon characters. The people around me looked nothing like the men in the cartoon; they looked more like O Lan or Anh Hai, except for their swollen and pale skin. They seemed to never be exposed to the sun. Old Dog said they spent most of their daytime underground in the network of tunnels.

The soldiers were all in their late teens or early twenties. Most of them spoke with an accent different from mine, out-of-town guests. Even though I didn't fully understand their accents, their guns impressed us. We were in love with their assault rifles, AK-47s. The gun shape and the curving of its magazine were in such a balance. The overall size was just right for a small person like Old Dog or me.

A Việt Cộng had let us touch the rifle and carry it on our shoulders. One of them even taught us how to use his gun, but we were not allowed to fire it. Now we laughed at our childish bamboo guns from earlier in the day. We wished to own a real one, even though we had not reached teenagehood yet. Many of my classmates would do just that in a few years.

## CHAPTER 5

# First Battle

One morning in mid-summer 1963, the buffalo boys and I woke up to face an ugly monster crawling through the village perimeter. It also passed through my garden, separating my house from the canal. The South Vietnam government had ordered the cutting down of all bamboo trees to build a twelve-foot-high wall with barbed wire reinforcement. That monstrous fence replaced the traditional bamboo tree lines, which had surrounded the village for thousands of years. I hated it. The buffalo boys hated it. And everybody in the village hated it. It was hemming in our playground and giving us a claustrophobic feeling that we couldn't stand.

Under the Strategic Hamlet Program, a fence was erected surrounding each hamlet's boundaries across South Vietnam to prevent the Việt Cộng's infiltration of the rural areas. I still remember drawing pictures of a strategic hamlet in one of my elementary classes a year earlier. I drew a village enclosed by a tall barbed-wire fence with four towers at each corner. It looked like a new settlement I had seen in a Western cowboy movie, except with bamboo tubes with barbed wire reinforcement instead of a wooden fence made of tree trunks. In the cowboy movies, the settlers built those forts to protect themselves against the region's Indigenous Peoples—"the Indians." Except for the beautiful women, all Indians were bad, and the white men were good. Here, there were no Indians, but there were VC guerillas, and they were also bad guys. I liked those Western movies, so I felt good about the new Strategic Hamlet Program. I tried my best on my sketch, hoping to get a high mark. But once the actual fence came to the village, I changed my mind.

The program's purposes were to pacify the countryside and reduce the communist influence on the rural population. On paper, the barbed wire would curtail the movements of VC. Still, in real life, the fences also separated the villagers from their rice paddies. It didn't make any sense to isolate the villagers from their lands, which focused on life and family activity in Vietnamese culture. The CIA, who had developed this program, didn't understand Vietnamese culture, and the Diệm government from the South agreed to implement it and became disconnected from its people.

Ngô Đình Diệm had grown up in Huế, located about six kilometres north of Dạ Lê. His youngest brother's compound, Chín Hầm, or "Nine Tunnels," was just west of the village border. Whenever the president returned for a family visit, we were the first to know because his convoy from the Phú Bài Airport passed through the village. When the buffalo boys and I heard the familiar and distinct siren, we dropped everything—even in the middle of a soccer game. We ran to the closest section of Route 1 to greet him and, at least for me, to see his convoy. "*Cụ ra, Cụ ra!*" we shouted (meaning "Sir is back!" or "Uncle is back!"), to tell the other kids as we raced for the best spot along the roadside.

And there was Mr. President, Cụ Diệm, in his trademark white suit, in the middle of the fleet of motorcades. He stood tall, holding the safety crossbar of the army Jeep with one hand, waving at the villagers.

People waved back and shouted, "*Ngô tổng thống muôn năm, muôn năm!*" meaning "Long live President Ngo!"

The motorcade added some spice to my childhood and made me dream about life beyond the bamboo hedges that enclosed the village.

That love changed to alienation when the Diệm regime poorly handled the Buddhist religious incident in Huế on May 8, 1963, which killed nine civilians. That shooting stimulated further protests, not only in Huế but throughout the country. On June 11, 1963, Thích Quảng Đức, a Buddhist monk, burned himself to death at a busy Saigon intersection to protest the alleged persecution of Buddhists by the Diệm regime. The photograph of a burning monk made headlines and shocked the world.

At the time, John F. Kennedy said that he had never seen any news picture in history generate as much emotion around the world as that one. That photograph was the first of many to come from the Vietnam War. Unfortunately, President Kennedy did not live long enough to see many more pictures that would shape world history.

The result was a coup d'état led by General Dương Văn Minh on November 1, 1963, to remove the Diệm regime. General Minh became head of the newly formed junta government. People called him Big Minh—a nickname he had earned because of his size. At over six feet tall and weighing one hundred and seventy pounds, he was much more prominent than the average Vietnamese man.

---

A few months after Old Dog and I met the Việt Cộng at the O Lan house, the South Vietnam government asked the villagers to build an underground bunker ready for war. Old Dog and I went out to dismantle the fence—the *Ấp Chiến lược* fence—around our hamlet. We wanted to use its iron poles to reinforce our bomb bunker. My mom and I had dug an L-shaped hole, over a metre deep, at the back of our house. We needed these iron bars to hold its roof up under two layers of sandbags. The hole looked like a grave, but a little wider.

"Fuck you," Old Dog, the buffalo leader, angrily said.

I looked back at my friend, who had just crawled through a dog hole we had opened on the barbed-wire fence to our soccer field. Old Dog kept hitting the barrier with his bamboo rod used for disciplining the water buffaloes. About a foot from the ground, a small piece of cloth was still hanging on the chain, and it looked like it came from Old Dog's shirt. Yup, I saw there was an inch-wide hole on the back of his T-shirt.

The barbed-wire fence was a forbidden place to us, after one of the buffalo kids had triggered a land mine and died while trying to cut a hole. But even that didn't discourage us from opening some rat holes in the barrier—we wanted a shortcut to our soccer field. We didn't follow the rules like the buffalo, who went through the gate to their waterhole. But the fence wouldn't be there for much longer.

Once the Diệm regime no longer existed, villagers began dismantling the fence in some areas under encouragement from Việt Cộng. We not only hated the barricade; we also needed its metal poles to enforce our bomb shelters. I joined in and helped my mother build ours with materials from that ugly monster.

The fence removal was still illegal, even though the new regime had unofficially abandoned it.

*Bang! Bang!*

Old Dog and I dropped down and rolled to the ground when we heard a gunfight.

"Is that sound from an AK-47?" Old Dog asked.

"I've never heard that sound before; it must be," I said.

The fighting was still going on, but we realized it was far away. We stood up and walked to the soccer field.

"Let's find out what's going on after the fight," Old Dog proposed.

"We'll go there tomorrow," I said. I wanted to go home.

---

The following day, the big news came.

Indeed, the prevention of the fence dismantling had initiated the gunfight. VC encouraged the removal, and that made the government soldiers intervene. The battle broke out between them on the west side of the village. The government soldiers won big, even with their inferior weapons from the Second World War. This battle in July 1964 was one of the South Vietnam government's early victories over the Việt Cộng. Nguyễn Khánh, the head of the South at the time, and General Nguyễn Chánh Thi, commander of the central region, came to the village to celebrate. People wondered why the government bothered to make such a big celebration in our hamlet. Old Dog and I went to the event at the village soccer field, even without an invite. After the celebration, we headed to Miếu Mõ Rẫy (a shrine built by the Mõ Rẫy people), where the battlefield had been.

When we got there, the place was already full of preteen kids like us. They stood near the trench bank, talking and pointing down into it. Half a block away, a farmer was transplanting rice seedlings, bush by bush, into her flooded paddy. I could tell she was a woman from her clothes (only a woman wore black pyjama bottoms rolled up to the thighs; a working man would wear shorts in the field). With a tattered conical hat on her head, she bent forward with her face down and moved her hands steadily along the water's surface. She was in her own world, even though she could see us gathering. A little farther away, a man balanced on a wooden roller pulled by a water buffalo. "*Đi, đi,*" he said, urging the animal to go faster. Old Dog and I approached the V-shaped trench, over a metre deep. In front of us stretched the aftermath of yesterday's battle.

Suddenly, I felt like I was going to faint. My hands turned sweaty, and my mouth went dry. I didn't want to see, but I couldn't move away, except to avert my eyes. It was too much to face—so many dead bodies in the trench.

"Thirty bodies, at least," one kid said.

"No, I counted twenty-seven," another boy disagreed. It was like they were playing a counting game. *Are they using this place as their playground? Do they have any feelings?* I wondered.

"They're all VC," the kid standing next to me said.

I took a deep breath to regain my composure before looking down into the trench. Corpses were randomly spread across the bottom of it, and the sidewalls. Some were missing their limbs or eyes. They all wore black pyjamas and tire sandals like the soldiers I had met at O Lan's house.

"Weren't any government soldiers killed?"

"What do you think? Maybe the government removed them already, if there were any," the kid said.

"Do you know any of them?" I asked in a shaky voice, even though I was trying to breathe steadily.

"Shush!" The boy put his finger to his lips. "Speak softly; people can hear you."

"Maybe they're from the North," the kid standing next to me said in a low voice. "That's why they got trapped in this trench; they didn't know their way around here."

I was surprised at the cool demeanour of the people around me. In a short time, the village had changed a lot. The rice farmer was still planting, and the man was still plowing. I gestured toward them. "Don't they know what's going on?" I asked my companion.

"They do, but who cares?" Old Dog said, shrugging his shoulders.

I understood. Gunfights happened all the time, and corpses and body parts were everywhere these days. People needed to work to feed their families, and the kids needed a place to play. Their lives had become shorter each day. Bit by bit, they learned to live with terror and adapt to the war—they had no choice. Life is too short, while death is forever.

I leaned closer, looking for the tattoo reading "Born North, Die South" on the corpses. I had heard that the Northern soldiers would have that motto tattooed on their bodies before heading south. But I didn't see any. Most of the bodies were teenagers.

The presence of the North Vietnam Army (NVA) infiltrators in the village was why the South Vietnam government made such a big deal out of the recent battle. The US used it as an excuse to land its troops and "allied forces" like Australian, South Korean and Thai soldiers in South Vietnam. A big mistake.

## CHAPTER 6

# Village at War

Big truck after big truck full of US soldiers jammed into the single narrow lane of Route 1. They were sitting on the back of each open-top army vehicle, laughing and waving at the students on the road. The soldiers were young, mostly teenagers, and having fun, as if they had just returned from a sporting event, except they were all in green camo uniforms and held rifles.

That was the first time the US Marines came to the village, even though I had heard about their landing in the coastal city of Đà Nẵng a few months before, in March 1965. Đà Nẵng, a hundred kilometres south, was the same place the first French arrived in Vietnam in 1858, starting France's one hundred years of colonial rule. I didn't think it was just a coincidence.

After landing, the US Marines started reinforcing the Phú Bài Combat Base. The traffic on Route 1 connecting Huế to the base with Dạ Lê at the midpoint got heavier each day.

The US first set up a Combined Action Platoon (or CAP) stationed in every village. The CAP platoon combined the US Marines and some Vietnamese Popular Forces (Nghĩa Quân). But I didn't see any CAP platoon with Vietnamese soldiers in the village. (Initially, its name was

CAC—the Combined Action Company—and not CAP, but the former acronym sounds like the word for male genitalia in the local language, so they changed it.)

The CAP was in charge of patrolling the village each night. I could tell when the force would pass through the road in front of our house. I noted their schedule so we could be ready to escape to the bunker in case of gunfire. People observed the CAP on the move on the village road each evening. They all walked in a straight line and looked ahead, then to the left, and then to the right, with a gun in hand—most carried an M16 rifle, but some had M60 machine guns. The distance between each soldier was very uniform and predictable. I believed that Việt Cộng could guess where the CAP would be on any given night. Even so, the CAP, with its firepower, was the first to cause some damage to the local guerrillas.

One morning, I was late for school. There had been a shooting in the village the night before—a big gunfight. Our family escaped to the bomb shelter and stayed there for a few hours. With the lack of sleep and unfinished homework, I was hoping that I would arrive to see there was no class that day. As I trudged along Route 1, my mind was looking for a reason not to go to school. *What if the school burned down in the gunfight? No, that's no good. I love that school. Maybe minor damage to the school? No, it will take too long to fix. How about a sick teacher, who'd be alright by the next day?* I decided I preferred that idea—just one day off—and thought about it as I walked. Then—*Oh no!*

Looking up at me was the disfigured face of a dead boy lying on the roadside. This was shocking to me: A young boy, a couple of years older than I, was dead. Some parts of the body were missing. I froze and felt sick to my stomach. Everything around him became a blur except the face. Although I had seen dead bodies before, this was different: I knew the boy. I disbelieved my eyes. My feet were numb as I stood there, facing the corpse. Even with that severely mutilated face, I could tell who he was from his remaining eye. But I didn't want the government to know I had been acquainted with the dead boy—I looked around to see if anyone had seen me, and then walked away as fast as I could. Mèo Lớn, or "Big Cat" (his childhood nickname and the only name I knew for him), was a local Việt Cộng who died during fighting with the CAP the night earlier.

I remembered the day that Big Cat had played a trick on me. I was about ten years old, and I was playing on the village road, watching water buffaloes and mobile street vendors pass by. The street vendors ranged from barbers and pig castrators to food merchants and straw sleeping mat sellers. At the time, I always had a hungry stomach, and the food vendors on the village road captivated me. One vendor, Mr. Lu, transported his entire *bánh mì* kitchen using a shoulder bamboo pole. At one end was a pot of Huế-style pork stew, under which a charcoal fire burned to keep it warm. The other end was a two-compartment glass drawer filled with meats and ingredients—fresh vegetables and herbs— and a thick bag of warm French baguettes. Every time Mr. Lu called out "Bánh mì!," my mind just froze. It was the smell. Yes—that smell! The smell of hot pork stew and baguette baking in the oven. I looked at the cart with my mouth hanging open. While Mr. Lu left his mobile kitchen unattended, Big Cat took a baguette and put it in my right hand.

"It's on me," Big Cat said.

It was just the bread—nothing inside. It surprised me, and I didn't know how to react. "I don't want it," I said hesitantly.

"Mr. Lu!" Big Cat shouted and pointed at me. "Someone stole your *bánh mì*."

Mr. Lu ran toward me. Without thinking, I sprinted away from him. The vendor chased me, but I was too fast for the older man. Like a rat at a dumpster that scurried away at a noise, I scrambled over the hedgerows, from house to house. My smaller size was also an advantage, and I managed to escape. I could hear Big Cat howling in the back as I was running. The whole scene was a good laugh for him and the other boys. Afterward, I told myself I'd return the favour and get him back another time, even though I didn't know what I could do—he was much bigger than me. But now I had no chance.

Big Cat was lying beside the village market. His remaining eye was wide open as though he was looking at me. In that lifeless eye, I could feel an innocent look of questioning. *Why me?*

I wondered whether his family knew about his death. Or maybe they were afraid to bring the body home for burial. I started to recognize that my problems were minor compared to the issues around.

That night I couldn't sleep. If I closed my eyes, the lifeless image of Big Cat appeared again and again. As an excuse to delay the darkness, I turned on the kerosene lamp and told my mom that I had to study for a test tomorrow.

---

A few weeks later, some local guerrillas wanted to settle the score and avenge Big Cat's death. Three local guerrillas, including Nguyễn Viết Phong, a teenager, ambushed a US Army Jeep on Route 1 close to where Big Cat's body had originally been displayed. Unlike the usual tactic of sharpshooting from a distance, they came out in the open this time. They executed two Marines at close range, sitting in their seats in a military Jeep on the main road, right in front of the village market. Then they left the scene, unharmed. The incident became the main talking point among the village teenagers, buffalo boys and school students, discussing it with excitement and admiration. Some of us disappeared from the village after that. Phong became a guerilla hero, and most kids looked up to him.

Everything about this war was confusing. It was nothing like the kid games that Old Dog and I fought on the rice field or in the canal. These battles—in which the buffalo boys and I attacked the kids from the neighbouring village—were simple. The boundary was well defined, and our team was on one side while the enemies were on the other. With this war, the real one, there was no physical boundary.

The village was more complicated, like a blend of sticky rice and beans, or *vùng xôi đậu*. This phrase is used in situations where you don't really know who is who and which side is which. Sticky rice—*xôi*—is white, and beans—*đậu*—are red. This means one could separate the bean from the rice, but it was difficult, if not impossible, to make it pure white again. Some rice had turned pink—no longer white. This was the state that Dạ Lê was in—red, white and pink—and nobody knew who anyone was.

Like a pot of rice, one didn't need many red beans to turn it pink, the communists just used a little propaganda arousing national pride, and pushing back against the new colonialism, to convert the villagers into communist sympathizers. Foreign soldiers stationed on the village land reinforced the claims of the communist propaganda.

Dạ Lê used to be an idyllic countryside village, but it had become part of a community with two official names, depending on what side a person was on. The village was also under two opposing administrations: one run by the South Vietnam government under the name of Thủy Phương, and the other by the Việt Cộng organization with the name of Mỹ Thủy. So, two different village chiefs with their respective councils ran the same territory simultaneously.

While the pro-South Vietnam government leaders were publicly known and active during the day, the other anonymous communist leaders ruled the village by night. Whoever got the village chief title in the South Vietnamese government—to carry out official duties during the day—knew it was like receiving a death sentence, just waiting for their own execution date. He would be the main target, certain to be killed or abducted. (One of my distant uncles had been executed in broad daylight after being the village chief for a year.)

People were forced to take sides, to do things against their will and to tell on others. The villagers couldn't trust each other anymore, even within their own families. Some family members could be pro-government, while others would be sympathetic to VC. And this divisiveness ran deep in each family. Old Dog's family, for instance, had conflicting loyalties: His oldest sister had left home for the jungle a few years ago, but his older brother enlisted as a soldier in the South Vietnam Army (SVA).

Our family was no exception. My cousin Anh Hai said he wasn't against the North, but he hated the communist ideologies. He hated all Vietnamese communists, whether it was the National Liberation Front of South Vietnam (NLFSV), or the regular North Vietnam Army (NVA). Anyway, they were both Việt Cộng; the NVA formed the NLFSV and directed it to liberate the South. Even the thought that Anh Hai might have to live under them one day made him sick. So he enlisted in the SVA, and believed it was honourable to die for Vietnam.

At the same time, Chị Mau joined the NLFSV, but the villagers always called it Việt Cộng, or VC for short. She claimed it was a glorious thing to die for Vietnam. I told Anh Hai and Chị Mau they would die for the same thing. But Chị Mau and her comrades believed that they—and nobody else—were patriots. Anyone who was against VC was an enemy of the people—*kẻ thù nhân dân*. So half of the villagers were the enemy of the people and unpatriotic. Brothers and sisters were killing each other—all in the name of nationalism or the fatherland. I wondered whether there was any other country in the world where siblings killed one another to protect their honour, as a so-called glorious thing to do.

Anh Hai was the only child of a fallen soldier, so he was excused from military duty. Nevertheless, he'd enlisted and requested to be on the front line. My mother attributed his stubbornness to the hair whorl on the right side of his forehead, where a tuft of hair stuck up that people could see at a distance. She said such a person would never work indoors or at an easy job, so she was not surprised that he'd chosen to become a battlefield soldier instead of an ornamental one.

Chị Mau was O Lâu's only daughter. O Lâu was a single mother and one of my two aunts. Her husband was also a government soldier who died young; I had no recollection of him. However, I was very close to both of them. O Lâu loved me as her son since I was a *dích tôn*, the oldest son of the first son in her clan. I treated Chị Mau like an older sister. She was three years my senior and liked to talk to me often because I was the only person who listened and looked up to her. With her long shiny black hair and pale skin, like a city girl, she had many admirers at school. Some followed her home, and others asked me to give her a poem or a letter they wrote. For the delivery, I charged a commission fee: a pack of Capstan cigarettes, which was a popular brand. The students wanted to be her boyfriend, but she ignored them all. She already had a boyfriend—a secret one she could not disclose, even to me.

Chị Mau said she hated the Americans and was against US imperialism and the Saigon government. I was surprised by these new strong opinions, because she used to scold me if I said anything against either Americans or Việt Cộng. She would warn me about participating in rallies.

"Why do you call the United States an imperialist country?" I asked her.

"Did we just fight off French colonization?" she answered with a question.

"Yes, we did. But this time, the Americans came to fight off the Communists, especially Red China—I learned this from a newspaper," I said.

"Why does China have anything to do with this?"

"Have you heard about what happened to Tibet, Mongolia and North Korea? The Chinese Communists have totally or partially over-run them. If we are not careful, the next one will be Vietnam," I said. I had heard that Red China was helping North Vietnam. Like most Vietnamese people, I inherited the thousand-year-old fear of a Chinese takeover of Vietnam, a fear born of a history of the terrible things they did to us. *We don't want to be a second North Korea*, I was thinking.

"If we are like Korea, we must select which side we wish Vietnam to be—North or South?" I asked her.

Chị Mau muttered to herself, then said, "What choice do I have? The French have trained many leaders in Saigon."

"Not all of the leaders. You can say the same for the North."

"True," she said, "but some of the generals in the South Vietnam Army moved up in rank because of killing our people during the colonial times." She paused for a second. "I don't trust them."

Chị Mau looked out the window at the rice paddy, but not at anything in particular. Then she declared emphatically, "Colonialism is out, and neocolonialism is in, plain and simple, and our barefoot peasants know it. A new form of imperialism—military installation and economic domination—is what Americans are doing in Vietnam. Not only that, but they also want to try out their weapons, including testing chemical warfare like Agent Orange."

"Agent Orange?"

"Yes, Agent Orange, an herbicide and defoliant that kills trees and woods, and destroys our crops."

"Is that true?" I asked.

"You will see."

I was too young to understand the war. Chị Mau knew more than my young mind could handle, but I still felt she was hiding something. One day, O Lâu complained that she had found a hand grenade hidden under clothes in her daughter's drawer. She didn't like having that kind of stuff in her house, and she blamed it on her daughter's secret friend. A boyfriend? *Tell me more, Auntie,* I whispered to myself.

"I hate that guy," O Lâu said.

"Who is the guy?" I asked.

O Lâu investigated my face. "You tell me."

I frowned and then shook my head.

"So you don't know," she said.

Chị Mau had fallen in love with an out-of-town guerrilla stationed in Rào, the next-door hamlet. Her boyfriend was the type of person who was fun and exciting to be around, like the one we had seen a few years earlier playing guitar and showing us an AK-47 in O Lan's house. He was fearless and had the attitude of an adventurer, just like Nguyễn Viết Phong had been. The buffalo boys idolized him.

The district police had arrested Chị Mau twice. The first time, my ba had sponsored her out, but the next time after, she wouldn't agree to the conditions of her release: that she must leave Huế. The police suggested she move to Đà Nẵng and stay with her other uncle. But Mau didn't want to go anywhere; she remained in the village with her mother. Even though she refused, the police still let her go after several months in jail because she was an only child of a fallen soldier.

A short time later, Mau confided in me. "I'm going away. You keep studying hard and don't do anything stupid."

"Where are you going?" I was concerned.

"You will know soon," she said sadly. "I can't do anything if I stay put."

"You go back to school, sis."

"It's not that easy," she said. "Do you remember a clash at the cross-roads close to my house a year back?"

"Yes, I heard some US Marines were injured." I nodded my head.

"I organized that," she whispered. "It wasn't just me; I worked with two other girls in the hamlet."

"What did you do?"

"I can't tell you," Chị Mau said.

I had heard about the cell of three girls, but I had no idea that Mau was one of them. I still didn't know who the other two girls were. Nobody told me. If I found out, I would be surprised then. One of the girls was Old Dog's sister. The other was the person who would later become, like Chị Mau, a heroine of the Revolutionary Armed Forces. The heroine had no formal education, not even a day in school. She looked after water buffaloes and pigs. I often saw her in the rice fields, cutting grass for water buffalo or collecting veggies for pigs. Cutting grass around military establishments or sports facilities was also the best way to spy. Now and then, the girl had given the buffalo boys some tennis or golf balls for playing. After ambushing the Marines, she'd left the hamlet and disappeared into the jungle. We lost the supply of balls.

A month later, in May 1965, my mother gave birth to another baby, my fourth baby brother. She now had five sons and one daughter. In opposition to the war, Mom named our newest sibling Hòa, as in *hòa bình*, which means "peace." This approach to naming also meant that she was anticipating having another child—who would be Bình—soon after. If she didn't conceive again, her wish would never be fulfilled, and the peace would never arrive.

## CHAPTER 7

# Propaganda

The beginning of the war was vague, confusing, chaotic and unsettling. How many of us, as kids, ever understood the war in the first place? How many lives would be sacrificed, how many families would be torn apart and how many children would be displaced before it ended? At the time, those questions were not for kids like us to think about.

The Vietnam War came to us like a game we played with the children of the neighbouring hamlet. It had started long before we could realize that we were in it. First, there was a division between North and South. One side fabricated or faked the events, while the other exaggerated or minimized the facts. They found every trick in the book to win the people's hearts and to break enemy morale.

The People's Liberation Front, or Việt Cộng, representing the North, organized many neighbourhood meetings at night to propagate their communist ideologies and arouse patriotism until villagers couldn't distinguish between the two. The conflict had changed. It had transformed from the war of independence to ideological warfare. *Communism is a torch that will light the way to lead the villagers out of poverty and oppression. The Saigon regime is corrupt and a puppet for the evil American imperialists, and most people in the South long for liberation.* Communists were using nationalism to appeal to the people of the South, and in opposition to the Saigon regime, who were making our lives poorer while Americans invaded our land. The communism of the Soviet Union and the Eastern Bloc was against the democracy and capitalism of America and its allies, and that's what the communists preached in the neighbourhood meetings. Our family was never invited to these local meetings, and I never knew why, but I believed it was because my father was a Saigon regime soldier. Even without attending, I still learned a few things through the buffalo boys.

Meanwhile, the South Vietnamese government and the Americans said they were fighting communism and preventing the domino effect in Southeast Asia. Like NATO in Europe, the US and other armed forces from Australia, New Zealand, South Korea, Thailand and the Philippines were here on a mission to prevent the communist expansion led by the Soviet Union and Red China throughout Southeast Asia. Thus, they fought the Communists, not the people. They claimed they came here to bring democracy to the country, not to take away any land. Meanwhile, the South Vietnam regime airdropped thousands of pamphlets on the hamlet at night to propagate their messages. Those leaflets rolled along the village roads the morning after, getting struck in the picket fences, blowing across the rice field and flashing white against the dark thatched roofs. They were everywhere. I picked some up. I liked the smell of fresh ink and the smooth touch of new paper; they reminded me of the first day of each school year. The hamlet kids raced to collect them. We could use them to make paper cranes, boats or even airplanes. But Mom said to throw them away and never keep them in the house; they were "*tờ truyền đơn Chiêu Hồi.*" They called the Việt Cộng to come out of hiding, saying, "Return now under the Chiêu Hồi program. There is nowhere to run … nowhere to hide," they said.

Before this psychological warfare, the South Vietnam government had imposed several orders on the villagers with little success. First was a curfew; nobody was allowed to be outside their houses at night. But Việt Cộng and its propagandists didn't follow the rule. The government instructed us to make noises whenever we heard a suspicious sound outside our house during the night. Our noisemakers—*mõ tre*—were made of big bamboo roots with hollowed-out insides. They gave a loud sound and a deep tone that could travel very far. An empty tin can could work if one didn't have a bamboo drum. Whenever I heard my neighbours playing a drum, I did the same, playing on an empty tin can. I didn't care or know about the reason—I just kept pounding. With the sounds of hundreds of beating cans, I was excited, as if I were in a jungle, running and hunting animals. My imagination ran wild until my mom told me to stop.

I waited to play again the next night, but the signal never came. Nobody dared to make noise again, because bad news kept on coming. One night, a man had been executed in front of his house, and the next, another villager disappeared overnight. I was curious to know whether the system of making noises and these disappearances were related. There were many things I didn't know then, and no one was around to ask.

After the drums, the South Vietnam government implemented other new orders to assert its influence over the villagers. When I was about eight years old, the government ordered each family to paint the South Vietnam flag—three red stripes on a yellow background—on the front of each house in the village to show that its owner supported the South Vietnam regime. Each household in the hamlet had to have their photo taken by a government official, and all family members had to be in the photo. Anyone absent member would be in trouble during future house checks.

Even though I struggled to brush the wet paint on the rough concrete surface of our house, I was happy to complete the task. It might be my first painting. The next day, a government official came with a photographer to take the family portrait—my first time standing in front of a camera. Mom told my younger brother Lanh and me to wear our newest outfits, a white shirt and a pair of black shorts we'd gotten for the previous Tết—our Lunar New Year—and we remembered combing our hair. I used fresh lime juice to smooth my stubborn hair and ensured that my side part was visible. I felt I looked good. The photographer told us to stand in the front yard below the painted flag. Mom was carrying my youngest brother, Tuấn, in her arms with my sister Hạnh at her right, holding the front flap of her *áo dài*, with Lanh and me on her left. After the official had written my mother's name and the house address on a small blackboard, he asked me to hold it in front of my chest. After fifteen minutes of standing under the noon sun, I could feel sweat flowing down my temples. The official told us to hold still and took a single black-and-white picture.

A few weeks later, Mr. Bá, the South Vietnam government village clerk, brought us the photo. When I saw our first picture, I thought it looked like an identification slide for a scene in a movie, but the adults said it was a prison snapshot.

Villagers learned about new orders from the village through Mr. Bá. He paraded around the main roads all day to announce upcoming events through an old-fashioned megaphone with a small handle. Mr. Bá earned the nickname Mr. Alo because he started every announcement with "Alo."

"Alo, Alo. Remember the photo to be taken at noon today!" Mr. Alo shouted through his megaphone as he walked past our house.

We followed him as far as we could, mimicking him with a rolled-up banana leaf.

"Alo, Alo. Listen to me. Listen to me," one boy announced, and the rest of us laughed.

And then, one day, Mr. Bá disappeared and the village officers started to use a handheld battery-operated megaphone, and I never saw him again.

---

Smouldering hatred was starting to build behind our ignorance. When we helped the adults dig out the ground for a bomb shelter, and then witnessed the deadly battle, we realized that the fighting was serious business.

Our buffalo gang began to talk about war instead of games or soccer strategies. We repeated what the grown-ups discussed among themselves.

"We'll be liberated soon," Old Dog started a conversation.

"Why do we need to be liberated?" one of the buffalo boys, Cu lỳ (or "Stubborn"), wondered.

"Once liberated, our village would become a city," Old Dog said.

"What does a city look like?" another boy asked. Like most boys, he had never been out of the village.

"Like Huế, where every house has electricity and tap water," Old Dog answered.

"What's tap water?" the same boy asked.

"Water just flows to our house whenever we need it," Old Dog proudly said.

"Cool! I would no longer need to carry it from the village well anymore," another boy said.

"Like what, Old Dog? Have you seen the tap water?" Stubborn kept asking.

"No, I have not," Old Dog said, and then rolled his eyes at Stubborn as if saying, "Shut your mouth." He then faced the other gang members and announced, "Anyhow, the Americans are here to kill people."

"And the South Vietnam government is no good. *Cõng rắn cắn gà nhà*—It brings snakes to a chicken coop," Young Dog added.

"That's not quite true," I said. "My cousin, Anh Hai, said the government didn't ask the Americans; they just came in to prevent Red China from overrunning the South. And they came during a coup after a coup; no one was in charge of the country. He also said that we don't need anyone to liberate us. Just leave us alone." I said.

With the presence of US combat troops in Dạ Lê, Việt Cộng had more reason to pressure the villagers to oppose US aggression. But nobody mentioned the North Vietnam Army also stationed in the area, or fighting for the communists. Their messages were "Unite the People," "Yankee Go Home," "Down with Thiệu Kỳ," and "Fight American Imperialism and Save the Nation." The latter slogan resonated with young people, and I was caught up in the whirlwind of the times.

My love of my country was my weakness. Like me, the buffalo kids loved our nation, even though they never went to school. We grew up knowing only real-life heroes from our history, not cartoon superhuman heroes like Superman or Catwoman. We didn't want anyone to invade our country, so we praised anyone who stood up and chased them out of Vietnam. After a thousand years under Chinese domination and a hundred years of French colonial rule, we have had many heroes and heroines, from the sisters Trưng Trắc and Trưng Nhị to Lê Lợi and Quang Trung—all ordinary people who revolted against the Chinese. During the period of French control, not only one but two teenage kings in the Huế court, Hàm Nghi and Duy Tân, risked their lives to rebel against the French. When they were just fifteen and seventeen, the kings were caught by the French and exiled to colonial territories in South America and the Indian Ocean. After thirty years of exile, the French let the younger king return to Vietnam, but his plane crashed in Central Africa on his way home. The older one was banished from Vietnam and died in France. With village kids like the buffalo boys, local brave guerrillas such as Nguyễn Viết Phong were revered as if they were one of these more famous heroes.

At thirteen, I joined my classmates and shouted, "Fight Imperialism and Save the Country!" That was the spring of 1966. We got involved in anti-war rallies, even though we didn't truly understand the causes, outside the rumours, deception and fake news. We were saving the country because we felt we must protect our fatherland.

But Mom, like most of the Vietnamese parents, had different hopes. She wanted peace—no more fighting. Another newborn, her seventh child, joined the family that spring, as if to fulfill her wish. As planned, she named him Bình, to complete the phrase "*hòa bình*." But not only did peace fail to come, the war worsened. My new brother was born at the worst time—anytime during the war was the worst time.

———————

I completed elementary school in the summer of 1966, but my mom didn't have money to send me to a private school in Huế. So I had to pass the entry exam for grade six at the district's middle school—which could accommodate only a single class of fifty students among several hundreds of elementary graduates in the area each year. With such a low passing percentage, I needed help. Uncle Dong was a well-known teacher who had tutored many fifth graders in his home. His proven passing ratio for his students was very high. Parents would pay Uncle Dong a handsome sum of money and give him complete authority over their child for the ten-week study period. They believed it was the best investment to prevent their boys from running away into the jungle.

Uncle Dong offered a discount to some selected poor students who could only pay part of the sum. The catch was that the chosen students must perform one assigned duty. Lam and I were two of those students. Lam was born three days ahead of me, and his father and mine were both in the same *đi tập kết* group. But my dad returned home, while his father continued to the North. He grew up as the only son of a single mom.

Each morning, I biked to Huế, a round trip of twenty kilometres, to pick up the tutor's newspaper. I borrowed a men's bike with a crossbar from Anh Hai. The bike was too high; I couldn't even stand up, but I curved my body to one side for pedalling. I was proud of myself for holding that position for such a long distance. I became the only young boy in the village to read the paper, and I read it every day. I was very interested in the news. Bad weather or sickness didn't matter; I must fulfill my obligation.

I preferred this over the chores that other students got—at least I could read the newspaper every day. Lam had to carry drinking water, while Tu polished Uncle Dong's Dural bike. Khang purchased and resold stolen US merchandise from the black market.

One morning, something I will never forget happened at Uncle Dong's house. The government suspected some Việt Cộng sympathizers among the students, so it sent a staff sergeant known for his brutality to the class to deter us from joining the insurgents. A rumour was going around that Sergeant Beo, from a nearby village, had done terrible things to the captured VC. Looking at his face, one could tell what kind of man he was. He had a square face with some scars on his left cheek. Even his name said something about him—beo, a leopard.

Sergeant Beo came to the class to demonstrate what he did to Việt Cộng, which we'd only heard rumours about. He ordered all students to sit in a big circle around him in the front yard of the tutor's house. Standing in the centre with a big knife in his right hand, the sergeant picked a student to face him. *Not me, not me*, I prayed. I forget which student was selected—all I cared about was that it wasn't me. The picked student's face turned green and pale. Sergeant Beo told the poor student to lie down. Instead of lying down, he just collapsed at his feet. Sergeant Beo lay the student on his back and then retreated five steps while demonstrating martial arts movements. Frozen with fear, we students watched wide-eyed and held our breath. His waving knife sliced the air, stopping an inch short of the student's stomach. "Ah," everyone exhaled at the same time.

The show did not halt there. Next, the sergeant exhibited how he cut the ears off VC fighters. He told the victim to stand, but the student could not get up. Sergeant Beo finished his demonstration without a subject. The terror of this event stayed with me, and I could not concentrate on my studies for the next few days.

Terrorizing us was all that he had achieved. Other than that— nothing.

When the school official posted the grade six entry result, my name was at the eleventh spot on the list of fifty. I passed, and eleven became my lucky number. Many of the students who had failed left home to join the guerrillas a few months later.

## CHAPTER 8

# Camp Eagle

Each summer, the winds of Laos swept over Dạ Lê. It was a hot and dry wind blowing down the side of a high mountain. It started with wet air from the Gulf of Thailand, and then its moisture condensed and caused rainfall before crossing the Trường Sơn Mountains. The remaining air became drier and hotter around Huế. Humidity could fall to 20 per cent, while the temperature could soar to over forty degrees Celsius on some days.

The leaves on the trees around our house turned brown. It was an unusual drought. Even the evergreen bamboo trees lost half their leaves, and the remainder became yellow. The shade disappeared along with the leaves. Water buffaloes and poultry took refuge under big bushes of banana and bamboo. Mom told us to watch out for stray dogs which could carry rabies, even though we hadn't seen any kind of dog in the village for a long time. It seemed everything stopped living except the crickets. I could hear the crickets chirping, as if they were complaining about the long drought. Some village elders told us that if we heard a toad, the rain would come soon. While my village prayed for peace, I also wished for the toads to croak.

My siblings and I were suffocating in the thin but hot air. The youngsters had nothing on, while the older ones, like me, wore only shorts. I liked to submerge in the mud of the canal behind our house like the water buffaloes did, because it was the best way to cool down.

The heat had slowed down the fighting and the war, but the other war continued—the war of fire. House fires, that is. A house in the hamlet had caught on fire just a few days back. The villagers couldn't do anything except rescue anyone trapped inside and comfort the victims. During the drought, water wells and canals dried out, and people had to travel several kilometres to get drinking water from the village's deepest well, which the Cham people had drilled over a thousand years ago. Once a house caught fire, nothing could stop it.

Besides the dryness and heat, I started to notice something else in the air that summer. A strange smell, like raw papaya resin, but different. This odour was not natural—it was an unmistakable chemical smell. The foul scent was being carried over the highlands to our hamlet by the hot winds of Laos. The stink was most noticeable in the early hours each morning. It was the thing that Chị Mau had told me about a year back.

The US military had sprayed Agent Orange on the western edge of the village to clear the bushes for building Camp Eagle for the 101st Airborne Division in late 1967. I once witnessed this program in action from the top of the pagoda hill, the highest point in the area. The camp would support the US airpower to the South Vietnam government, covering its most northern area. Dạ Lê became the centre of the conflict. Planes were spraying the whitish chemical on the bushes in the wooded area that provided coverage for Việt Cộng around the perimeter of the future Camp Eagle. The other purpose was to destroy the ability of peasants to support themselves in the VC-controlled countryside. The military thought that lack of food would drive the peasants to flee to regions where the US military or South Vietnamese government dominated. This would deprive the guerrillas of their rural support base. But the displacement did not come as expected. The US military had dropped several million gallons of chemical herbicides and defoliants in Vietnam's central provinces—the more Agent Orange was dropped on the farmland, the more hatred of the US grew. One of the herbicide spray-mission areas was the A Lưới district, encompassing the mountainous A Shau Valley bordering Laos, west of Huế and over fifteen kilometres from the hamlet. Many well-known battlefields of the Vietnam War, like Hamburger Hill, were there.

---

A few weeks after the heat of summer and the fighting subsided, the village would enter a prolonged rainy season: a monsoon. The rain could go on and on for months until the soil rotted—the ground was saturated and nothing could grow. In October 1967, when the annual flood arrived, our house was cut off from the rest of the village and became an island. Due to its high foundation, the main floor was still a couple of inches above the water level. The house could withstand the regular floods, but not the big ones that usually took place in the Year of the Dragon, a twelve-year cycle. In those years, our family had to evacuate to higher ground—the highlands, west of the railroad tracks. This year, we kept our eyes on the water level, ready to move at short notice and hoping the flood would be over soon. My uncles and close relatives sailed past our house every other day to check on us.

My school closed during the flood. All day and night, the waves gently lapped the walls of our house—*Zeh zah, zeh zah*—and the wind blew—*zee zee*—against the thatched roof. The sounds cast a hypnotic spell on us; we all felt sleepy.

"Oh! Oh!" Hòa suddenly screeched in panic, pointing up at the ceiling. "Snake, snake."

I awoke. My younger siblings were close to me. The two youngest were shaking. One held my right arm tight, the other the left. Their breaths were heavy while the hissing sounds of rats skittered around in the thatched roof above us. There were many rats. All the rats on the ground had moved up into the ceiling during the flood, along with what's known as either a cave racer snake or a beauty rat snake.

Whenever I heard hissing sounds, I imagined the snake-chasing-rat scene above us. We must be in a state of readiness. With the fact-paced chase overhead, the rodents or even the snake might drop on us anytime. My siblings were afraid of both. We huddled in the middle of the bed under the mosquito net, even though I knew it wouldn't hold up the weight of that cave racer. But my siblings felt much safer like that, and I felt their grip on my arms loosen.

We were lucky. The snake never dropped on us, while the rats sometimes did. And the net was strong enough to hold them off.

Even though I was nervous, I did like to look up at the scene. The rat ran for its life along the house frame while the snake was close behind, circling the roof purlins. Like the villagers avoiding the fighting, the rats changed lanes from purlins to rafters. Still, they couldn't get away from the racer.

Our family had no boat, but we needed supplies during the flood. So I waded through the toxic water with my clothes inside banana leaves, held up high to keep them dry. Yes, the water was poisonous, but I didn't know that then. I enjoyed playing in the water. The Agent Orange washed from the trees and soil in the highlands and drifted downstream into the rice field and the floodwater surrounding our house.

Even though that year's flood was not the biggest one we had experienced, its effect on us was the most severe and most memorable.

Mom and I got a skin rash that has affected us on and off ever since. We could not get rid of it. The rash was on the nape of my neck, my hands and feet and generally worse in the summer months. That is why I used to go to the beach in my shirt with a high collar and long sleeves, and wearing socks. But the severest of skin disorders was on my youngest brother, Vinh. He was born a few months before the flood started, and his skin rash was all over his scalp; not a single hair could grow. His head was more prominent than average at his age, and when we looked at him, his head was all we saw. His hair finally began to grow at five, and it grew faster, darker, thicker and curlier—far more hair than any of us. That was also when we recognized that he had some concentration and memory problems. Vinh never really grew up; he was developmentally delayed his whole life. He passed away when he was almost thirty, but his mind was still like a baby's.

---

In addition to the Agent Orange affecting the village's land, air and water quality, the presence of the Americans at Camp Eagle also had many other adverse effects on its habitants. Soon after they arrived, a black market appeared to supply the camp with workers from nearby regions and to distribute the stolen or leftover food. (Since the Americans considered the village residents a security risk, the base refused to employ immediate locals, even for demeaning jobs.) Many children became garbage pickers around the camp. One of my former classmates, Khang, had become a broker in the black market of stolen goods. He and his gang even hijacked a US convoy carrying food supplies. They'd taken advantage of the vehicle slowdown at a traffic elbow to jump into the open-top US trucks loaded with food parcels. The boys grabbed and dropped off the goods at prearranged locations hidden from the drivers' view. One day, the next truck driver saw what was happening and called the guard, a GI with a machine gun, to go after them. The boys jumped over a barbed-wire fence and disappeared into a dense forest. The railing was well over two metres high, but the kids somehow sailed over it. The GI returned to his truck, shaking his head. The kids bet their lives on a few small boxes of food, and some died because of such hijackings, including my schoolmate, who fell off the food truck on the Bạch Hổ bridge over the Perfume River.

―――――

After our last talk, Chị Mau had disappeared. I didn't know when she left and where she went, but I had to walk alone to school for the next few weeks. One day, I was alone on the Tram Trail and missed her.

In front of me, a team of US soldiers was using metal detectors to find any land mines hidden in the layer of red dirt on the trail. They were on foot, walking in formation starting from Route 1 and moving west toward their base a few kilometres away, in the westernmost part of the village.

Several days before Chị Mau left, I had experimented, out of curiosity and stupidity. I removed a big rock from the trail and then concealed an empty, flattened can under a layer of dirt while Lam kept a lookout for soldiers. Even with thoughtful planning, my heart pumped too fast to keep my hands steady. After a few minutes, I completed the job and retreated to watch from the school grounds to see what would happen. The students had made a bet on the effectiveness of the machine. The soldiers detected the flattened can successfully and removed it. I don't know how Mau found out about this foolhardy act. She had warned me: She said the US soldiers would have assumed I was planting a land mine and might have shot me on the spot if they caught me in action.

65

"Hey! Do you want chewing gum?" someone asked me as I was walking alone on the Tram Trail, jolting me out of my reverie about my cousin Mau.

I looked to my left. A young girl, a few years older, smiled at me. She was sitting by the window of a makeshift house on the roadside.

"Me?" I pointed at my chest and asked.

"Yes, you!" the girl nodded.

I liked chewing gum, but no way would go inside that house—it was a brothel. I knew a classmate, Ky, who had been in that house, and no girl at school had talked to him ever since. It was not going to happen to me. So I looked the other way and kept walking.

"Catch," the girl called out.

I turned back just in time to grab a pack of chewing gum. I smiled and waved back to the girl.

Those thatched huts appeared after the Americans, hoping to prevent sniper shootings, had bulldozed all houses and big trees along the road, leaving only the middle school and the district hospital. (They still couldn't stop the sharpshooters, who continued to target US vehicles on the trail that linked Route 1 to Camp Eagle after crossing the school.) I had to walk past the brothels on my way to class, and even though I didn't want to go inside, I was still curious. Just last week, Lam and I had gone around to the back to look, but we couldn't find a door or window. We saw nothing.

Those brothels and bars existed because of Camp Eagle, the headquarters of the Screaming Eagles of the 101st Airborne Division. The Americans gradually built the base to accommodate nearly ten thousand US Airborne members and their support, while the village population was only about three thousand. Even so, the camp was a makeshift structure that combined plywood, aluminum, sandbags and camping materials. This was unlike the French colonists, who built their camps with concrete and iron rebar, which remained long after they were gone. My elementary school used to be one of their outposts. With these temporary structures, were the Americans indicating that they would not be here for long?

The Airborne took over the dirt trail, the only road that connected Route 1 to my school. The traffic became unbearable, and students competed with the military for school access. Bicycles were brushing up against heavily loaded trucks, and hundreds clogged that red-dirt trail daily.

Every time the search team had completed landmine detection on the trail, a water truck with sprinklers would follow for dust control. Nevertheless, within a few hours, the American trucks would raise a cloud of rust-coloured dust again.

We found our classroom was full of the red stuff—red floors, red tables and red walls. If we blew our noses, red mucus would come out. Even our school uniforms turned red, and we felt sorry for the girls. The dust was tough on them, because there was no way they could keep their school-uniform dresses—white *áo dài*—dust-free.

*Screeeeeeech!*

I looked back at a Jeep as it came to a halt about twenty feet behind me. Two US military policemen (or MPs) jumped off their Jeep. They rushed into the brothel where the girl had just thrown me a pack of chewing gum. The MPs looked for any US soldiers abandoning their posts to come here. As the military police went in the front, several GIs ran out the back and into the bushes. So there *was* a door. *How had Lam and I not seen it before?* I wondered.

After fifteen minutes, the MPs exited the brothel, with two soldiers carted away in the back of the Jeep.

The escaped GIs would be lucky not to run right into the hands of Việt Cộng, or a bamboo trap or a land mine. The village land was full of tunnels, except for some low-elevation areas prone to flooding, like the land surrounding our property. VCs were hidden everywhere—at the back of people's gardens, under bamboo bushes or inside the complex of underground tunnels. Most villagers just closed their eyes. We didn't want to know; we didn't want to see. We knew nothing, saw nothing—that was the safest option. It seemed nobody knew the exact locations.

That was not entirely correct. "You can figure out where VCs are," Old Dog once said. "Go to the village market and observe what the women buy. If they buy too much food for the size of their family, you can bet that their house has some mystery guests." When I heard that, I could tell that Old Dog knew more than most kids his age. Someone must have shown him how to make an observation like that. At the time, all sides—the government, the CIA and VC—tried to recruit children as spies and saboteurs. The buffalo boys were the ones that were best for the job. I had expected some of my friends and classmates, or even my cousins, were also undercover. So I listened to them, but I didn't talk much. I acted as if I knew nothing, like anyone around me.

Besides bulldozing the houses along the trail, Americans also designated Rào, the hamlet next door, as a free-fire zone (FFZ), meaning that the US Marines could shoot anything that moved. Dạ Lê was now sandwiched between Camp Eagle in the west and the FFZ in the east.

## CHAPTER 9

# Free-Fire Zone

One early spring morning in 1967, loud explosions woke me.

"Go to the shelter. Now!" Mom yelled.

With quick reflexes, I got out of the mosquito net and then rose from my bamboo pallet. In the dim half-light of dawn, I saw my mother grabbing my youngest brother, Vinh, with her right hand, holding my sister Hạnh's hand with her left, and heading to the bomb shelter, which was an extension to our house. I shook the feet of my five other siblings to wake them up.

"Follow me—quick!" I told them and led them toward the shelter's entrance.

Once inside, I counted all my siblings to make sure they were all there. Then I changed my mind. I wanted to see the action. The explosions and the airplane flying overhead were not close by—they were distant sounds. From all the noise and the shell whistles, I could tell the battle was over on the other side of the rice field, away from our house.

"Stay here," I told my siblings while climbing out of hiding to look outside. "I'll be back."

"No. Get down here!" Mom ordered.

"I'll be back in a minute, Mạ," I answered, even though I could no longer see her. She was sitting in the dark at the back of the bomb shelter.

The house was silent, with all doors and windows closed. I peeked out from behind one of the small gaps between the concrete back wall and a window, which overlooked the paddy field to Rào, the free-fire zone. Over the flat rice field, two big white fighter planes criss-crossed the blue sky at a distance. I felt terrified but excited, too. *Are they A-37 Dragonflies or A-1 Skyraiders?* I wondered, as I tried to identify the aircraft, but the sun's rays made it impossible. I lowered my eyes to avoid them. A light breeze brushed the rice plants, creating paddy waves like ripples on the sea surface. The farmers were trying to return to the village, leaving everything behind—even their water buffaloes. In peaceful times, this would have been unheard of, since the beasts, if left alone, could eat and destroy the rice fields. The villagers didn't care. They wanted to be safe, and they wanted to be home as soon as they could. When the wind gusts blew off their conical hats, they kept running without bothering to pick them up. The hats landed on the rice paddy and bobbed in the waves.

*Boom, boom!*

I looked up. About two kilometres away, the planes had dropped bombs and napalm on a small green strip of a lonely hamlet below; the area looked like a fence in the middle of a rice paddy. This is why people called it Rào, meaning "the fence." The hamlet runs along the riverbank of an artificial channel, a tributary of the Perfume River, Lợi Nông. In the old times, before building Route 1, Lợi Nông River had been the leading commercial route from the village to Huế. During the war, the river system was unsafe for travel. Like Việt Minh had during the French colonial era, Việt Cộng used the waterway to transport ammunition and weapons in the dark of night. The hamlet became a VC sanctuary and was now the free-fire zone, where VCs lived among the villagers and were indistinguishable from them. Networks of secret tunnels connected house to house; no enemy force could penetrate it. The Saigon government had ordered the people of Rào to move away before sending heavily armoured trucks to enter the area, so that the VC's human shield tactics would no longer work.

The people of Rào had evacuated to this side of the paddy a year earlier. During the mass displacement, I saw a long queue of people and animals on the dirt road of the rice field. The refugees brought along their rice crops, water buffaloes and poultry. They took everything they could. Anything remaining was destroyed or burned to the ground to prevent it from falling into the guerrillas' hands. Any villagers who were reluctant to leave their land had to evacuate at gunpoint. Those who remained in the zone became unfortunate war casualties or lived underground as local guerrillas. Half a dozen of my classmates had lived there, and none of them appeared to leave the hamlet—they just disappeared. Uncle Dong's nephew, Binh, my close friend, joined the Việt Cộng and stayed back in the hamlet. I never regained contact with him.

Several long trails of black smoke rose from Rào, protruding like a long island into the middle of a green sea. Guns sounded in the distance. *Oh! That was an M16. And AK-47s.* I identified the type of gun after hearing the gunshots. "Napalm!" I said out loud when I saw a big flash of fire rising. After each flashing, the artillery explosions echoed like thunder after a lightning strike.

I recounted what was going on to my family.

"Be careful," Mom said. "You could get hit by a stray bullet."

"It's too far, Mạ," I replied, while my eyes were fixed on the battlefield.

"Who knows!" She was doubtful.

After my mother had realized the fighting was on the other side of the rice field, she no longer restricted me to the shelter. Still, she ordered everybody to stay inside the house and keep away from the back windows. She hoped the concrete wall would make us safer.

I heard people talking outside. "Look, look," a man shouted. "The Southern army is coming."

I opened one of the windows. The projectiles of the gunfire from the aircraft crisscrossed the hamlet horizon behind the clouds of black smoke. Even under the sunlight, I still saw the flashes here and there. With some help from the wind, I could smell some light gunpowder burning in the air and taste a little, bitter and pungent, in my mouth. To the left of my view, an armoured convoy approached the hamlet from Huế using a trail along the Lợi Nông River. The airpower had destroyed the area first, before the army marched in. I turned to look at the neighbouring houses. People were standing outside, even some on the roofs, watching the fighting like an outdoor theatre. They pointed their fingers, nodded their heads and covered their eyes from the sun's rays.

After ten minutes, tears started to swell in my eyes, and my nose started to run. I wondered whether those consequences were due to the contaminated air or the heartbreak of what I was experiencing.

All day long, the US and South Vietnam armies battered the Việt Cộng. By late afternoon, the green island had turned brown. All the bamboo trees and empty houses disappeared; only brown dirt remained. The VC sanctuary no longer existed, and I wondered what had happened to its tunnel system.

Soon after being declared a free-fire zone, the hamlet of Rào was gone. With their houses burned and their families destroyed, most local guerrillas hailing from there would become more extreme and aggressive. Some surviving guerillas from that FFZ would later take revenge—a greater revenge than people could imagine.

The war spread so quickly that I worried my hamlet would be next.

# PART 2

# *Division*

Calgary, Summer 2017

Dear Da-Lê,

You called recently and seemed shocked that so many Vietnamese refugees, particularly from my generation, would support Trump. You were wondering why there was growing division between parents and their children in the Vietnamese diaspora.

I believe it is because my generation is still living with the divisive trauma of the war that brought us here. We keep living with the past and hiding how it has wounded us. We hear what we want to hear. I know of many Vietnamese parents whose adult children no longer talk to them. Even when we do talk, there are insurmountable barriers to understanding each other's perspectives. We have differences in upbringing and life experiences. Like me, most Vietnamese who survived the war don't want to discuss it with anyone, especially their children. We don't want you exposed to the trauma and terror, or to let you experience the pain we faced.

When the Việt Cộng and the US Marines came to Dạ Lê, my childhood was cut short, and the hatred and division has germinated in my mind ever since. The effects of all the propaganda—the division and hostility—have continued long after the war, for the entire diaspora: Many older South Vietnamese outside of Vietnam have such a positive, wistful connotation for the old Southern regime. Even though the war ended over forty years ago, this cancerous nostalgia will be here to stay as long as there is no conciliation among the Vietnamese.

We came from the land of perpetual war. Some of us worship the strong leaders who defeated the Chinese invaders or chased away the French colonialists. With that mentality, we look up to whoever we believe is the strong man who can beat the Communists and bring democracy to Vietnam. In the 2016 US election, Trump might have given many older Vietnamese people in the diaspora that illusion. Or, for many in Vietnam who have lived under the Communists for so long, the image of a strongman like Putin has made him the best person to challenge the Americans and the West. I have no idea why they are against those same democratic countries where they still wish to buy homes or send their kids for education.

Today's divisions bring me back to those days during the Vietnam War. The similarity includes generational and geopolitical gaps—older hard-liners versus liberal youths, and divisions between the city and the rural folks, or between the northerners and the southerners of Vietnam. There is a lack of information inside Vietnam, and many rely on propaganda, live on lies and fake rumours and get sucked into a system of hatred. When I was growing up, there was a blur between colonialism and multilateralism: We hated the French colonialists and, thus, any of their alliances with foreigners, including America. Our love for our fatherland was powerful, but the problem was that some of us also unintentionally equated communism with it; loving the country also meant loving the Party.

Whenever I hear echoes of this love for our fatherland, I get anxious chills, as I'm transported back to my childhood living under the constant terror of war.

Da-Lê, you may know that the majority of South Vietnamese people came initially from the North.

We moved south many hundreds of years ago when the country expanded along the coast of Southeast Asia. This migration is the same phenomenon as the early movement of people from Europe to North America. The newcomers explored the new land and formed new settlements. The tension between the newcomers and the natives was comparable to that between Canadian Indigenous people and white settlers. Most pioneers were adventurous and open-minded and easily adapted to the new environment. Our accents and skin tones have changed since we began living among the Indigenous peoples—the Chạm people of the lowlands and the Montagnard, who lived in the highlands—and when the first division between the North (Đàng Ngoài) and the South (Đàng Trong) started.

This history means that we used to be colonized by China, became colonizers of the Cham and then returned to being colonized again by the French. And since the Vietnam War ended, we have been colonizing ourselves. Someone does something terrible to us, and we do the same thing to others who are weaker. This practice is not isolated to the Viet but is also in many other countries worldwide, of any size. Some do it in the name of national pride, and others in self-defence, or both.

Two hundred years after the first separation, the king of the Nguyễn dynasty in the South united the country without discrimination against the North. Instead, he encouraged the northerners to move south to help the fatherland with further southern expansion until the French came. During the French colonization, the divisions worsened. The French divided Vietnam into three colonial territories (Tonkin, Annam and Cochinchina) and ruled it under the name French Indochina. Even with all that turbulence, it was uncommon to meet any Vietnamese people living outside the country before or during the Vietnam War.

With the fall of Saigon in 1975, twenty-one years after the second separation of Vietnam (1954), the country was reunited. It was time to connect and celebrate, but why were more people than ever trying to leave the country? Nowadays, you can meet people like us in any corner of the world. Most of us are either refugees, guest labourers or their offspring—like you, Da-Lê. And just like inside Vietnam, the Vietnamese diaspora is also divided into two factions.

Da-Lê, you have asked me about the country's flags. The red flag with the yellow star that you see in all the guidebooks represents the former Democratic Republic of Vietnam in the North—or the Vietnamese Communist faction—and has been the flag of a reunited Vietnam since 1976. The yellow flag with three horizontal red lines you see in Canada and the US represents the noncommunist South Vietnam faction. The refugees brought this yellow flag with them. That is the flag that I grew up with, the flag that existed before the Vietnam War. It's the flag that was painted on the front wall of my house, and the flag that I saw on my first day of school.

In the early 1960s, at nine each morning, all students from five elementary classes in my Dạ Lê school stood in lines in the schoolyard, forming a circle with the flagpole in the middle. Once that bright yellow flag with three horizontal red stripes was raised, we sang the national anthem. Everything froze in time. On the main road, Route 1, people stopped walking and biking; they stood straight and faced the flag with their hats lowered. This ritual made me aware, even as a child, that there was something special about flag-raising. The villagers respected the new flag and national anthem. That image is the first memory that comes to my mind when I reflect on the good times I had in the village.

But that image only lives in my memory; it no longer exists in real life. Now when I see those two types of flags, I feel uneasy and sad. They remind me of the division and the war, with millions of people dying under those flags, on both sides. They remind me of the 1968 Tết Offensive in Huế, when many died in the act of raising or removing one of these flags.

Love, Ba

## CHAPTER 10

# Under Crossfire

O ur house was right on the canal that connected to the Rào water-way system and the free-fire zone. There was a small bridge and a dock at the southern edge of the property. From that vantage point, one could observe all movements from the rice field and the free-fire zone. Because of the water network and the surveillance advantages, our house had become a militarily strategic fort.

Since the raid on the FFZ took place, our property had turned into an ambush ground for the US Marines. From our backyard, the platoon could spot any Việt Cộng guerrillas who tried to sneak into the village from Rào Sanctuary. We were surrounded by a potential battlefield each night. Mom did not allow us to go near the back garden, outhouse or bushes during the day. She believed US Marines might have planted their land mines there, or that we'd step into punji traps built by VC fighters, with many sharpened bamboo sticks buried in an unmarked hole.

Roughly one night a week, the US Marines occupied the place. Their schedule was unpredictable—sometimes they came one or two nights in a row, sometimes once in two weeks. They took positions behind a row of rocks under the bamboo bushes along the property edge, waiting for Việt Cộng infiltrators from the rice field. They were quiet and patient. For some time, my family didn't even know when the Marines were coming and going. I first discovered the ritual when I stumbled upon some empty C-ration cans they had left behind. There were some newly dug foxholes along the rock structure that my dad had built along the canal.

At first, I treated it as an odd occurrence. But then after the third night, I collected some more stuff. From that time on, we were afraid to go outside after dark. Mom told us to be ready to run to the shelter once the gunfire started. Even in heavy silence, we waited. And when we slept, we were only half-asleep: One part of us was always awake and listening. But one thing we couldn't keep quiet was the baby. Whenever Vinh got itchy, he cried. My heart jumped each time he squawked, and his cries went deep into my soul and out into the dark silence.

One night, there were loud knocks at the door.

A sizable shadow darkened our front door, and a smell I had not experienced before blew in and filled the room. It was the smell of sweat, like dead skin and old warm cheese. I lit a kerosene lamp nearby and inched the door open. A giant US Marine stepped in, bending his head to enter the house. I was shaking and didn't know what was going on. *Does the soldier want us to tell the baby to be quiet? What is "quiet" in English?* I tried to remember the English words that I recently learned at school. We were all worried, but Vinh didn't care; he kept crying.

The Marine turned his back to me. A piece of barbed wire was hanging from his combat uniform. I understood. I put the oil lamp on the table to remove the wire.

"Thanks," the Marine said.

With a smile, the Marine left the house. I knew he didn't mean to harm the family. Somehow, he must have heard the baby's crying and seen a sliver of light shining through a gap in the wall from the small kerosene lamp by the bomb-shelter entrance. The Marine needed help and we were glad to give it. But even this simple action might have caused potential trouble for our family; nobody wanted to associate with either side during the night. Many eyes were watching. If one of our neighbours saw a US soldier come to the house at night, the family—especially me—would be in trouble with Việt Cộng. They would suspect me of being an informer for the CIA or the Saigon government. And if something else, like the killing of a VC, had also happened that night, I might not have survived the next day.

I examined the piece of barbed wire; it came from the fence installed under the Hamlet Strategy Program. That fence was long gone now and had been replaced by a front line of US Marines, supposedly to protect the village from VC.

Our family was lucky. Nothing else happened that night.

---

A week after, what we had feared might happen did happen. Gunfire behind the house jolted us awake. As usual, I took care of my four younger brothers while Mom guided my sister, Hạnh, and the youngest, Vinh, underground. Lanh could go alone. We all slid into the bunker as if it were an emergency escape from an airplane. Once inside, I ensured all seven of my siblings were there. I had forgotten to check more than once before, and I hated going up and looking for any of them during the gun battle.

The Marines used the roof of our shelter as a base for their machine guns. The sounds of the gunfire infiltrated the sandbags and it felt like a thousand pins penetrating my head. We sat with our heads bowed to our knees and we used both hands to plug our ears.

*Bang, bang.* The sounds of each round were so loud and close that we couldn't hear anything after a while. It was changing from thundering sounds to just some buzzing in my ears. And finally, silence. I noticed that the shelter was full of gunpowder smoke and it was a little hard to breathe.

The skirmish lasted only fifteen minutes, but it felt like hours.

The following day, my backyard looked like a battlefield. Indeed, it was—a most violent typhoon had passed through. The starfruit trees' branches and pieces of honeycomb lay all over the ground. I had no doubt that some of the bees had escaped.

When I met Old Dog later in the day, he whispered to me that the Marines had shot down two local VC guerrillas on the canal bank about a block from my house. What hit me the most was that one of the bodies was my distant nephew (even though he was much older than me). The other dead boy used to live in Hamlet 4. Our backyard was full of bullet shells. The Marines suffered no casualties.

Following that successful ambush, the Marines kept returning for weeks and months. We waited for another gun battle to break out any minute. The most dangerous time was from nine to eleven at night, when Việt Cộng slipped into the village. We waited in our beds, like cockroaches out looking for food who are ready to retreat in an instant, scurrying away to safety. The mosquito net was in bad shape, full of holes from the kids scrambling out and ripping the net in a panic. As we lay there listening under the buzz of the mosquitos, the waiting game became more intense. If this continued much longer, we might all go crazy.

Our mom was afraid that one of us might sleepwalk or go outside to pee. The outhouse was at the far end of the garden, where the heavily armed Marines were on guard. The use of that outhouse was now out of the question, even during the day. We learned that claymore mines and gas canisters had been scattered around all perimeters of any US military installation and the same for Việt Cộng areas. They also planted land mines and bamboo traps anywhere the CAP soldiers frequented. That meant our property.

Whenever my younger siblings played in the yard, Mom asked me to keep an eye on them. They would venture anywhere to retrieve their toys, regardless of the dangers. One day they were throwing a tennis ball back and forth. I knew that sooner or later, it would bounce into the bamboo bushes. Instead of watching over them, I told them to stop. They looked at me.

"Why?" Tuấn frowned.

"Because I told you so," I said.

"But Mạ told us to play," Chương, my four-year-old brother, argued.

"Play inside the house, then," I ordered. I tried to maintain a serious and firm face even though I felt sorry and sad for them.

The kids stomped back into the house and ran into each other at every turn. *They need space to play catch, just like I miss playing with the buffalo boys*, I thought. Now I could only recall distant memories of soccer matches on the rice field, or of hunting fish in the water canal. Day after day, we had to sit, just looking at the walls and listening to the silence. *I don't know why they put dangerous things around us to lock us inside our homes. Did we do anything wrong to receive this punishment?* I wondered.

We used the rice paddies as our restroom during the day and a bucket at night. Mom placed a one-gallon metal bucket in the corner next to her pallet, with the doors and windows closed all night for safety and privacy—no fresh air. The smell of wet shit and urine was unbearable, and it followed me to school. Because of that, I kept myself apart from other students. I traded my seat right behind Hương, a popular girl, for a place at the back of the classroom. At the beginning of the school year, a classmate had offered me a pack of cigarettes for the seat. Now I gave it up for free. I shrank from not only the girls but also the boys.

Living with a foul smell was still better than being shot dead in the outhouse, Mom kept telling us. And that did happen: One of my aunts had been shot dead on the rice field just before I was born.

The family prayed every night that nothing would happen: No fighting. No casualties—especially no US Marine casualties. We'd heard many rumours about the damage that US troops could inflict if any of them were killed. Some of them would get mad and shoot buffaloes, chickens or anything that moved. Then they would bring in artillery to bombard or burn everything in sight. Although that kind of rampage had not yet taken place in the village, it had come close. The raid on the Rào hamlet, a couple of kilometres from our house, was a good lesson for us. US troops had bulldozed the area along the red-dirt trail so snipers had no place to hide. If the Marines burned the hamlet, our home would be the first target. I felt sick at the thought that this scenario could happen anytime.

But nothing happened. For many months, the family lived in an anxious state of waiting, ready to escape to the bunker. No fighting. I was tired of waiting and wished they would settle it once and for all.

The guerrillas still infiltrated the village more often than not. They selected the nights that the Marines were absent. It was as if the VC and the CAP had coordinated their schedules and taken turns to "guard" the hamlet. When the Marines were there, the VC stayed away. When the VC visited the village, the CAP took a night off.

As it turned out, this wasn't a coincidence. There was a signal— something Old Dog told me about much later.

After the Marines had shot down two local guerrillas, VC recruited a village informer who lived in a house with the best view of my property. From inside the comfort of his home, he could see when the Marines came and retreated. He lit a kerosene lamp at a strategic location if there would be an ambush. The Marines couldn't see the light, but the guerrillas on the paddy could. The signal worked perfectly to save many lives—those of Việt Cộng, the Marines and my family.

## CHAPTER 11

# Tết Offensive

"*Giải phóng! Hết chiến tranh,*" the kids yelled at an early hour, just outside of our home on the second day of the 1968 Lunar New Year. "We've been liberated! No more fighting." They ran happily up and down the street while some strange Vietnamese adults strolled along with guns on their backs. My neighbours were nowhere to be seen.

I stood behind the window, looking out, still in a state of half-sleep after staying up late. I didn't know what had happened or what their shouting meant. But I heard someone call out "Liberated!" and the first thing that came to my mind was thinking about the lifestyle our village would soon have: Everyone in the village would have food to eat, tap water to drink and electricity to light their houses and streets. People would no longer be hungry and live in the dark. And most of all—no more war. A little joy flickered in my heart.

My mạ had woken up long before me. She was outside talking to the neighbours; they said Việt Cộng had taken over the village during the night. The loud bangs people had heard late at night were not firecrackers for the New Year celebration but gunfire. Some parts of Dạ Lê had been under VC control by night for a few years. Now they would be here to stay, night and day.

What troubled me most was that the fighting occurred on the first day of the Tết festival. The Tết celebration of the Lunar New Year is the most important holiday in the Vietnamese calendar. Most people believed that anything we did on the first day of the lunar year would repeat itself for the next three hundred sixty-four days. People tried to do only good deeds on that day; doing anything bad was a huge taboo. And killing was unimaginable. Thus, there was always an informal ceasefire for Tết, even during wartime. This new year's holiday was no exception, but fighting had broken out all over the South. Had it happened before midnight last night—still on the first day of the lunar year—and someone died as a result of the fighting? That would be a bad omen.

Some of the neighbours had advised my mom to bring my dad home. He was home on leave but had returned to the city the evening before, after celebrating the lunar festival and the ritual of ancestor worship with the family.

It was never safe for anyone associated with the government, like the village chief, civil servants, clerks and soldiers, to stay overnight in the village. Even older students did the same; they didn't want to take a gamble. Like these people, my dad biked into the city late in the day and would return home to our family the following day. People spent the night with relatives or friends—even with relatives of relatives, or friends of friends. Whoever they could find to stay with overnight.

The family anxiously waited for Dad to return. By ten in the morning, he was supposed to be home already. But he was not.

Later in the day, I learned from the rumours that the people in the South had had an uprising, and VC had been controlling not only Huế but also the whole South. In our village, we believed that peace had come at last. But there was no celebration, and the village was strangely silent—as if people had just disappeared.

By nightfall, Dad was still missing. I found out that nobody who had commuted into the city the night before had come home yet. His younger brother hadn't come back either. Mom was unable to keep still. She said her stomach was burning. She wanted to go to the city to look for my father and urge him to come home.

I suggested I go instead. Deep down, I wanted to do it—an adventure that I had been looking for for a long time. I convinced Mom to let me go.

"I know where Ba stays," I told her. I had accompanied him one night to a military compound of the district subdivision in Huế. We had slept in a big room—an office—on top of a desk, with several people on other desks. I guessed they were soldiers in the Saigon government army, on leave from a rural area like my father. The neon ceiling light shone directly on my face, and I wondered why they didn't turn the light off. Even though lighting the house with a flick of a switch was my dream, I craved the dimness of a kerosene lamp.

"Are you sure you want to go?" Mom asked.

"Yes, Mạ."

I went to bed and hoped for a good night's sleep to prepare for tomorrow's trip.

———

The next day, I woke up early and biked into Huế via Route 1 to find the compound where my father used to hide. I was alone on the road—no cars or traffic. An eerie feeling came over me, and I was shaking a little, but it was too late to change my mind. I must keep going. I could see many eyes looking at me from behind closed doors. They probably wondered why a young boy was wandering on the road at such an anxious time.

It took me about twenty minutes to reach Ngự Bình Road, which passed through a scenic mountain of the same name in the southern suburb of the city. Ngự Bình Mountain and Perfume River were Huế's best-known landmarks, and symbols of its beauty. I took that route to check one of our relatives' houses. My father wasn't there. I went to every place on the city's south side to find the military compound where we had stayed, but I couldn't recall the exact location. I biked around Huế—from Ngự Bình and An Cựu to Bến Ngự and Phú Cam—hoping to find my dad and uncle.

The streets were tranquil, just the *click, click* of my bike pedals and my heavy breathing as I climbed uphill. Nobody was outside. As I approached the Trường Tiền Bridge, built by Gustave Eiffel over the Perfume River, I finally saw some movement. People were in a hurry—they weren't walking around leisurely.

That was my last view of the bridge intact. Over a week later, the Communists would blow up one of its six arches to cut off any reinforcements from the SVA in the South coming across the Perfume River to the trapped troops in the Huế Imperial Citadel. From the southern side of the bridge, I saw the VC flag flying on the flagpole of the imperial palace, a symbol of Huế and a testament to a period of history associated with patriotic figures. The new rulers had replaced the South Vietnamese government's flag, reinforcing the authority change over the city.

Without stopping to eat, I kept moving all day. I had to find my father. His former comrades were returning from the North as conquerors. I worried that they would label my father a traitor for his decision to turn around and return South. My dad was now a staff sergeant assigned as the district's liaison non-commissioned officer for the SVA, which meant he was on the losing side. I worried what they might do to my father if they found him. While biking, I imagined arguing with his former comrades:

*My father is not a defector nor a traitor. He just wants to stay in the South, his home. Are South Koreans and West Germans also traitors to their country? For thousands of years, the right thing to do for us was to fight the invaders—whether French, Chinese or whoever. But now, the reality is more complicated. The Americans have not come to invade us, but to fight the Communists. Who are you to decide what is right and what is wrong?*

I tried to stop thinking about it any further.

In the early afternoon, I was hungry but kept going. I went to my cousin's residence. From the house's second floor by the An Cựu bus terminal, I could glimpse some long trails of black smoke rising into the sky on the northeastern horizon. The fighting was still going on. The cousin told me my father was hiding at the old An Định Palace, the former home of Prince Bảo Đại and his mother, Queen Từ Cung. When Prince Bảo Đại became the last king of Vietnam in 1926, he moved into the imperial palace on the north side of the Perfume River. Although he had once confessed that he would rather be a citizen of an independent country than an emperor of an enslaved one, he still enjoyed a lavish European lifestyle, earning the nickname "playboy emperor." Bảo Đại returned to the An Định Palace in August 1945 when he gave up his throne to Việt Minh. He stayed there for a short time before leaving to live in France for good.

The old palace of An Định, next to the Huế Cathedral, was deserted when I arrived. I entered through an open gate on the north side and biked along the ponds and canals, looking for someone to ask for directions. Nobody was in sight. I dismounted and carried the bike through the debris of a collapsed wall. Suddenly, someone called my name.

"Cu tý, over here." A man waved at me from behind a column.

"Uncle," I called and left my bike.

He was surprised to see me. "Someone told us there was a boy outside," my uncle said. "We didn't know it was you."

My dad was nowhere to be seen, so I asked him where he was.

"Follow me." My uncle signalled with his right hand for me to follow him. "Your father and I have been hiding here since yesterday."

We walked through the rubble and picked our way into a room at the rear of the building. Dad was talking to a middle-aged man whom I didn't know. The man left when I entered the room. My father said that he and others from the village had been hiding there.

"Don't tell anyone that," he said.

I tried to convince him and my uncle to come home, but instead, they asked me to stay with them. They worried that the Việt Cộng and South Vietnam government soldiers might already classify me as an informer because I'd left the village and wandered around Huế. That might get me a death sentence or a jail term, depending on which side got hold of me first. I told them I must go back. My uncle asked for my wallet. I wondered why he needed it, but I handed it over anyway. After my uncle had taken all the pictures of him and my father from my wallet, he returned the rest. This severing of ties between us cut me to the quick, but I understood the need for precautions. There was no kinship when it came to survival.

My dad and uncle didn't want to go home, where they would inevitably have to surrender, so I returned alone. But I was happy that they were alright.

---

"Stop!"

"Stop there!"

The shouting came from the government soldiers at the Lê Lai army camp gate on my way back to the village. I almost fell off my bike.

I couldn't believe that a transportation unit of the SVA was still intact and guarding this section of Route 1. This is how I knew that the total uprising had not taken place after all.

"Bomb, Bomb! He's carrying a bomb!" the gate guard shouted and pointed at me.

I was shaking and I felt the sweat running down my back. *What bomb? I don't have any.*

"Put your hands up!"

I raised both hands above my head. The bike leaned on my hip.

"Now, move slowly away from that bike."

I followed the instructions.

*Crack!*

All the soldiers dropped to the ground and rolled away to hide.

But nothing happened.

It was just the sound of my bike falling on the pavement.

One of the men stood up. *Click, click.* He adjusted the trigger and put his handgun to my head.

I felt cold metal on my left temple, right on the black scar.

"What're you carrying?"

"Nothing," I said in a shaky voice.

"What's in the bike carrier?" the soldier asked.

Oh! My father had given me a pack of French biscuits to share with my siblings, and I had eaten some to control my hunger. "A package of biscuits, sir."

A soldier approached the bike to have a closer look. They soon realized there was no bomb and let me go. I was so lucky—they could have shot first and asked questions later. From a distance, the package did look like a block of TNT, a powerful explosive commonly used to destroy bridges. Most of the bridges in the South were gone because of that.

On the way back, the road conditions on Route 1 were not the same as they had been that morning. A couple of blockades had appeared in the middle of the road to prevent vehicles from passing, and I had to make some detours on village roads. From the curve of the trail leading to my house, I could sense the black silhouette of my mother appearing behind its window. I dismounted and left the bike against the front door. My mother pulled me inside the house. Once we were in the kitchen, she whispered just loud enough for me to hear, "Did you see your father?"

I told my mother that my dad and my uncle were safe in the city and that they were not coming back. I could see the worry on her face dissipate.

"You must be hungry," she said. I looked at the kitchen table; food was waiting for me, making me remember the package of biscuits. I returned to my bike, but the cookies had already disappeared. The cookies had been distributed among my siblings.

Later that night, two Việt Cộng came to the house. They asked whether Mom had communicated with Dad and told her that she should urge him to return home. She explained that I had been in Huế the whole day looking for him, with no luck. "As soon as we find him," she promised, "we will convince him to return." I doubted they believed her.

---

The following afternoon, Anh Hai appeared in the house. I was not surprised.

Hai was a lieutenant in the SVA and had requested to be on the front lines. VC said he became an enemy of the people, the kind that should be eliminated first.

He went out with O Lan on the first night of the Lunar New Year. After the fighting broke out, Anh Hai ended up staying in the village. At first, he was at her house, but he left because the house was so busy, with many people entering and exiting.

At the time, we were still under a ceasefire. But even if we weren't, he wouldn't have cared. He was rarely on leave, but when he was, he stayed in the village whenever he wanted, instead of retreating to the city at night, like everyone else. Nobody knew or expected that, so it was hard to believe he stayed in the village overnight. But he had done it again, and he might be in a mess this time.

One day, he'd said to me, "If anyone wants to get me, they must pay a hefty price." I admired his confidence and rebelliousness, and his attitude affected my views on life and war. As a child, I was drawn to adventurous or dangerous missions. I was different from my siblings, who just wanted to stay home. And my outgoing personality frequently gave my mother heart palpitations.

Hai stood behind the door of the lean-to kitchen. He asked the family not to tell anyone he was in the house, and my mom asked him why.

"I don't believe them, the newcomers." He looked at her and shook his head.

"They said, 'The war is over.' Sooner or later, it would be best if you went to report to the new government," she told him.

"I'd rather kill myself than surrender," he said firmly.

"Don't say that." She stared at him, wide-eyed.

"Don't worry," he said. "I will wait to see what's going on before deciding what to do next."

"Does Lan know you're here?"

"She does. But I don't think she will turn me in."

"Don't be sure about that." My mom shook her head. She sat on the floor, looking up at him. "Is she a spy?"

"We have never talked about the fighting, or about politics."

My mother turned to me. "You go be a lookout by the front door," she whispered in my ear, "and wave your hand behind you if someone comes in the gate. But don't look back."

"Okay," I said, and left for the front door. I sat on the top step to look out, but I could still listen to the conversation.

"Do you know that her father has returned from the North and stays somewhere in the village?"

"I know," he nodded.

"But why do you still date and trust her?"

"I've dated her for a few years—I know her well."

"She was here last night asking for your uncle!"

"That's her job: to go around and ask for the people she knows. The VC take advantage of her because they know she's a well-liked and trusted person in the hamlet."

"You mean her father?"

"Whoever looks after this kind of thing."

"I should let you know she did look up in the direction of the attic when she was here last night," Mom said.

Hai had no answer. He just stood there silently, thinking.

## CHAPTER 12

# Forced Labour

Night had fallen on the village. It was the third night after my adventure into the city, looking for my father and asking him to surrender.

My siblings and I sat quietly, anxiously watching Mom prepare dinner under the light of a kerosene lamp in the east corner of our front yard. She used dry rice stalks to feed the open flame, and the stuff burned fast. She kept feeding the fire, producing a lot of smoke and many small burning pieces flying in the dark, like colourful butterflies playing. No mosquito could come near us under such smoke.

She was frying several slices of *bánh tét*—a sweet rice cake inside a banana leaf. This type of food, which we used for the Tết festival, came in the shape of a circle (*bánh tét* in the South) or a square (*bánh chưng* in the North). Both symbolize perfection and wellness, and they are offered to our ancestors on the first day of the Lunar New Year. Each household in the hamlet had prepared a big pot for consumption for a week or two during the festival. We kids had already eaten them for the whole week without seeing any good fortune—only adversity—and now we were fed up with these symbolic foods.

"You all are lucky. You have something to eat. Many people wish to have some, but they don't." Mom looked at us. Our faces must have indicated what we really thought about the food.

Suddenly, the front gate opened, and Thai, a former buffalo boy who was now a contact person of the newly liberated government, and a replacement for Mr. Alo, entered the yard and approached Mom. He whispered into her right ear. Despite the growing darkness, I could see her face turn pale.

"What's wrong?" I asked.

"I have to go to a special meeting right away." She looked at me. "You continue the cooking." She followed Thai out of the gate.

Once outside, she said, "Have your meal. Don't wait for me."

After we finished eating, I brought my siblings back into the house to wait for Mom to return. It felt just like when she had been in labour. Each time, we all sat by the door and longed for the local midwife to come out of the delivery room and say "*mẹ tròn con vuông*" (literally, "circle mother and square baby"), an idiom that means that both were alright. But today, there was no midwife.

We all looked at the front door, waiting for it to open and for our mom to step in. But it was a silent doorway.

"I have a bad feeling," said my younger brother Lanh. "Is this because of Dad refusing to go home?"

"Let's hope not," I said.

"Or is Anh Hai hiding in the house?"

I didn't want to think about it. I walked around the room and then stood by the door. I sat and lay down on the floor. We stared at each other. Even though we did not have clocks or watches, we kept up with the time. My younger siblings were like nature's clock: I knew time had passed when they grew hungry, or when they cried. First, the youngest started to whimper—the kids were hungry. After they ate, they lay down, and finally, they all slept on the floor. Neither Lanh nor I bothered to carry them to our shared pallet bed.

It felt like the meeting was going on forever.

It was late; the flame had long since gone out, and the makeshift oven had turned completely cold.

———————

At last, the rear door opened, and Mom appeared. Her face looked sad and worried, and we quickly surrounded her.

She said that Việt Cộng had ordered each family in the hamlet to contribute the equivalent of forty cans of rice and some labour for undisclosed missions. She was worried about who would carry those missions out.

The local Việt Cộng organization again pressed our mom about when our dad would get home. They were calling for him to come back and surrender. Three men from our hamlet had just returned home from hiding in Huế. They had returned home after their family convinced them; I had tried but failed. I hoped those three men hadn't seen me there with my dad, or even if they had, that they wouldn't say anything. That would protect our lies. The returnees were not government soldiers, but a village civil servant and two low-ranking clerks—one of them used to be my preschool teacher, Chú Han.

Because my father hadn't come out of hiding, not only the local VC but also some of the neighbours were now treating my family with suspicion and hostility. The atmosphere became more oppressive each day. Everywhere we went, people avoided us. No one liked to talk to any of our family members. The neighbourliness that we had built for so many years just disappeared overnight. Not only would people have nothing to do with us, but they watched our every move.

Because of the distrust, we had to do whatever the local VC organization ordered. So when it asked each family to contribute food and labour, as the oldest son in the family I accepted the task so that Mom could stay home. That was a better scenario. Since Dad was no longer with us, Mom must be the one to look after the kids, and I knew I had to be the one to go. I became the man of the house at fourteen. Nobody knew what would happen had the family declined the order; we wouldn't want to take that risk. Part of me saw the mission as an adventure and a challenge. *I am going to explore an unknown place. Will that be exciting? Yes, it will. On the rice paddy? I don't mind. In the jungle? I haven't been there. And at night?* That was what I had dreamed of. But I kept that thought and excitement to myself. After I asked to go, I knew she wouldn't have any peace of mind, and that she wouldn't be able to sleep later. At dinner, she had urged me to have more food; that was the Vietnamese way of saying she loved me very much. She handed me a second bowl of rice.

"I don't need that much, Mạ," I said, putting half of the portion back.

"Be careful and look out for yourself." She looked into my eyes. "You're too young for this kind of thing."

"Mạ! You worry too much. I'll be okay," I assured her.

The next day, Mom collected all the family's rice and even borrowed more from the relatives to make the ration. She used an old condensed milk can as the rice unit for measurement, a common practice in the village. She poured the rice into a bag she had sewed that afternoon from a burlap sack, tying the rice bag at both ends with a rattan rope. That would be my backpack for tonight.

I put on an extra layer of clothes and then repaired my tire sandals, ensuring they could survive the long trek ahead. Outside, Thai paced back and forth, shouting, "Hurry up! Hurry up! Go to the ancestral family chapel at once!"

I arranged the rice bag on my back and headed to the ancestral clan house. As a practice in the Vietnam War, any new occupier would select a school, a temple, a church or a community house as its makeshift base.

Bright stars sparkled above the landscape of rice paddies and reflected on the irrigation canal. The water was still. A group of villagers had already gathered at the shrine, all talking in low voices. They were people from my hamlet, and I knew them all. Some leaned against the wall, and others sat on the floor, waiting for further instruction. There were also a couple of girls, a few years my senior, whom I used to play with when we were children. I was the youngest person there.

After receiving the signal to hit the road, we marched in a single file. I didn't know what to expect from that first journey. I had no idea where we were going or how long we'd walk. I just followed the person in front of me and knew we were heading west, an uphill hike, and not east to the free-fire zone. From the houses along the route, people looked out at the caravan. Even in the dark, I could see their movements under the dim light of a small kerosene lamp on each of their altars, which must light up for the first few weeks during the Tết festival.

After several minutes of walking, we crossed Route 1 and then passed the railroad tracks where the bombs had exploded fourteen years ago, three days after I had been born. I unconsciously touched the black tattoo on my face and reimagined my mother's tale of my first escape, when I was just three days old.

The caravan climbed the rocky road up the hill behind the village pagoda. I heard a Zippo lighter open and then a click. A light came up. Someone in front of me was having a cigarette. Nobody said anything. I, too, felt the urge to smoke, but I did not dare light one. Would such a spark put our lives in danger as a bomb target? I was surprised that the guerrilla, our guide, said nothing. So, smoking was allowed after all.

To me, this confirmed that the war was no longer here; liberation had come to the village. There would be no more Marines and government soldiers on patrol each night. But I had thought otherwise because of the biscuit incident a few days earlier.

After a half-hour walk, we left the residential area and entered an open space, an enormous graveyard. At the boundary, I faced several Việt Cộng guerrillas. What surprised me the most was that one of them was my former classmate Long, from the hamlet of Rào. Long was thinner and taller than I remembered. Studying under Uncle Dong had been the last time we saw each other. He was the son of the village official gunned down a year earlier by a local Việt Cộng. Now, Long had become one himself! He wore black pyjamas with a pair of tire slippers and carried an AK-47 on his shoulder. I wondered whether he'd joined the organization before or after the assassination of his father. How did he react to the news at the time? Had I not seen all of this unfold with my own eyes, I might not have believed it. But this was not the first abduction in the village. Old Dog had told me about other killings. In one case, a son had asked to meet his father, a low-rank village officer, and then he executed him on the spot. But that young guy was somebody I hadn't been acquainted with, unlike Long, who was a close friend and a distant cousin.

Understanding the complexity of the family relationships during the war was like looking through the mist of the Perfume River. It blurred my vision and wet my eyes, unsure of what I saw and what to believe in anymore. Preoccupied with my thoughts, I passed Long without saying hello.

As the night went on, I was more surprised at the exposure of the local guerrillas out in the open. They were mainly my former classmates who had failed the middle school entrance exam. But they couldn't stay home, and they couldn't leave the house to work. They would become the target of suspicion on both sides if they did. Now, they must feel safe enough not to bother covering their faces. *Will they trust or have confidence in an old classmate like me? The one who has ventured into the city? The one whose father is a South Vietnam government soldier? If the offensive fails, will they assume that I'll tell on them? What will they do with me then?*

We came to a village of ghosts, or *làng ma*. Not a living soul. Not a single sound. Entering the graveyard, I felt a chill as if someone was blowing cold air on the back of my neck. This was a place where I would never walk alone at night. That eerie feeling was getting stronger and stronger as I walked through tomb after tomb. It was not uncommon for some people in Huế to try to compete with each other when building their ancestral graves. The bigger, the better: Some of them were huge, like temples. They even cost more than their own houses. But looking at these structures, all I felt was pity: pity for the living who believed they had sacrificed so much to elevate the spirit of the departed in the underworld. I really didn't know whether people did that to show off their wealth to living souls or to demonstrate their love of their ancestors.

Looking at the tombs around me, my mind wandered. *This village of the dead is only for the accounted-for ones. Some spirits leave the earthly world but have no home to return to; they wander around the village roads. They hang under the branches of the giant banyan tree. They lie on rough rocks. They cry. They laugh. They stand. They float. They scare the weak. They are everywhere but inside the homes of the living souls. Some of them used to be rich, and some were once poor. They came from different ethnicities and races, due to many wars on the land. But every spirit is the same, homeless and bodiless. They have nothing. The Huế's area is jam-packed with more wandering spirits than human beings. The dead are more crowded than ever and will be more overcrowded still, as more lives are cut short.*

Once we reached the far side of the cemetery, I saw an area of bright lights several blocks away on my left. Electricity hadn't yet come to the village, but there was now a jungle of electrical lights within the village boundary in Hamlet 5, where my paternal grandmother had taken me to visit her childhood home. I remembered the hills near her house were full of *trái sim* (wild blueberries). I loved those and spent most of the visiting time picking them. The US Army had confiscated the property when it took over the land to build Camp Eagle. The Saigon government compensated families with a symbolic amount to move their houses and ancestral graves away from the property.

The Americans sprayed the chemical defoliant on the entire area around the camp perimeter to get rid of vegetation. And the wild blueberries and those rolling hills were already gone.

That village of lights was Camp Eagle.

*So, this is Camp Eagle*, I realized. It was still here! Nothing had changed.

The night was quiet. No searchlights were shooting up to illuminate the dark ground around the base's perimeter to detect penetrators. The caravan did not stop or even slow down when we passed by Camp Eagle, as if it didn't exist. Some people kept smoking. The Americans might have been aware of our passing, but they didn't care either. That made me wonder whether the US had kept quiet and let Việt Cộng and the North take over the South, or at least Huế. Was this a trap?

The group left the open hills of Camp Eagle and came to a ravine traversed by a long bridge made of small tree trunks and rods. What I saw was a black hole—no bottom in sight—even under the light of the new crescent moon and stars. Far below, the faint sounds of a stream. I wondered what the bridge looked like in the daytime and what would happen if it broke when I was on it. My legs started to wobble. The man behind told me to relax and look ahead, not down, while slowly dragging my feet on the foot bar and holding tight to the hand rod. I followed the advice, concentrating on the black dot in front while feeling my way across, step by step.

After passing the ravines, we stopped for a break, and I had my first smoke of the night. We were in a dense forest. *Was this the place we called Lụ, where the villagers once came to cut trees or gather deadwood and herbs for sale at the market?* A few years back, it was not unusual for villagers to report an elephant or wild pig rampaging their vegetable gardens here. This side of the village—a hilly region to the west and near the woods—had been inhabited by wild animals, so I wondered, *Where are they now?* When I was about five or six years old, a tiger had killed an herb picker, and for a time, no villager was courageous enough to go into the woods.

Finally, a young man named Nhi went into Lụ himself. For several days, he waited for the tiger to come. He was patient and fearless, and in the end, he killed the beast. Nhi brought the dead animal back to the *đình*, the village's communal temple, for display. One of the tiger's ears had three scars. People muttered that it had killed three people—one mark for each. Thousands of people visited the đình to see that tiger and meet Mr. Nhi, who instantly became the village hero and our idol.

But that way of life was long gone. Now, nobody dared to come here; they were afraid of triggering a land mine, getting caught in the crossfire or walking in the rain of the Agent Orange spray. I thought of wild animals—here was their home—and wondered whether they would survive the bombing, and the Agent Orange.

The forest had supported the villagers for a long time. People used wood for building houses, deadwood for cooking and herbs for drinks or medicine. Mom bought those dry herbs in the village market for resale in Huế's suburbs for a small profit. The most precious medicinal plant was a species of jasmine, *Jasminum subtriplinerve*, known as *lá vằng*. *Lá* means "leaf," and *vằng* refers to the healing herbs of the forest. The villagers used *lá vằng* to make tea for a new mother. Postpartum, Mom had to drink only *lá vằng* tea; no other drink was allowed after each delivery. She had already done that eight times. Thanks to the medicinal *lá vằng*, she was still strong enough to walk thirty kilometres a day, carrying goods for sale.

*Lá vằng* was also associated with the Basilica of Our Lady of La Vang in the province of Quảng Trị, about seventy kilometres to the north of Dạ Lê. According to a legend, many Catholics took refuge in the woods of Quảng Trị Province, north of Huế, in 1798 when the Huế imperial court persecuted them because of their faith. While hiding in the jungle, many became ill and started to pray to the rosary. One night, a lady appeared above the *lá vằng* bushes, wearing the traditional Vietnamese *áo dài* dress and holding a child in her arms. The lady told them to boil leaves from those shrubs and drink the medicine. As a result, the refugee villagers survived the ordeal.

My mind was wandering, but the guide signalled to walk on, as the group still had a long way to go. The rice bag cut into my right shoulder, and I shifted it to the left. In the thick forest, it was too dark to see anything a few feet away. Gauging by the thickness of the canopy, Agent Orange hadn't yet caused any damage. Maybe the rains in the previous fall had washed some of the chemicals away. Although I could find no evidence of destruction at night, the daytime might have told a different story.

Walking through the canopy, I felt the humidity, the hotness and the smell of dead leaves. It reminded me of the steaming pot of boiling herbs my mom would make each time I got sick as a kid. She would use the pot to create a sauna effect for us under a blanket.

From time to time, cannon shots would break the silence of the night, a long distance away. Suddenly, the group heard the smooth sound of mortar flying nearby, a low-pitched *whump*. A few of us, including me, ran for cover in the dark and then rolled downhill to lower ground while the rest kept walking. Afterward, I learned from one of my walking companions that most villagers could tell how far away a mortar would land from its sound. The sound we had heard was a mortar passing us by—nothing to worry about. It made a resounding *thump* sound if you were close to where it'd land. Anyway, if you heard it, you knew you were still alive.

A short time later, I heard people talking in a foreign language—a different dialect—and I couldn't make out anything. *Are we already in Laos territory?* I wondered. *That can't be possible. From the village to the international Laos border is about forty kilometres. We haven't walked that far—maybe halfway,* I thought. Or close to the Hồ Chí Minh Trail? It couldn't be. Anh Hai said the trail was not inside Vietnam but in Laos territory. The voices became louder and louder, but I still couldn't understand a single word. I guessed they must be Montagnard, the highland Indigenous people.

I walked down two flights of dirt stairs and edged my way along a dirt wall. It was a cave or tunnel; I couldn't tell which. "Drop your rice bags here," someone said, directing us to an adjacent room where the group received guns, grenade boxes and ammunition cases. He instructed us to bring the weapons home. Because I was the youngest person in the group, I carried only the rifles back to the village.

We returned along the same trail, but the load was heavier than before. Again, I had to cross that unstable bridge on shaky legs.

At daybreak, we were back where we had started the night before. We unloaded all the items at the clan house's hall, and someone would deliver them in small boats to Rào, the free-fire zone, on the other side of the rice field. I didn't care. I was hungry and tired and wanted to go home. An all-night-long walk with nothing for my hungry stomach was more than enough.

I didn't want to wake the family up at that early hour, so I entered the house through the add-on, where I could open the door from the outside by simultaneously lifting and pulling it—all other doors were locked from the inside by a crossbar. I tiptoed on eggshells to the living area and was speechless to see Mom sleeping while sitting upright by the front door. I touched her shoulder.

"Mạ, are you sleeping?"

"Oh, *con*—my son. You've come back," she shouted for joy. "Are you alright? I waited to open the door for you, but I must have fallen asleep. How did *con* get in?" Mom kept asking.

"I'm fine, Mạ," I said. "I got in through the lean-to kitchen door. Has Mạ waited for *con* all night long?"

Without answering, she went into the lean-to to prepare food for me. All my tiredness just disappeared, and I felt safe.

## CHAPTER 13

# The Front Lines

The local Việt Cộng kept telling us that if Dad didn't come home soon, our family would be in danger. But we knew Dad had made up his mind.

At that difficult time, Chị Mau returned to the village after a year-long absence. As a local guerrilla, she came to see the family. I was not home at the time. Even though she did ask my mom about me, I felt she was trying to avoid me. But perhaps that was alright, since I did not want to meet her either. I was afraid that she would ask me to join her.

"Auntie," she asked Mom, "where is Uncle?"

"Your uncle hasn't come home yet," Mom said, looking worried.

To relieve some of the pressure from the local VC, Mom asked her niece to accompany her to Huế to see her two uncles. She reasoned that Chị Mau's organization would believe her because she was one of them. She wanted her niece to verify that we did try our best. Chị Mau agreed to go with her aunt. They walked for an hour from the village to Huế, where my dad was staying. As a local guerrilla, Chị Mau knew all the checkpoints on Route 1, so they had no problem getting through.

The girl convinced her uncles to come home. She promised she'd do anything to protect them, as they'd done for her. Dad's younger brother said he would follow what his older brother decided. Dad told her they'd come home in a month or so. They were biding their time, waiting to see if the government could regain control of Route 1. Both still followed the news from the BBC radio broadcast, so they knew the war from the outside, not the rumours or fake news, as the people in the village did. Mom and her niece returned home alone, just the two of them. We didn't know what Chị Mau had said to her organization, but Việt Cộng eased up on the family. However, the pressure was still there.

Most of the villagers believed that the war was over. At the same time, I felt something was not right. Even though Việt Cộng occupied Huế and the surrounding area, the Phú Bài base and the government army camp near An Cựu were still intact. Most of all, Camp Eagle, located in Hamlet 5 of the village, was still there, like a giant tiger at rest.

The Americans, if they wanted to, could fly their Cobras anywhere. Whenever I saw them approaching in the distance, I preferred to keep out of their sight. A few months earlier, one of them caught me using a small sampan boat as an outdoor toilet. I had no place to run. I was behind a tall bush so that nobody could see me from the village, but I couldn't hide from the sky. Soldiers fired at me from a helicopter, like hunters shooting at their prey. Splashes of water encircled the boat and showered my face and body. I jumped into the water full of my feces and dove under a cloud of water hyacinth. I still wonder whether they intended to kill me or make fun of me. Of course, I was lucky. Some farmers had died on the rice field because of such a shooting. Even though I eventually got out of the water safely, my heart still pumped faster and heavier than the norm.

Each of those choppers was deadly. It could shoot you without any provocation or reason. At times like that, the best solution was to run for cover.

There was no liberation going on. The shoeless peasants had only rumours, but they believed them. They didn't realize that the US Marines, 101st Airborne Division and South Vietnam Army had stayed put around the village, and that the people should brace for more fighting to come.

———————————

A few nights after I had marched into the jungle with the rice supply and brought ammunition back to the village, I again went out for another adventure at night. I followed the villagers with a pickaxe on my shoulder and a curved machete in my right hand. The work took place in the dark, but tonight was not that dark. I could see my hands. I wasn't going to kill anybody: The new authorities had ordered us to demolish the pavement of Route 1 and to erect some road blockades on it. The purpose was to cut off any reinforcements from the Phú Bài base or the South Vietnam government to the trapped troops in Huế. Việt Cộng wanted to isolate the city from the rest of the country, and Dạ Lê was at the front lines. The detonation of one of the Trường Tiền bridge arches across the Perfume River in Huế was also part of the same plan.

Although I had seen several blockades when I returned to the village from Huế less than a week prior, I didn't know what to expect. One part of me believed it was a sort of adventure, while the other thought it was not up to me, a feeling of guilt. *Don't blame me*, I whispered.

Many things raced through my mind. The French built Route 1 during the colonial era long before my time. It guided me to school every day. I remembered the first time I'd gotten out of the village—beyond the bamboo hedges. Everything was new and exciting. My childhood dreams. An adventure. I took a bus with Anh Hai to Huế. The trip was like I had imagined it, whenever I watched those buses pass by the village. Everything from houses and trees to people and buffaloes kept moving past the bus window. My playmates and class-mates walked along the roadside and saw me waving. When the bus passed by the pagoda hill, I saw Old Dog and the gang looking after a herd of water buffaloes. They looked up and saw me waving at them. Old Dog pointed at the bus and called to friends, "Look. Look. Cu tý on the bus." They all looked at me while the bus kept moving, leaving them behind. They got smaller and finally disappeared in the distance.

Not long ago, I had stood at the roadside and waved to then presi-dent Diệm on his way to visit his family in Huế. Villagers used to call him Uncle Diệm. The gang and I would have dropped everything and rushed to greet Uncle each time his convoy passed Route 1 from the airport to his house.

Because of this road, Mom could bring and sell goods in the city. Now, I would destroy the road and in doing so, erase some of these memories—my past and my childhood. Could I do that? I was unsure. My vision blurred, and I tasted bitterness in my mouth when I struck the surface that Mom's bare feet had imprinted. The farmer tool I brought was no match for the hard asphalt, and my hands and wrists ached with each impact. I had not done that type of work ever in my life. The villagers had a name for the type of person I was: *đứa học trò*, or a student who was not expected to do any hard work, but to just read a book.

The pickaxe cracked after several strikes, so I stood on the road-side and looked at the shadows. The villagers worked in silence, and the sounds of metal striking asphalt were loud. It delighted me—I felt the vibrations and wondered how far they could transmit, like music, on a silent night. Each time the tools hit the road surface, tiny sparks flew up in curves like fireflies playing hide-and-seek under the dark sky.

I climbed up the hill to help carry tree trunks for the blockade. While climbing, I saw a couple of the local Việt Cộng. One of them,

Lai, was my former classmate. Lai was one of the best students—I had envied his intelligence. He was the one who taught me how to build a bamboo machine gun.

On his shoulder was not a bamboo machine gun but an AK-47, a real one. It could kill over a dozen people in a minute. As I passed him, I said hello. He looked at me with a cold expression, as though we were strangers. We had last seen each other a few months prior. Lai looked a little paler and was acting more mature than his age. I knew that Lai, like me, liked guns. I wondered whether one of the reasons he joined Việt Cộng was to own that deadly machine gun.

Suddenly, I heard the noise of flying artillery heading toward us, a whizzing sound. *Whizz ... whizz ...*

I could tell that the mortar was going to drop nearby. I rolled down into the ditch along the roadside, landing in a thorn bush, yet I didn't feel a thing. Protected by the shrubs, I settled into the side of the ditch. Lots more artillery fire followed, explosion after explosion. The earth trembled beneath my back and my ears rang. I thought of our family; I thought about how I might not get home that night. The bombardment seemed to last forever.

When the explosions paused, I was unsure if I was still alive. I felt some pinching on my shoulders and back. *Have I been injured? Hit by shrapnel?* I tried to ignore the pain. Once the thundering artillery restarted, the pain disappeared. I had been so lucky—the first artillery shell hadn't exploded when it hit the ground. If it had, most of the labourers and I might not have survived.

I went home without any tools; I left them behind. Mom was waiting behind the door with a kerosene lamp in her hand.

"Are you alright?" she asked.

I smiled. "Yes, I'm okay, Mạ."

She looked at my right arm.

"Oh, you're injured!" she screamed.

I looked down. There were some black spots on my shirt. Blood and some thorns were sticking on my right arm and back. My mom pulled them one by one out. It hurt, but thorns in your body are much better than shrapnel from exploded cannons. She anointed the wounds with oil. I could feel her relief, as if she had just lifted a big rock that had been crushing her.

---

I went to bed, but sleep didn't come. And when it came, it was cut short. I was jolted awake in the early hours of the morning by an explosion. Later that morning, the news came that two of my distant cousins, Du and Một, had died. A land mine had blown them up when they'd tried to remove one of the road barriers. The US Marines had made some villagers clear them in the early morning before any army convoy came. Villagers put the blockade up. Villagers removed it. Villagers died.

The victims this time were around my age—in a few months, they would have been fifteen—and two of them were the only child of my second uncles. I felt even more depressed and confused over whether I would still be alive tomorrow. If I were killed as my cousins had been, I would be just one more victim in the crossfire. My dreams of higher education and world travels had vanished. For now, my desire, if any, was simply to survive—to exist another day.

CHAPTER 14

# Bombardment

Ten days after the 1968 Tết Offensive, the fighting intensified.

The roadblock plan didn't work. The US Marines and the South Vietnam Army (SVA) took over Route 1 during the day. Military convoy after military convoy passed through the village on their way to Huế. Their goal was to reinforce the trapped units of the SVA and take back the city.

The fighting restarted. Villagers could hear the gun sounds if they concentrated hard on listening.

Once the roadblock on Route 1 had been opened, several small groups of refugees also appeared, passing through the hamlet. They were mainly children, mothers and old people from Huế who were temporarily staying at the Buddhist temple.

The refugees gave us many tales of things taking place in Huế.

One man said a group of young men from his ward had come to his house with a list. His son's name was on that list, since the son was a government army officer. They'd taken the son away along with some of his neighbours. His wife asked the group to visit her son, but they refused. Ever since she heard people talking about possible executions, she had become despondent. Another man said everyone must stay in their homes. All the streets were empty. The SVA had returned, and fighting had broken out here and there. They said when the airplanes started to bomb the city, people ran—they just ran without knowing what would be ahead. The only thing on their mind was staying alive, and going south was a safer route. *Yes. Go south.* I kept wondering why no one wanted to run north to the other side. Even without knowing where they were headed, they just walked and walked, always heading south. They didn't know where they would sleep for the night. Their kids asked where they were going.

"We go to a safer place, with no war," was all they could say in response.

Like most kids in the hamlet, the displaced children had also gotten new dresses and *li xì* money for the Tết festival, but they must have hidden, with their new gifts and clothing, in their bunkers the very next day. They had no time to enjoy themselves. And now they were refugees, walking as they thought about those left-behind gifts.

The refugees realized the fighting had expanded and kept moving on, further south.

*How many lists do they have?* I wondered. *Is there one for each ward or each hamlet? If so, my dad's name should be on one of them.* Even though he hadn't yet returned, three others had.

Once the returnees were back in the hamlet, they reported to the local rebel committee. They were told to go home and stay there for further instruction, a kind of house arrest.

But Anh Hai gave a different opinion. He told Mom she should not trust the new authorities. It was just a trap. This time, none of the returnees were being executed, but some refugees had heard of this happening in Huế. One said he saw a makeshift court martial in his neighbourhood school.

"Don't ask your husband to return yet. I think he is safer there than here," Anh Hai reasoned to my mom.

"So what should you do then? Your name may be on this hamlet's list," she said.

Anh Hai said he was thinking of disguising himself and fleeing to Route 1, then finding a way to rejoin his unit. He must have heard the gunfights, and overheard me talking about the refugees we'd seen.

"No. That's too dangerous. You should remain here for a few more days," Mom disagreed.

But that night, Anh Hai left the hideout and disappeared without a trace.

———————

The hamlet had now become a free-fire zone when sharpshooters from the nearby houses along Route 1 had started to target the US military vehicles. Crossfire and bombings were more frequent. Mom had us all retreat into the underground bunker.

Nine of us packed into that L-shaped bomb shelter, three square metres in area, like sardines in a can. Its walls and floor were moist soil. Inside was dark with high humidity all day and night, even with a sliver of light shining through the small kerosene lamp at the bunker's entry. The young kids tossed and turned all night. They seemed to sense the seriousness of the situation and kept quiet during the night, except for Vinh. He cried anytime he wanted; he didn't care when. With the rash on his scalp, he couldn't do anything except cry. Mom covered both his hands with thick but soft cloths to prevent him from hurting himself. His cry was loud and desperate in the middle of the night, enhanced by the echoes from the bunker's walls, making my heart jump faster. I felt the same itching he was experiencing, and if possible, I wished it were me instead of him. In this dark fantasy, I would scratch as much as I could so the itch would no longer be there, scratching until all the itch-infested blood came out of my body and there was no more poison left.

We hardly went anywhere except to come up for food, fresh air or the washroom. To entertain us, Mom related stories about the time she and Dad met or when we were born. Of course, the story of the French colonists' raid of the village three days after I was born was her highlight. She had many other tales about how she delivered each of us, like my sister Hạnh, who was born while Mom was heading out to sell her wares, or my brother Lanh, who arrived without a midwife. When I wasn't pacing inside the empty house to release the tension and numbness in my legs, I took turns telling jokes or old Vietnamese myths.

The temperature within the bunker wasn't that hot—a little uncomfortable, but manageable. Dạ Lê had two seasons: monsoon and drought. The weather in February was dry and mostly sunny, but cool. The daytime temperature was about seventeen degrees Celsius.

The siege had been going on for over two weeks, and we had spent about ten days and nights underground, to the point we lost track of time.

People in the hamlet were desperate for food and faced starvation in the late stage of the siege. No one expected this to happen to us, living next to the rice paddy. But since we had carried our contribution to the VC rice reserve deep in the jungle two weeks earlier, we had less food than usual in the house. My mouth was full of saliva each time I remembered *bánh tét*, the festival food I had been tired of eating a few weeks ago. Now I wished I could have even a single slice.

Without rice, our family lived on garden produce—a couple of giant pumpkins and squashes—that my grandma had reserved for a rainy day. She'd covered their stalks with white lime liquid and stored them in a cold dark room. She said a combination of the lime, coolness and darkness could delay them from rotting for a year. After the family consumed those reserved fruits, we foraged for edibles in the garden. We ate the soft inner part of the banana stem, reserved for pigs.

It was low in nutrients but kept our hunger in check. Banana trees were abundant around the house. We also picked vegetables and dug up some yams left behind in the garden. We were not concerned about the land mines anymore. That was how we'd fought back the hunger, day after day.

One day, the first daytime raid came to the hamlet, catching the villagers by surprise. The strikes had typically occurred at night when people had already settled inside the bomb shelter. But this time it was early morning, and the artillery came without warning, when some people in the hamlet were out looking for food. As soon as I heard a flying cannonball overhead—that same whizzing sound—I dove for the bunker. But it was too late for me.

*Boom!*

The pressure of that explosion pushed me down. I fell onto the dark and watery dirt floor near the bunker entry. *Too close to my home. Did it hit my neighbours' houses?* Without further thinking, I plunged into the shelter. The rest of my family members were still there; they hadn't left the bunker yet.

Explosion after explosion, the ground above and around us shook as if in revenge for something we had done wrong. Someone was angry. Very angry. Some of the explosions were so close it seemed they would blow the bunker apart any minute. The children were all in a panic. The smaller kids screamed and held tight to the older ones, who covered their ears and kept quiet. "Pray. Pray to Buddha. Pray to Guan Yin," Mom kept saying, while many thoughts raced through my mind. *Is this attack in retaliation against those snipers, guerrillas or VCs—whatever we call them—firing along Route 1? But we are the villagers, not the guerrillas! They should distinguish between the two. They can't kill us all—that is unfair!* Even at age fourteen, I knew this. *But nothing in war is fair anyway*, I told myself.

I didn't know how long the artillery strike lasted. Fifteen minutes? An hour? When it was over, I snuck out of the bunker and then the house. Around me, it looked like an earthquake's aftermath. I heard shouting and saw smoke coming from the direction of Uncle Chai's house, two doors away. I ran over to find out what the fuss was. It was difficult to make my way through the still-smouldering ruins. There was a smell that was like a mixture of rotten cheese and butter, blood and acrid fumes. In the front yard between the houses lay three dead bodies: Uncle Chai and his two neighbours, O Manh and her daughter. Uncle Chai's house had collapsed, but O Manh's was untouched. Several adults were busily digging through the debris with their bare hands, looking for missing people. When people pulled bodies out from the wreckage, blood was everywhere: on the corpses, on the ground, on the rubble. The artillery shell had been robust; it destroyed the house and penetrated deep into the shelter where they were hiding. The neighbours rescued two injured children, a girl and a boy, both about seven years old, covered in blood. The boy was the second youngest son of Uncle Chai, and the girl was the youngest child of O Manh.

A month earlier, that boy, Can, had been standing by a royal poinciana tree, in full bloom with vibrant red flowers—it's also known as a flamboyant tree, flame tree or phoenix tree—in front of the ancestral clan house. He waved at me as I returned from school. I was curious.

"You wait for me?" I asked the boy.

"Yes, Chú—Uncle," the boy said, smiling. "I [go to] school next year."

"You want to ask me about school?" I asked. The boy nodded. Even though he had several older brothers, none went to school. They had to stay home to look after the family buffalo herd or work on the rice field. He would be the first boy in the family to have a chance for an education. So, I told him what school was like. Now, Can was in critical condition.

The neighbours handed the injured kids to two older women. It was a village superstition that parents or siblings were not allowed to hold dying ones—they should not even go near them. People believed that being with a loved one would satisfy the dying soul; that it would have no will to survive. But if strangers, like those women, held the babies, they might have a chance. O Manh's sister-in-law, O Doi, briefly examined the little ones and then ran off to fetch supplies.

A few minutes afterward, the neighbours brought out another baby girl. She was already dead—Uncle Chai's first grandchild. The child's parents—Uncle Chai's oldest daughter and son-in-law—were not there; they were hiding in Huế.

One of the artillery shells had killed Uncle Chai, the head of the family, instantly. His wife sat beside his body and her grandchild's, crying, while their surviving kids stood around them. Uncle Manh, O Manh's husband, was sitting between his wife's and daughter's bodies with a heartbroken expression. He stood up and walked around to cover each body with a straw mat.

A toddler, Bi, sat alone next to a collapsed kitchen, his skin layered in black soot. He looked like a big piece of charcoal, with two holes for the whites of his eyes and a small bubble of white saliva at his lower lip. Those static, unmoving pupils inside those holes touched me—I wanted to hug him, but was afraid of hurting him. Looking at the boy closely, I saw bloodstains on his right sleeve. I pulled it up for examination. He had a small cut on his right forearm. Nothing serious. I asked, "Does it hurt?" The child shook his head without saying anything and stared off into space. I followed his gaze; there was nothing to see except the rice paddy flattening out to meet the darkening sky. Did he understand that his father had gone away forever, and his older brother was dying?

I sat with Bi looking at a collapsed pigsty not far away. O Chai
fed her pigs with US army camp cafeteria leftovers she'd bought from
a food dealer. The stench from the feed was so intense and unfamiliar
that I could smell it from my house. In one corner of the pigsty, a dead
pig lay as if it were just sleeping. The rest had escaped or been sold
before the Tết for a high price.

Half an hour later, O Doi returned with a pail of warm water, a
large piece of clean white cloth and two bottles of liquid, one red and
one white. The red liquid was iodine, and the white was homemade
rice wine. Every house in the hamlet had these remedies in case of an
accident. O Doi tore the cloth into several pieces and used one to clean
the injured boy with warm water. Blood kept dribbling down the dirt
floor. The cut on the back of his head was so deep that I could see the
bone. I felt faint and dizzy. The child, Can, didn't react when O Doi
cleaned the wound with wine. He looked at her face without flinching,
as if asking where his mommy was. O Doi tied an iodine-soaked cloth
around his head. Still no reaction. She turned to the injured girl, who
had dried blood covering her face. O Doi washed the girl's body with
warm water and cleaned the small cut on her face with rice wine. These
were all the treatments they got. No ambulance. No medics.

The hamlet had no doctor, but we did have an on-call medic, Chú
Kim. He acted as a nurse, a doctor and a pharmacist, but he was away
at the time.

The boy died a day afterward—no more dreams of schooling. The
toddler, Bi, and the injured girl survived, but she was rendered deaf
and mute.

A total of five civilians died: two older adults and three children—
and not an injured or dead VC in sight.

Our house also sustained some damage; a deep trench, twenty
feet in length, had appeared in the front yard. It just missed my aunt's

shrine in the right corner of the property. The back wall was full of shrapnel holes ranging in size from a fingernail to a dinner plate. The bamboo hedge in the backyard had slid into the irrigation canal, where I found a headless chicken. Flying shrapnel must have cut off its head. The hen was the only livestock our family had left. Mom had sold a couple of pigs and most poultry before the Tết festival, when the price of animals would have been at its peak. She was not angry or upset, even though she needed that last hen for her egg supply. Eggs were the only source of protein Mom had for my siblings. There would be no more from now on. Instead, she was happy that all of us were safe and sound, and she thanked our ancestors for that.

I must have been the luckiest person; a big piece of shrapnel had ripped right through the bamboo pallet I shared with my younger brothers. The mosquito net was in shreds. If I had laid down on my pallet that morning instead of walking around, I might have had a big hole in my chest.

CHAPTER 15

# Death Cheater

A few days after the daylight bombardment, my family started to
stay outside the bunker for much longer periods. We were much
paler and thinner than in the days before Tết. We moved slowly, like
living ghosts, and we all felt dizzy when we walked. Our limbs were
heavier each day. We hardly spoke to each other anymore; Mom had
stopped telling stories to entertain us. Even though we were all hungry,
we kids kept quiet. We had no energy to move or talk, and even Vinh
stopped crying.

For about a week, ever since the US Marines had begun to control Route 1, airplanes had dropped parachute flares all night long to
illuminate the rice paddy behind our house. We felt like we were living
in the Arctic, where the sun never sets in the summer months. Under
the constant light, the Marines could detect any Việt Cộng movement
through the rice field and cut off any food and military supplies that
VC might bring to the village. Each flare was attached to a white parachute—as big as a village house—to delay its landing.

During the day, the paddy field was quiet except for the noise
from a herd of ducks. They belonged to a duck farmer. Nobody knew

whether the farmer had left the village or died, but the birds ran wild. The ducks must have laid eggs in the field, and we were interested in those. The eggs would supply us with much-needed protein. A few buffalo boys and I planned an expedition to the rice field to retrieve them. We set a meeting at the hamlet's dock, by my house. Old Dog was nowhere to be seen, and nobody knew where he was.

The following day, I was out of the bunker, heading to the paddy field and breathing in the scent of new rice plants under the rising sun. The air had a sweet scent: I could smell the land, the soil and the grass. For the first time in three weeks, I was free in the open air and feeling invigorated, even though it was a little chilly. Because the rice plants were still short, I could see a long distance without standing on my tiptoes. There were no fences, no boundaries, just miles of rolling rice paddies and water canals meandering through the fields and under single-beam bridges. Blossoms of blue hyacinths floated like small clouds on the water's surface, and I felt as if I could reach out and trace them with a fingertip.

A group of us, ages twelve to fifteen, started to head to the rice field, in a single file on the narrow dirt bank. At first, we talked to each other in a low voice, but gradually, we started to shout when we were far apart. Our shouting overwhelmed the *quack, quack* sounds carried by the gentle breeze. A raft of ducks gathered about halfway between the village and the free-fire zone. We divided the field into five areas and assigned each by a draw. I got the longest stick for the farthest section, close to the free-fire zone. I approached the ducks' nests in that area, walking along the edges of the canals and across the footbridges. In less than fifteen minutes, my bag was full of fresh eggs. Some white parachutes had landed nearby, reminding me of our shattered mosquito net: We could use one to mend it. I advanced farther into the field to pick one up and used it as an extra bag for the eggs.

When I looked up, my friends had left the field for the hamlet. They were about four blocks ahead of me. I saw the old royal poinciana tree that I used as a marker to locate my house. I didn't see anybody—just a quiet hamlet behind a line of bamboo trees. But when I was halfway to my house, I heard it:

*Whizz! Whizz! Boop! Boop!*

It was like a hundred neighbour kids closed upon me and simultaneously released their slingshots. The rocks didn't hit me, but they sent the water and the rice leaves flying all over my body. *Was I daydreaming?* No. And it wasn't the neighbour kids, it was soldiers; instead of slingshots it was rifles; and these were not rocks but real bullets. It was the sound of gunshots. Bullets were whizzing and dropping all around me, randomly splashing the water up.

*Are they trying to shoot me?* I wondered.

Oh! Yes. I was in the middle of an ambush. The shooting came from the village, the south side of the hamlet.

*Boom!* My plastic hat, a replica of a tan safari hat, had been hit by a bullet and flew off my head. I fell into the water.

*Oh no! Was I hit?* I asked myself.

The memory of one of my aunts getting shot down a long time ago on this field went through my mind. I felt dizzy; I lay down on the dirt bank. The shooting stopped.

After a few minutes, I sat up but kept low to the ground. I felt pressure on my left temple and something running down from my forehead into my eyes. *Is it blood?* Did one of those bullets hit my old scar? I examined it with my left hand. No blood, just black mud from the rice field. I felt so relieved. The rice plants were too short to hide under, so I crawled like a snake in the shallow water. After ten minutes in the mud, my limbs turned numb with cold, and my fingers wrinkled, like an old person's. I had no energy left in me.

The paddies were silent, just a light breeze following the waves of rice plants and blowing into my face. I felt a chill through my body, but it gave me some strength. I waited five minutes, then stood up. Nobody was on the rice field beside me. All four of my friends must have reached the hamlet.

*Crack! Crack! Boom! Boom!*

The gunfire started again. A rocket blasted from an M79 grenade launcher exploded less than a block in front of me. I dropped down and crawled toward home. The soldiers might have singled me out for shooting because they mistook me for a VC guerrilla from Rào, assuming I was following the kids in order to infiltrate the village. But why me? I needed to get out of here.

As usual in a planting season, the ground was covered in a foot of mud. I hardly kept my head below the rice plants, so my movement was undetectable. There was little room to manoeuvre. Dozens of leeches bigger than my thumbs were gluing themselves all over my body. I didn't bother to detach them. Big ones were not, typically, the problem. Tiny leeches, the size of a toothpick, were the most dangerous in the rice field, because they could get into people's eardrums. They swam in schools and multiplied fast when the rice plants flowered.

That reminded me of a game that Old Dog and I had played a few years back. That day, we couldn't bathe in the canal since its water was full of silt. Kids from the nearby village swarm upstream, sending muddy water down to us. Old Dog decided to teach those kids a lesson by giving them a surprise visit. It was late spring; the rice plants were shoulder-height, in their early flowering stage. We couldn't walk through them without being detected. So we crawled, snakelike, in the mud under the rice leaves, following the bank.

It was only a couple of blocks from their playground, but it felt much longer. The rice stalks and leaves would itch on our naked skin, and there were lots of leeches. To overcome the itching and prevent the bloodsuckers from attaching to us, we covered our bodies with a thick layer of mud that made us feel warm and protected. As we approached the target, the sounds of laughter and water splashing became louder. The kids, who were about ten, were playing under a bridge, the girls bathing on one side and the boys swimming on the other. They left their things on the dry bank and swam naked. Old Dog and I collected the boys' clothes. "Ha, ha," Old Dog teased them. To the girls, he signalled kisses—"*mwah, mwah*"—and said, "I love you." As we were covered only in a layer of black mud, and no pants, the girls glanced away or covered their eyes with their hands. The boys shouted at us while they swam naked. They were too shy in front of the girls to chase the intruders.

But now, everything was silent. There were no other children; no jokes or banter. This was not a playful prank between kids. I stood up, and the firing resumed. I dropped down again.

This sequence was repeated several times. Someone was playing a shooting game with me. The last few times I stood up, I saw a line of people behind the village bamboo bushes, looking out in my direction. My family must be in that group, along with our neighbours and my four friends who had just left the rice paddies. A year ago, we had been watching the battle of Rào, just a kilometre from where I was. And now, they were witnessing a potentially deadly shooting of one of their family members, but could do nothing except watch.

The shooting must have been coming from the government barracks, a few blocks south of the hamlet. Whoever they were, they were cheering when they saw me fall. From the sound, I could tell that the shots were fired from an M1 Garand, a single shot at a time, not an M16. US Marines used M16s, whereas the local government troops still employed M1 Garand guns. Although the M1 couldn't compete with an M16 in a gun battle, it was still a deadly weapon for long-range shooting.

Many things were going through my mind. *How long will they keep shooting at me? Until I die? Do they want my dead body as a trophy? Sooner or later, one of those bullets will hit me. If not, they will send out an attack chopper to finish the job, the same scenario that I have witnessed on this rice paddy many times. If I die, the villagers will say, "A poor child," and then forget. They have nothing about me to remember, just one less boy to worry about—I would never steal from their fruit trees again. I can't die now. I am too young to die—I haven't experienced anything yet. I wish I had been born ten years earlier, so that were I to die, I would be a combat soldier like Anh Hai, who fought for his beliefs; or an excellent engineer who could fix the broken Trường Tiền Bridge; or a skilled doctor capable of saving lives. I must be somebody before I die. I must escape before the killing chopper comes.*

I looked at the rice paddy around me. I didn't see any field of water hyacinths on the canal nearby that I could use to hide under. *Where are they when I need one? How about a hole? Can I dig one into the dirt levee?* But I had no energy left, and my hands were too weak. *I want to disappear!*

*Think! Think of something, quick!* I kept repeating in my head.

I lay on the mud bank, trying to find a way out of this mess. Time had frozen, and I was transporting myself back to my childhood games on this field. This time, I was playing games with the real killers. I started to cover my body with mud. I remembered the pile of clothes that had been on the dirt bank, which gave me an idea. Suddenly, I had the feeling of being alive.

Slowly, I collected the broken hat, the parachute and a bag of eggs. With those materials, and mud from the irrigation canal, I built a dummy about my height on an embankment. After placing the hat on the figure—this was the finishing touch, to push the dummy's head above the rice plants—I slid into the channel and dove down along the bottom as far as I could.

When I surfaced to gulp for air, I still heard the guns firing at the dummy, but I was already far from it. Too cold and tired to dive any farther, I breathed deep and held the air to float. I rested on the water's surface to regain strength and used a dirt bank for a bulletproof wall. The touch of the water was sensuous, enfolding my body in its soft, close embrace. After some time, I no longer heard any gunfire. The soldiers had probably flattened the dummy and reckoned they did shoot a VC down. They didn't need to call for a gun chopper to finish the job. I resumed diving short distances and coming up for air. Exhaustedly and slowly, I crawled back to the village, following a zig-zag pattern through the field.

After an hour, I made it back to the house with no duck eggs, but a good-sized goose egg on my left temple. If the bullet had moved an inch to the right, it would have lodged in my brain instead of just grazing my head. Leeches coated my body. I felt sorry for them, since I had nothing in me, and the blood of a malnourished teenager must have been terrible. They were just like the war, sucking the life out of people.

"I almost had a heart attack," Mom told me when she met me at the village gate. Her body was still shaking. My siblings held me tightly, smiling, their eyes filled with tears. I was a death cheater—*thằng giả chết*, as people started to call me—and I collapsed on the dirt road. I had no energy left.

---

After escaping the ambush on the rice field, I became known as a death cheater. I was like the young rice plants behind my house; they would ripple to create those paddy waves under a light breeze, but even under the strongest wind stirred by a helicopter's blades, they would not break. After the chopper flew away, they would rise again. *I should stand up before it is too late. I should run from this terror and control my destiny.*

But my legs were too weak, and my head was too heavy.

I woke up with a pounding head and strange sensations in my feet and upper arms. The sharp tingling started deep in my bones and reverberated through the muscles and outer skin tissues, like agitated insects invading my body. I felt twinges on both knees. The stink of liquid chives, a homemade ointment, covered my whole body, which brought me back to reality.

I felt cold and kept shaking.

My mom began to feed me rice porridge with honey.

Later in the day, I could walk around inside the house. Peeking through the front window, I saw no one outside. The road was quiet. While I was bedridden, the US bombers kept flying overhead during the day, and airplanes continued to drop parachute flares on the rice field all night long. Nothing, not even an ant, could escape the planes' surveillance, but they couldn't detect the movements of Việt Cộng, even though they quietly came and then left the hamlet during the night without a trace. They were withdrawing from Huế to their base, and some passed through Dạ Lê. The US Marines had been busy securing Route 1. At the same time, the SVA concentrated on the counterattack to take Huế back from Việt Cộng.

I had started to feel a sense of constant fear because I knew my body could be taken from me at any time and by anyone. A Marine. A soldier. A VC. A friend. A neighbour. Frustrated with our lives in Dạ Lê and seeing no future ahead, I told Mom I would leave her for Huế, as soon as I was strong enough to reunite with Dad. She agreed with the idea—she had expected it, even though she needed my help to keep my seven siblings in line. That was what had kept me home until now. As the oldest child in the family, especially the *đích tôn*, I was responsible for looking after my siblings when my dad was not at home. I had to live a life for my siblings to follow, to support them when they were weak and guide them to success. Other important duties were to keep my eyes on the ancestors' tombs and graves and organize the anniversaries of the day each died. With such a role model, my siblings looked up to me more than they looked up to my parents. Mom sensed my difficulty. She said her main concern was my safety; the local VC might think I knew too much to keep me from leaving the hamlet. She went to the ancestral altar at the centre of the house and prayed with burning joss sticks. She didn't forget to get outside to my dead aunt's shrine. She asked our ancestors and her spirit to forgive me for leaving and to protect me, a *đích tôn*.

While I decided whether to leave or not, I was still sick—I was unconscious for over a day. My limbs jerked, and I made some strange noises. My mom couldn't tell what I was talking about—she thought it must be a nightmare.

But I was having a dream full of hope, not a nightmare. *I'm a kite flying above the village rice paddies. On the steady wind, I am gliding smoothly. When I look down, I see farmers working in the field. They're singing while they work, and I hear their idyllic songs. Some are planting rice, and others are bailing the water from the canal into their fields. Old Dog and the other buffalo boys keep the beasts off the rice paddies, and they cannot fly like me. I feel sorry for them. I try to slide close to Old Dog, but I can't. I'm free, but I'm not. Something is holding me back, keeping me in the air and tying me down. The rope, that's it! I hope to get free. Free to fly anywhere. Free to glide high or low. Free to carry no weight. Free to all.*

*Suddenly, I get what I wish for. The rope breaks. I soar for about ten seconds and then lose my balance. Headfirst, I plummet down.*

*Thud*—I hit the ground, and that was when I woke up. I was on the dirt floor.

I clambered onto my bamboo pallet again and tried to go back to sleep. I hoped to dream of another flight so I could fly far, far away from the terror.

Two days later, I took my bike and left home without any luggage— just the bike and myself. I put on some extra clothes. If someone saw me that day, they would have thought I had bulked up. That was all. In reality, I was thin and pale, especially after my near starvation the last couple of weeks. People used to call me "sugarcane."

"Where are you going, death cheater?" Thai, standing in the middle of the road, asked.

I stopped and dismounted. Thai had an AK-47 on him.

"Hi, Thai. I'm in a hurry, looking for Ông Tho," I lied.

"What is the matter?" Thai looked at me, examining my body.

"Not me. My mom has a dislocated hand bone," I said with feigned sadness.

Ông Tho was a village medicine man, or more like a kind of chiro-practor, to be precise. Anyone with a sore shoulder or ankle, or any problem with a dislocation, would call on him. With rice wine soaking his hands, he worked the bones into place in no time. He had once fixed my dislocated shoulder after I'd missed a jump from a wooden sampan to a canal bank during a helicopter raid on the paddies. The treatment hurt, but my shoulder was back to normal.

"There is something different about you," Thai said. "You look funny. You look sick." My childhood friend started to laugh.

"What's new with you?" I changed the subject.

"I want to talk to you." Thai pointed at me.

I smiled. "Sure. Let me see Ông Tho first."

"Where are you going?" The messenger was furious.

To get to Ông Tho's house, I should make a left turn instead of heading to Route 1, the direct route to Huế.

"*Chào*," I said, and made a turn in the right direction instead. If Thai was suspicious of me, he didn't show it. Once I was out of his sight, and in order to continue bypassing him, I took the canal route heading to the neighbouring village.

I heard someone arguing when I was approaching the village boundary. A group of people stood on the road below the bamboo bushes at the intersection. I stopped, dismounted and tried to figure out what was going on. One thing that came to my mind was that they might be the VC's captives. Were any of the three returnees in the hamlet among them? But the scene didn't make much sense. I couldn't find anyone, not even a local guerilla I knew. Besides the guerillas with guns, the civilians gathered. They were not villagers. I could tell from their clothes that they were city people or from other villages near Huế. Among them was a young girl about eighteen years old. She was dressed in a red shirt with white trousers. By her actions and the way the girl kept talking and arguing, I could tell that she didn't seem afraid of the guerrillas. *Are they prisoners, and the VCs are taking them to their base?* I wondered.

I backed off by carrying my bike to prevent any noise. I didn't want to be mistaken as one of those prisoners. I retreated slowly away from the scene and returned the previous way. Thai was no longer there; my heart pumped much faster than usual. Route 1 was busy with traffic. I biked alongside the army trucks filled with soldiers in full combat gear heading to Huế.

## CHAPTER 16

# Huế, 1968

By the time I arrived in the city, the battle of Huế—also called the siege of Huế—was still going on.

Given its central position, Huế was a strategic location for fighting during the French occupation and the ongoing war. The old imperial city is located at the midpoint between Saigon and Hanoi. Huế was the fulcrum, with heavy weights on either side: Saigon with the Mekong Delta on one side and Hanoi with the Red River Delta in the north on the other. That precarious balance was an easily conjured symbol in any Vietnamese village, where bamboo shoulder poles are crucial to survival and daily tasks. They are used to carry merchandise to the market and to bring products home. A farmer would use it to transport the rice stalks on the paddy bank, and a street vendor walked around with a heavy load on her shoulders. Both a fulcrum on a balance lever and a bamboo shoulder pole must be strong enough to endure the weights on both ends, just like Huế had persisted, against all odds.

Perhaps to compensate for such geographical burdens, the scenery around Huế is beautiful. The river flowing through Huế, Sông Hương (Perfume River), is named for good reason. The vegetation and rock formations upstream give the river a fresh and relaxing smell around

Huế. The Sông Hương's water comes from the Trường Sơn Range and flows through the highland west of Dạ Lê village before entering the city of Huế. It bypasses the Huế Imperial Citadel to meet the East Sea at the mouth of Thuận An.

The counterattack forces, the SVA and the US Marines, had pushed the NVA and Việt Cộng out of Huế. I suspected they had headed south to their base, as I had seen them a few days ago in the hamlet. The forces fought house to house, one block at a time, to retake the northern part of the city, the Citadel and the imperial palace from the VC forces. Beautiful Huế, the forbidden city, was now in ruins!

Marine A-4 Skyhawks, which I knew by their distinctive aircraft markings of a white star on a dark blue circle, kept dropping bombs and napalm on the north side. But the Citadel could resist the heavy bombardment, due to two-and-a-half kilometres of brick walls that were four metres high and one metre thick. From the south side of the Perfume River, I could not see the flares, but I could tell where they were, marked by columns of black smoke. Now and then, the planes flew over my head on their way south to Phú Bài Combat Base. The thunder of those iron birds sent people and dogs running for cover among the ruins. Disoriented sparrows in an old banyan tree next to the bridge dispersed over the river in all directions. Once a person was already facing the aircraft, it was too late to hide, so I stood on the road and looked up. The antenna at the nose of each bomber tore through the air. These hulking machines had just emptied their stomachs and were probably on their way to get more ammunition.

I headed to the old An Định Palace, where I had last met my dad. Getting there was not an easy task. In the aftermath of combat, the city resembled an ancient ruin. Many blocks were unpassable. Everything all around me was black, and a stench permeated the air. House after the house had been burned or flattened to the ground. The few buildings that remained standing were without a roof, just bare skeletons full of holes in the walls. The streets were deserted and covered with brick rubble. The sidewalks were nowhere to be seen—obliterated or buried. I carried my bike on my shoulder and climbed the debris to get through. The scene reminded me of the Champa ruins in central Vietnam, not far from Huế.

After struggling through the streets full of debris, I finally arrived at the old An Định Palace, severely damaged. My dad had left the palace, and its old caretaker told me where to find him. He had changed his hiding place for security reasons and was staying with a friend in the Thủy An commune, a southern city suburb. The house faced Route 1, a convenient place to get news. On the other side of the road was a famous paddy field, where rice was once planted for the Annam kings.

A few days after settling in the city, the US Marines and the SVA started to secure the Citadel. Huế went back under the Saigon government's control. The Black Panther Company of the SVA 1st Division and Task Force X-Ray (US Marines) took down the Việt Cộng's flag. It had flown on the imperial palace since the battle started on January 30. They raised the South Vietnam flag in its place—three red stripes on a yellow background. No celebration. This changing of hands had cost many lives on both sides.

---

A few days after I had arrived in Huế, my dad received a message from my mom that I must come home—it wasn't about him this time. If I wouldn't, I would be treated as an informer, and our family remaining in the hamlet would be in trouble. She also mentioned that Old Dog came asking for me the day after I had left.

With that threat, my father decided to evacuate the rest of the family to Huế, even though Huế was still in chaos. My young father didn't yet know where we would stay, but he arranged for my mother and siblings to be picked up at the front of the temple on Route 1, where the Marines were in control. As planned, Mom and my siblings arrived two days before the US and government forces regained control of the entire city on February 26, 1968.

My grandma didn't join us. She told Mom she would stay and die on her land. If she needed anything, her daughters—my aunts—lived nearby and would be there for her. She had no enemies, and she said no one would bother her.

After retaking Huế, traffic on Route 1 became heavier each day as people returned to the city and soldiers departed south after completing the mission. Restrictions on movement were lifted. I welcomed this freedom and went out to explore. Walking along Route 1, I passed an army convoy.

"Stand there! Raise your hands."

I froze when I heard a man shout from behind. The voice sounded familiar.

In a strange coincidence, this was the same place where, four weeks earlier, I had been asked to dismount my bike and raise my hands on my way back to the village after meeting my dad. I turned my head.

"Don't look," said the voice firmly. "Raise your hands."

As I did, people laughed. The sound relieved me, but I didn't think it was funny.

I turned around. Several government soldiers at the back of an open-top army truck were looking at me. Their unit insignia—a snarling black panther superimposed over a red triangle—adorned the right chest pockets and left shoulders of their combat uniforms. These soldiers belonged to the elite Black Panther unit under the command of Lieutenant Colonel Trần Ngọc Huế. This fighting force had recently restored the Southern flag to the Huế imperial palace.

The officer who laughed the hardest at this prank was Anh Hai, sitting in the front passenger seat of an army Jeep. He jumped off the vehicle and hugged me; I felt the coolness of metal against my right cheek, from two yellow flowers pinned to his collar.

"How's your mạ?"

"She's okay, and staying near here."

"She's here?" The officer widened his eyes as he looked at me in excitement.

I nodded.

"I want to see my aunt. Take me to her."

---

After hearing about the family's dilemma, Mr. Phung, my father's barber, offered to share half of his house with the family. Nothing was better than that. We had left the village with nothing and were very appreciative of the kindness.

Mr. Phung had a barbershop near the An Cựu market, and his house was a block from his shop. He and his wife had five children. A total of seventeen people—thirteen children and four adults from two families—jammed into the small four-bedroom house. My family lived there for free until my dad could find a new place.

Two days after settling in, I was awakened in the middle of the night by the sounds of someone knocking on my parents' bedroom door.

"They're coming!" Mr. Phung shouted. "They're coming!"

"Who's coming?" Dad asked.

"Việt Cộng! Việt Cộng!"

"Where?" my father asked nervously.

"Outside the temple. We must escape. Quick! Follow me ..."

I heard the door of my parents' room close and then the sounds of running.

"This way," the host whispered. "We go this way."

I stood up and moved closer to the door, listening intensively in a wait-and-see mode, ready to escape. The sounds of hurried footsteps from Mr. Phung and my dad disappeared into the night. Inside, the house was silent. Outside, no sound was heard. Nothing. A heavy silence.

I concluded they must be having nightmares. I returned to my sleeping corner and fell back to sleep.

The same drama took place a couple of nights later. The third time, my dad was the one who woke Mr. Phung up. They both kept having nightmares that Việt Cộng had come looking for them. Dad attributed those to our host's obsession with relating all the horrible stories he had heard from his customers at the barbershop and my father's month-long period of hiding. He reckoned that getting away from each other might help, and my father found another place for the family to live.

———

Our family occupied a tumbledown house, an abandoned French colonial villa on Hàng Đoác, or Sugar Palm Street, close to the American Cultural Center Library, where a giant picture of President Lyndon B. Johnson hung in the centre front hall. We felt like we'd instantly become rich! We lived in a villa.

We didn't know or care who the owner of the house was. Since it had been abandoned, we just moved in. Half of the two-storey brick building had collapsed, but the other half was livable. My father returned to his post in the Vinh Lộc district.

The house, which had plumbing and electrical lines, was like the one in my dream, even though the power had been cut off. The bath-tubs were full of mice excrement and dead cockroaches, and broken light bulbs littered the floor. With our bare hands, we picked up the glass shards. The family slept on the floor.

At the back of the building, there used to be a swimming pool. But it now contained contaminated water and functioned like a garbage dump. The brackish water reeked. Worse than the smell were the swarms of mosquitoes that invaded the house each night. At dusk, they flew up from the pool and buzzed around my head, looking for skin to bite. I hated that sound. Even with a mosquito net, nobody escaped the biting. Each morning, we all had over twenty red spots on our bodies, and more if we could actually count them all, especially on our hands and feet.

After settling down in the new house for a month, my mother decided that Lanh and I should return to school in the village if conditions allowed. My brother had a couple of months left to finish the fifth grade, while I was in the seventh grade at the district middle school. My other younger siblings were temporarily allowed to stay home. Lanh didn't have to go back to the village; his elementary school had been blown up in the Tết Offensive, so he was allowed to continue studying in Huế. *Why had that school been destroyed?* I wondered. Nobody had the answer. My middle school in the village was still intact. By April 1968, US Marines and government armies had complete control of Route 1 around Huế and the Tram Trail, where my school was. So I went back to my class.

The twice-daily school trip was hazardous. The distance—seven kilometres on the bike—was not a problem, but the drivers of US convoys were. They drove their trucks so fast and recklessly on a shared single-lane road. I had to look out whenever I heard the sound of a vehicle behind me or saw it approaching from a distance. I didn't want to become roadkill. A person's life was just a statistic in the name of war. And I couldn't do anything except be aware of the danger.

On that section of Route 1 that passed through the village, Việt Cộng launched ambushes and sniper attacks daily. US Marines atop open army trucks indiscriminately returned fire on the village houses. During each night, there were still clashes between US Marines and Việt Cộng. And in the morning, I often saw corpses of local guerrillas lying on the side of Route 1 on my way to school. Sometimes I identified the victim as one of my former classmates. This morbid display was a warning sign for any village girl or boy like me who ever thought of joining the guerrillas. *This is how you will end up if you follow them.* As I walked around a dead body, I would try to keep my composure and avoid calling attention to myself.

But when this kind of thing becomes frequent, abnormal becomes normal.

When I came back to class, a third of my classmates were missing, even though students in my grade were just fourteen or fifteen years of age. The oldest class, ninth grade at school—Chị Mau's class—was severely devastated. It had forty-five students before the Tết Offensive, but only twenty-five showed up in the aftermath. If they were alive, they had enlisted in the government army or, like Chị Mau had done, disappeared into the jungle to join Việt Cộng. The latter was more likely.

The students all felt so sad when we heard that our science teacher, Cao Thị Hồng, had died in Huế. Her bomb shelter had collapsed during the Tết Offensive. She was five months pregnant.

A few months later, a mother displayed her son's coffin in the schoolyard over the weekend. The mother didn't know who had kidnapped and killed her son while he was on his way to school—someone had found him dead in a shallow ditch on the hills west of the village. The mother brought his body to the schoolyard in protest; she didn't know what else to do or where to go. The school had no answer, and nobody knew or had cared why a student had been missing.

## CHAPTER 17

# Huế Massacre

A year later, after the Tết Offensive, our family was chased out of the rundown villa on Sugar Palm Street. The owner came to claim his property and decided to demolish the building. People started to rebuild their houses and their lives. We moved again.

This time we moved to a new house—a single-room thatched hut—that my dad himself built in O Lai's backyard. As our aunt, she was kind enough to lend us a small piece of land alongside the railway tracks next to the An Cựu train station in Ngự Bình Ward, a suburb of Huế.

One afternoon after we'd just moved in, an older boy came out of nowhere, facing me as I walked along the rail tracks by the new hut.

"Are you from Dạ Lê?" he asked.

I looked at the boy to see if I recognized him. "Yes, I —"

Suddenly, he slapped my face hard. I didn't have time to react.

"You're from a VC village," the boy said, laughing at me. Like many people in Huế after the Tết Offensive, that boy hated Việt Cộng and anyone related to that organization. In this case, it was Dạ Lê, a VC village, and I was from it. There was no distinction between the guerrillas and the villagers.

Shocked and angry, I ran a short distance and picked up a rock from in-between the rail tracks. I turned and threw it, hitting the boy squarely in the back.

"Oh!" the older boy cried in pain.

He ran after me, but I escaped without a problem. The boy, however, followed me home and sat on one of the rail tracks facing the hut with a knife concealed inside one of his sleeves. The boy sat there quietly, waiting for me to come out.

In the evening, my dad drove an army Jeep home with his visiting soldier friend, Canh, from Cần Thơ, south of Saigon. When the soldier saw the boy with the concealed knife, and me looking out concerned from behind the thatched wall, he comprehended the situation. Canh took his M1 Paratrooper, a collapsible semiautomatic rifle, from the military Jeep, approached the boy and aimed it at him.

"Drop your knife. Now!" Canh shouted. "Don't ever come back here again. I'll shoot your legs off. Run!"

The boy dropped the knife and ran. I never saw him again.

This hatred between Huế people and the VC sympathizers was magnified after discovering the dead bodies of missing people in the early days of the Tết Offensive.

In the spring of 1969, over a year later, the US and the SVA found many mass graves in Huế and surrounding areas. Many believed people had been buried alive with their hands bound behind their backs. Some had close-range bullet wounds. Relatives bowed over bags of their loved ones' bones, crying. People arranged funerals for the remains recovered. These scenes were everywhere in Huế and haunted me day and night. I felt their grief and sorrow.

An unofficial tally showed three thousand bodies in those mass graves. Another three thousand residents in Huế and surrounding areas were still missing. The US and the SVA charged the Việt Cộng and the NVA for the massacre, claiming that the guerrillas had committed genocide during their capture and occupation of Huế. The North claimed that the Americans and the SVA committed those atrocities.

Although none of those graves were in the village, several were found within a radius of ten kilometres—Đá Mài ravine to the west, Bãi Dâu and Gia Hội to the north, and Phú Thứ to the east. Those locations were near, or along, the riverbanks of the Perfume River, or one of its estuaries. The river became the witness to all the horrors the war had brought to the area, which is what the songwriter Trịnh Công Sơn described in his song, "Hát Trên Những Xác Người," or "Song for the Corpses."

Sơn was a local, but famous in Vietnam and internationally. Joan Baez had dubbed him the "Bob Dylan of Vietnam" for his moving anti-war songs. Everyone in South Vietnam knew or loved at least one of his songs. The "Song for the Corpses" was written in mourning the Huế Massacre, but it also reflected the feelings of everyone who had lost loved ones in the war yet who saw the killings as the only way. In the song, Sơn is passing through Bãi Dâu singing over the corpses, and he sees an old father holding his dead child, surrounded by many mass graves. Everyone is clapping their hands; a mother celebrates war while another cheers for peace. Some want revenge, while others are repentant. We were full of contradictions and divisions.

One afternoon, O Ba met me on the road. She hugged me tightly. I felt embarrassed but still, I let her hold me. The passersby glanced at us and then walked away. She looked like a drunk or homeless woman. Her clothes were messy with brown dust, even though she wore a black *áo dài*. She exposed her neglected and dried-out hair by carrying her tattered conical hat in her left hand. She was my mom's age.

"My boy! I am so miserable, *con ơi*," she cried, her tears dropping on my right shoulder. She was not my mother or aunt; we were not related, but she called me her boy, *con*, and I called her Auntie, *O*.

"What is this about, Auntie?"

"I have tried to look for my younger brother's body, but I have had no luck."

*Oh!* Her younger brother was Chú Han, my preschool teacher and the one who returned home while my father stayed hiding during the Tết Offensive. They had hidden in the same place.

"I went anywhere that a mass grave was discovered," she continued. "Day in and day out, but I couldn't recognize his body. All the corpses looked the same—disintegrated." O Ba cried and wiped her nose with a handkerchief. "I regret calling him home. Why did I do that?"

I felt her shaking as she sobbed.

"This is my fault. All my fault."

I gently patted her back. "Not your fault," I said. "My mom and I did the same to my dad. We did what they told us." I tried to convince her, but I wondered about the role we had played as well. When I thought of what it would be like to look for my dad's remains, my whole body shook.

"But I still feel I was at fault," she said.

Relatives of the victims used dental records to identify the bodies. The city people were lucky to have such a record, and at least they could say goodbye to the victims for closure, unlike for O Ba's younger brother, who had no dental work to identify his remains. She needed to find his body to lessen her pain, but she had had no luck.

Had I been one of the victims, I would be easy to find. I had two buck teeth, and between those two front ones was a small and pointed tooth. Behind that, a similar one grew out of my upper gum; I had used it as a hole puncher when I bit a piece of paper. I did not know why I had that crazy thought about someone else identifying my body. It had to do with my guilt about participating in the Tết Offensive.

During the Tết Offensive, Việt Cộng occupied and established its authority over the so-called "liberated zone" of Huế for four weeks. The people of Huế had received more than a push, but a final uprising was nowhere to be seen. Việt Cộng had to withdraw back to the jungle when the US Marines and the SVA moved in. A tragedy did happen in Huế.

People didn't realize that all the roads around Huế had been packed with wandering souls, and were now more crowded than ever after the Tết Offensive. The newcomers were getting lost and more desperate, looking for their families. The dead needed a proper burial near their homes, which might put their wandering souls to rest. Their relatives wished for closure.

## CHAPTER 18

# Anti-War Rallies

On Christmas Day in 1969, the Bob Hope USO show came to the village of Dạ Lê to entertain the US troops at Camp Eagle. The show featured the actress and singer Connie Stevens, astronaut Neil Armstrong and others. Almost twenty thousand US soldiers and their friends attended the concert in a village of three thousand people. The villagers were not invited.

The show demonstrated US confidence that Dạ Lê was a safe place and could challenge any VC attacks. The 101st Airborne Division also focused on pacification programs in the more populated lowland areas, to build people's trust. At the same time, it continued to conduct normal tactical operations in the highlands, dropping bombs, burning VC hideouts and spraying thousands of gallons of Agent Orange on the forests.

In the summer of 1970, Mom and my siblings moved back to the village, thanks to the strong presence of Camp Eagle. I stayed back in Huế to attend Quốc Học High School. To finance my studies, I got a job as a private teacher for a family living inside the imperial palace walls. I tutored three children ranging from ages eight to twelve, and in return, I received complimentary lodging and meals. Besides tutoring,

I also wrote short stories and articles for the *Trắng Đen* newspaper in Saigon. For each piece of writing, I received eight hundred *đồng*, or about ten US dollars. To get to school on another side of the Perfume River, I biked on a new floating bridge that the US Army Engineers had constructed to temporarily replace the Trường Tiền Bridge—which had been partially blown up during the 1968 Tết Offensive.

At the beginning of the '70s, the hippie movement had reached Huế; the most visible place was the high school yard. We had school uniforms, and heavy enforcement of blue pants and white shirts, but some of my classmates started to don the enhanced bell-bottom pants and shirts with bell sleeves, and they wore peace-sign necklaces. But the most noticeable change in styles was the male students' long hair. The school tried to discourage the trend while students were on the premises. One day, the head supervisor requested those hippie students come to his office one by one. When they returned to class, a piece had been cut from their bell-bottom pants and their hair had been trimmed, with a large section of hair missing at the back.

The following morning, my class sang the national anthem and raised the flag in the schoolyard's centre. Almost all my classmates, including me, arrived at the school wearing hats. After forming five lines and standing under the school flagpole, we removed our hats and let our bald heads shine in the morning sun. We looked like newly enlisted soldiers happily singing the national anthem, and the school officers and other students looked at us, dumbfounded.

After the flag saluting, we were asked to see the school's general supervisor. One by one, we went into a room with a closed door.

"Is Lui the instigator?" asked the school officer, who faced me at the other side of the table.

Lui was one of my close friends. He was known for his trouble-making in the past and was now an advocate for hippie fashions. I wouldn't say I liked the counterculture movement, but I was not against it either. Not all the long-haired students at the school were hippies—some of us had long hair just for the sake of saving money, or not having the money for haircuts. And our decision to shave our heads was more about solidarity and resistance against the school meddling with our personal decisions.

"No, he's not, sir," I said.

"So, who is the leader?"

"No one, sir. This protest is the whole class's decision."

"To protest what?"

"We are against the haircut. The school cut off the students' hair, and it feels like a warning sign of the draft."

The school ignored the incident, and the students turned to other things of interest, like new movies and music. They admired French actor Alain Delon and worshipped The Beatles. I liked hearing the students speak but knew nothing about what they were talking about. Some of them formed a music band to play English or French songs, and they went to my village or to Phú Bài to entertain the American soldiers.

---

Until my sophomore year in 1971, I was busy working and studying and tried not to join any mass rallies. But one day, my beloved teacher, Ngô Kha, didn't show up to teach his civil rights and civics education class. Instead, a classmate showed us a letter he claimed Thầy Kha—Teacher Kha—had written from the Thừa Phủ prison. Teacher Kha, who was also becoming a well-known poet, had quoted from his anti-war poem "The Sunrise," saying that Vietnamese don't have Egyptian pyramids or the Acropolis, like the Greeks, but are full of martyrs.

Yes, we, the students, would be the martyrs of the Vietnam War. Kha—an inspirational teacher and a poet—was also a close friend and the ex-brother-in-law of the songwriter Trịnh Công Sơn. Both men were well-known anti-war activists and grew up in Huế. Their work influenced each other back then.

The subject that teacher Kha taught was only a minor; we received just one credit for his class compared to four for math. Even so, such a contemporary and controversial topic drew the students in like a magnet. The class examined economics under capitalism and communism and discussed the advantages and disadvantages of each system. These were sensitive topics because these systems violently clashed right outside our classroom. And for us it was more than just philosophical or theoretical; people were arrested and sent to jail; others were shot dead or kidnapped in the middle of the night. Thousands and thousands of people on both sides had died. The Vietnamese killed one another, even though most peasants did not give a damn about those economic and political systems. They just needed enough food, and safety for their families. They would follow anyone who spoke their languages, which was love for their country and a hatred of any invaders. America sending its troops onto Vietnamese soil didn't help their cause.

We also discussed the difference between patriotism and nationalism. Like most of my classmates, I thought they meant the same thing. But one of my classmates, Dai, said they were not the same; nationalism is a kind of excessive, aggressive patriotism. He used the case of Phan Bội Châu as an example of patriotism.

Phan Bội Châu formed the Vietnamese Restoration League, modelled after Sun Yat-sen's republican party, which later ruled Taiwan. He had sent many young Vietnamese to Japan from 1905 to 1908 for learning and had drawn up a plan to get the French out of Vietnam. In 1925, the French arrested and convicted him. He spent the rest of his life under house arrest, a few blocks from where we were sitting in class in Huế, until he died in 1940. More than once, I had seen Teacher Kha attending, and sometimes acting as the master of ceremonies, at Phan Bội Châu's death anniversary.

In our classes, Dai said that Phan Bội Châu was like most anti-French activists devoted to Vietnam: He had a certain sociability in his struggle. In contrast, he argued that "a nationalist doesn't work with anyone who disagrees, or who doesn't share the same ideology, but labels them 'traitors.' He is the only leader. Do you see the differences?"

I was more confused.

But my classmates and I didn't have a chance to discuss this further. Our teacher was in jail again.

Because of his anti-war activism, the South Vietnam government had first imprisoned Ngô Kha after the student uprising in 1966, five years prior. This time was his second. The reason? I didn't know. That was a troubling time. What happened was that the South Vietnamese president Nguyễn Văn Thiệu was competing for a second term—except there was no challenger in the upcoming election. Students charged that the president had forced the opposition leaders out of the race. We organized rallies to denounce and call attention to the fact that it was not a democracy. Across the South, police arrested student leaders and political dissidents.

A coalition of all student associations across South Vietnam held a meeting in Huế at the time. The purpose was to decide on a united action against Nguyễn Văn Thiệu's government—we had condemned it as a police regime. We demanded immediate cancellation of compulsory military training classes, which was a graduation requirement for senior high school students. In that class, students learned how to assemble, clean and fire a gun. Any male student over eighteen with an education draft waiver had to join the People's Self-Defence Forces and spend one or two nights a week on duty, guarding against the Việt Cộng's infiltration wherever he lived. Most guard locations were relatively safe, but the potential for a gun battle was still there. The coalition also requested the release of students in detention or jails across South Vietnam. It advocated for political democracy and citizen's rights. Slogans like "Down with the police regime," "Down with the militarized school," and "Yankee, go home" appeared on many cloth banners hung around Huế.

In the middle of this political turmoil, a US military vehicle ran over a student right on the Huế main street in front of those slogans. The boy died, and the American driver left the scene. That caused a further uproar among the youth of Huế.

A student protest was nothing new to me.

My first rally was when I was thirteen years old, still living in the village. This also would have been Teacher Kha's first arrest, but I didn't know him at the time. One day in the spring of 1966, when I was in the last year of elementary school, I left home for school but didn't arrive. The scenes of death I'd witnessed and an adventurous mindset might have affected my view of the war, so I got involved in anti-war rallies, even though I didn't truly understand their causes. Lam and I both skipped class to listen to the older students from Huế. Some of them were young poets who had self-published their booklets and given them to us for free.

The students had organized rallies in Huế against the Saigon government. They arrived at the middle school near my elementary school to oppose the US troops' arrival in Vietnam. The protest spread to my village by sneaking behind the blockades on Route 1.

Around noon, Lam and I were on the back of an open-top army truck with older students from Huế, going to Huế for a rally. Lam and I liked the adventure.

Buddhist altars were placed in the streets to block military and civilian traffic. We joined the protest on Lê Lợi Boulevard. We marched and shouted, "Down with the United States," "Yankee, go home," and "Down with Thiệu and Kỳ." Thiệu and Kỳ were the top leaders of the South at the time. The city was paralyzed.

At thirteen, I admired those students who recited many beautiful poems and sang many rally songs, including "Gia tài của mẹ," or "A Mother's Fate," another song composed by Trịnh Công Sơn. In the lyrics, Sơn says Vietnam has been under a thousand years of Chinese domination, a hundred years of French colonization and twenty years of civil war. What is left for our future? A sad Vietnam. He called the Vietnam War "Nội chiến," or civil war. At that time, most students like me also treated the war as *nội chiến*: families divided, and brothers killed brothers. But our favourite song at the rally was "Kẻ Thù Ta (Our Enemy)," an adaptation by songwriter Phạm Duy from the first two lines of one of Zen master Thích Nhất Hạnh's poems. Nhất Hạnh was another local poet and a Buddhist monk.

> *Kẻ thù ta không phải là người,*
> *Giết người đi, thì ta ở với ai?*

This slogan would later appear on a giant banner on the Chicago streets in 1967, along with the English translation:

> *Men are not our enemies,*
> *If we kill men, with whom shall we live?*

Dr. Martin Luther King Jr. himself had led that anti-war march in Chicago and walked under that long banner.

The South Vietnamese government started cracking down on the dissidents after the rally. But by then Lam and I were back home acting like nothing had happened, getting ready for our junior high entry exam. We were too young for anyone to notice. The authorities arrested Ngô Kha and, a year later, released him. But many other rally leaders, well-known and respected educators, escaped to the jungle. They were called *lên xanh*. Some returned two years later with the infiltrators during the 1968 Tết Offensive.

Five years after my first protest rally, my schoolmates and I at Quốc Học joined students from other schools in Huế on the street to request the release of Ngô Kha. We wrote a manifesto denouncing the election and demanding that local police immediately release the teacher and other leaders.

At the Lê Lợi–Duy Tân Square, I met Lam, my childhood friend, attending another high school in Huế. Lam stood at the front of the crowd, holding a white cloth banner with the slogan "Down with the police regime" and chanting "Down with America." He had forgotten his promise to the district chief back home.

Two years back, when we were still junior high students in the village, Lam had promoted a walkout to support the prison release of a Saigon student leader, Huỳnh Tấn Mẫm. He had organized the protest after receiving a leaflet from the Student Association of Saigon.

The walkout was a success; all students were out of classes. Someone had painted the word "walkout" in big red English letters on the school wall facing the trail that linked Route 1 to Camp Eagle, so the Americans could see.

The next day, the school principal called Lam to his office. Lam was terrified to find Major Dao, the district head, waiting for him. Lam thought of the district's tiger cages or the Thừa Phủ prison, which he'd heard about. To his surprise, Major Dao smiled at him and said, "You're too young to get involved in this kind of thing. Don't let anyone take advantage of your youth. I'll let you go this time, but you must promise me you will finish your schooling. Once you've completed high school, you'll be mature enough to decide for yourself what to do."

Lam had agreed and promised. I was struck by the chief's compassion and thought deeply about what the district head had said. My friend was lucky. And that chief taught me that war might not always be brutal.

But now Lam had changed his mind. He was back in the streets, despite not yet completing high school. I forgot the lesson and did the same.

The demonstrators marched past the spot where the Huế Buddhist crisis had taken place eight years earlier, where nine people had died. We approached the Trường Tiền Bridge. A line of riot police stood in the middle of the bridge, waiting for us. Without hesitation, we broke through the blockade and crossed the bridge over the Perfume River. Lam, in the front line, led the charge. The police fired tear gas at the crowd. We ran away, leaving the banners and signs scattered on the road under clouds of black smoke. Suddenly, I heard gunshots.

"They shot me," Lam screamed. Clutching his tummy, he fell on the bridge.

I couldn't believe it—Lam, in front of my eyes! It was a real thing, not a game or on the news. For the first time, I felt anger rising within me—a rage that I hadn't had before. I wanted to fight back at the police. I didn't have much, but I threw a rock, a poster and shoes at them. They returned fire with tear gas.

Lam, still holding his belly in pain, rolled on the bridge pavement, and his eyes caught mine. That encouraged me to run to him and call, "Lam, hold on."

Right beside him, a tear-gas shell started to release. In no time, the smoke engulfed us. I tried to get close to Lam, but an invincible force was holding me back—I could not stand the tear gas. I ran away and left my friend behind. From afar, I saw two men, their faces covered with gas masks, come and carry Lam to an ambulance and then drive him to a nearby hospital.

Later, Lam told me a doctor operated on him to drain the blood from his stomach and fix his liver. A tear-gas shell had hit him in the abdomen. Two years later, he accompanied me to Đà Lạt and then to Saigon. Whenever someone saw the twenty-centimetre-long scar on his tummy and asked him what had happened, he always said it was just a street fight. We did not want anyone to know what we had done in our youth. In those days, it was not wise to tell the truth; we lived with fake stories.

After many weeks of demonstration, the government released Thầy Kha from jail and returned him to the classroom. But he vanished again, for the third and last time, before the end of the next school year in 1972.

Over fifty years later, his family still could not find his body. Nobody knows who was responsible for his disappearance, but the new government recognized him as a martyr as his poem had predicted.

His martyr soul might wander somewhere in this overcrowded underworld along the Perfume River, waiting for his "Sunrise" with all the other martyrs killed in the past.

# PART 3

# *Runaway*

Calgary, Spring 2020

Dear Da-Lê,

You may have heard that the US government signed a peace agreement with the Taliban in Afghanistan. This event brought me back to almost a half-century ago, when the Paris peace treaty was signed in 1973 to end the Vietnam War. The 1968 Tết Offensive was a turning point. At the time, America's interest had also changed from isolation to strategic and economic alignment with Red China.

With pressure from China and the US bombing Hanoi, North Vietnam agreed to the treaty with a promise of compensation from the US. The US ignored the input from the South Vietnamese government. That was the end of "the domino theory"—that if one country became communist, others would surely follow. The superpowers had finished using Vietnam as one of their surrogate battlegrounds. Since then, China has transformed from a backward country to a modern one with the world's second-largest economy. Without financial and military support from the US, the South Vietnam regime collapsed with the fall of Saigon; the fallout from this would have the biggest effect on me.

My flashbacks from those years are vivid.

US president Richard Nixon introduced a policy to end US involvement in the Vietnam War in late 1969. The plan, the Nixon Doctrine, was to build up the local government forces to take over the defence of South Vietnam. This policy became known as "Vietnamization," as the US transferred its combat roles to South Vietnamese troops but continued its military supply and air support.

I was nineteen in 1972, when the war was at its peak. It was also the year the US had just withdrawn its troops and closed its bases. Because of the Vietnamization policy and the increasing military launch attacks from the North, the demand for soldiers in the South increased dramatically. The South ordered total mobilization to speed up the military draft. I wanted to follow my dreams of further education, and the only way to continue was to pass a grade each year. My goal became about more than just learning—it was about how to pass the exam. The war taught me to be practical: day-to-day-survival.

When I left Vietnam in January 1975, the SVA still held strong, even though the US had withdrawn its troops more than two years earlier. But suddenly, the North occupied Huế. In three months, the North took over the rest of the country, ending with the fall of Saigon on April 30, 1975. I lost contact with my family.

Da-Lê, I am afraid of a similar displacement. You and your brother always complain that we are too protective. Yes, we are protective parents. I haven't told you often enough of that fear—and where it comes from. I always want to connect with you two. Having you and your brother home, living under the same roof with us during the COVID pandemic, has felt like our wishes came true, in a way.

Calgary, Fall 2021
Dear Da-Lê,

History repeats. Now, the Taliban has taken back control of Afghanistan from the US-backed government, captured all major cities, including the capital of Kabul, and ended two decades of war with the US, Canada and other Western allies. The US-backed government collapsed while the US troops were leaving the country. People were stunned and could not believe that the regime collapsed so fast in a matter of weeks. Nobody in the Western media predicted that, even though it was just a matter of time. Saigon's and Kabul's governments were like leaking balloons with a continuous air supply. Without such a feed, they just collapsed and fell.

Now, the war in Afghanistan has ended. The last US military with its troops, diplomats and allies left Kabul, ending America's twenty-year involvement there. Like the Vietnam War, many Afghan army officers or civilians collaborating with America and its allies are left stranded, and many thousands of American soldiers will come home with PTSD. Unnoticed, each war also imposes that disorder on millions of children in the affected areas. They will survive on their own without any help, like your mom and me. But its effects don't stop there; it carries forward for generations.

I hope Afghanistan won't build any reeducation camps, or be placed under a US economic embargo like what happened in Vietnam, so that its people will avoid the same grave repercussions and conditions that forced Vietnamese people to leave their own country.

Love, Ba

## CHAPTER 19

# Vietnamization

*What do the Americans mean by the label "Vietnamization"? Isn't this the Vietnam War?* I wondered. It was the summer of 1972. *If that is not the case, we are not fighting each other, not our own war, but we are fighting for someone else's international war. We, in the South, have died for America or the West, and in the North for China and the Soviet Union. Is this why many leaders in the North have proudly claimed all along that they fought for the Communists? They refuse to call this war a civil war, or* nội chiến.

By late 1971, Nixon had reduced the number of US military personnel in Vietnam as quickly as possible. Camp Eagle at Dạ Lê was the first to go. The Americans had built the base in late 1967 to accommodate nearly ten thousand US soldiers to support the air power to the south. It covered the most northern area—from Huế to the DMZ, or demilitarized zone, the 17th parallel. My mom said she saw columns of black smoke rising from the base, and later I learned those were the locations of the burn pits. The Americans burned or buried on the spot anything that couldn't be carried back to the US. They left in a hurry. They had no regard for the people who remained living there.

Now that the US airpower no longer existed in the South, the NVA crossed the DMZ to take over Quảng Trị Province, north of Huế, in the late spring of 1972. The battle was known as the Easter Offensive, or the Summer of Fire, since it dragged on until it ended in the fall.

The North used a version of China's trademark invasion strategy—the human wave tactic—for the first time. The human wave tactic describes a military assault in which soldiers attack in dense groups to overrun the enemy by engaging in face-to-face combat. This tactic had no regard for human life and was nothing new: China had used this military scheme for each invasion of Vietnam. The first occupation lasted a thousand years, from 111 BC to AD 938, but the Vietnamese refused to assimilate and become more Chinese. Once Vietnam had gained independence from China, it spent another thousand years guarding against China's reinvasions. And that had happened frequently. The guerrilla warfare tactics successfully countered China's human wave attacks every time. This ongoing conflict reminded me of the beehives in my backyard. Even with the giant swarm's daily bullying, the smaller one kept its ground—until the human bullets destroyed everything. The bullets, in this case, represented the Westerners.

The North employed the same tactic, sending three army divisions with over forty thousand NVA troops to overrun the former US bases and the city of Quảng Trị. What a gamble that was! The North bet that the US airpower would not return. But it did, and the SVA took back the city. Thousands and thousands of people died.

People in the northern part of Quảng Trị Province ran south to Huế, away from the fighting. Many died on the road, and survivors became refugees in their own countries. The classrooms at my school became temporary shelters for the refugees from that province. School closed. And again, people ran south.

At the time, I was in eleventh grade and preparing to take the first round of the national exam required for my high school diploma, which would take place across the South in four months. I had to pass the exam; if not, I would be drafted soon after. Without a classroom, I studied on my own for the test. But I could not close my eyes to the needs of the refugees taking over my school for shelter. To help them, I joined the local Red Cross Youth at Thương Bạc's headquarters by the Perfume River. My team of six, all boys, collected food for the refugees and offered basic first aid.

After a short stint at the Red Cross, I was back to studying for the national exam.

---

I woke up under a bright light. I raised my hand to block the sun, which had risen above the bamboo treeline and beamed through the back window into my eyes. I had a hangover. Although I recognized I was lying on my old bamboo pallet, I had no idea how I got there.

"Cu tý, are you awake?" Mom asked.

"Why am I here, Mạ?" I closed my eyes against the light.

"You came home at the Hour of the Rat last night," she said. "You collapsed at the front door. I was worried."

The Hour of the Rat was around midnight. She still used the twelve zodiac animals to name the hours of the day.

*Last night? What happened last night? What did I do?* Many things raced through my mind. *Tri. Draft. Wine. War.* I started to recall. I remembered that Tri, my classmate, had come to my boarding house yesterday afternoon. Tri and I had both passed the national exam after completing grade eleven. Still, Tri was going to be shipped south in two days for military training, along with two other classmates from Dạ Lê. Our friends held a farewell party at a bar in the neighbouring village where the military curfew was more relaxed than ours. Our restriction was from an hour after dark to an hour before dawn. Between those hours, soldiers on all sides could shoot any moving object, no questions asked.

It was late in the summer of 1972. Because of the Vietnamization policy and military invasion from the North, the demand for soldiers, especially officers, had increased dramatically. The Defence Ministry had issued an order for total mobilization of the South to speed up the military draft and further restrict draft deferments for educational, medical and family reasons. Some students who had passed the exam, like Tri, but were over eighteen years of age without a draft waiver, had to join the SVA. They had to enter the Thủ Đức Military Academy, an officer training school, and those who failed the exam were to enrol in the other school, which was for non-commissioned officers, Đồng Đế. After six months of training, the graduates would be ready for the battlefield. By 1972, these military schools had more than doubled in size compared to their totals before the Vietnamization policy. I wondered whether the South Vietnam government was drafting so many young people into its army to keep them under its control. It would mean fewer people and fewer rallies in the streets.

"Have you seen Cam lately?" Tri asked me as we biked across the new bridge on the Perfume River. Cam was one of my childhood friends who would also join the army. Cam and Tri wouldn't have a chance to complete grade twelve; on paper, they were older than me by a year. (Since we were born in a rural area under French domination, the village officials had not yet certified our birth certificates at the time. We got one only when we needed it. People lowered their kids' age by a few years for registration. We all had two types of age: one actual and the other just on paper, and the former didn't count.) So, I had another year to study.

"No," I said. "What's Cam doing?"

"He got married last week," Tri said.

I stopped pedalling and let my bike glide. Cam was the best soccer player our village had ever produced. He had the most accurate and powerful left shot in our junior high school.

*Why didn't he invite me to his wedding?* I wondered.

Tri read my mind. "His family organized it in a hurry," he said. "Cam himself did not even attend his wedding."

"What?" I turned my head to face Tri. "Has he left the city already?"

"Yes, he's in Thủ Đức for military training," Tri said, while criss-crossing the road. "After the wedding ceremony, his parents sent his wife to join him." Cam's parents wanted a grandchild before something happened to him on the battlefield.

We biked in silence. After a while, I asked, "When will you join Cam?"

"In a few days," Tri answered sadly.

"You still have time to get married then," I joked.

Tri laughed and started singing "Kỷ Vật Cho Em," or "Mementos for You," a song about a young combat soldier who, as he is leaving for the battlefield, is asked when he will return. His last words, loosely translated, are, "You ask me when will I return? Let me reply that I will soon return: I will return as a decorated war hero, winning many battlefields, from Pleime to Bình Giã. I will return when trees rustle under a strong wind, in a wooden coffin covered with flowers, or on a stretcher on a helicopter painted white in mourning."

It had been one of the hit songs from Phạm Duy that you could hear anywhere you went in the South back then. The lyrics were from a poem written by Linh Phương, a second lieutenant of the SVA Marine Corps and a combat soldier. The song's sadness didn't help morale—the songwriter had changed it to a softer version—but people preferred the initial lyrics, especially after there was a rumour that the poet had been killed in battle.

Tri sang as if he were saying goodbye forever; his future was not up to him.

Tri and I arrived at the farewell party around six o'clock that evening. Several friends were already there. A village house was converted into a bar serving local beers and white rice wine. Like the sake of Japan, Vietnamese rice wine was made from fermented rice starch. People used rice wine in feast offerings to ancestors. I had tasted it once—too strong for me. I didn't like it. But this time, I enjoyed sipping rice wine from small cups with my friends and got drunk without even knowing it. We chatted about our childhood, laughed about the good times and grieved our losses.

We talked about our village elementary school that had been blown up by a bomb during the Tết Offensive. Nobody knew who had done that. It collapsed under a massive pile of rubble—my first school and also my first refugee camp. Over half of the graduates with me at the school had disappeared or died already. Some were dead on the roadside. Some even in front of that same school. Some at the village market. I had seen some, but not all, of their dead faces. And for those I did see, I still felt that their corpses were all looking at me.

Now more graduates were leaving school to join the fighting, and the rest would follow soon if the war continued much longer, including me. I hated the war, but at the same time, I envied my friends and I was ashamed of myself for delaying the draft by studying hard. I recited the poem "Sunrise," which Thầy Kha wrote and dedicated to his classmates at the same military academy that my friends were going to attend.

Late at night, we began reciting anti-war poems and singing anti-war songs. The owner had closed the bar but let us stay inside past the curfew. I felt sick and queasy; I rushed outside and vomited. That was all I remembered that night.

Mom handed me a warm glass she'd prepared to cure the hangover. "Drink this," she told me. "Hot lemonade with ginger."

I knew that remedy well; it tasted unpleasant—a combination of sour and spicy hot. I frowned and held the glass out to my mom. "Mạ, can you add some sugar?"

"No, this is medicine, not a treat," Mom said. "I didn't know you had started drinking."

I tried again. The remedy was terrible, but I felt better after finishing it.

"You walked home from where?" she kept asking.

I told her what had happened.

"What were you thinking?" She sounded angry and disappointed. "See what happens when you start drinking? You could be shot, and you were lucky. How far did you walk?"

"Just over three kilometres."

"All that distance under a night curfew—it's a miracle you didn't get killed." She paused. "Your dead aunt must have protected you; I'm going to make a feast thanking her."

She left the room and went outside to my dead aunt's shrine. With some burning incense sticks in her hands, she thanked my protector.

Everybody in the family except me believed that my aunt—the aunt who had been shot in the rice field during a night curfew—had saved my life many times, especially during the Tết Offensive. I hadn't recognized the miracles or honoured the graces I had received.

## CHAPTER 20

# Prison Exchange

The Americans wanted to leave Vietnam honourably and bring their prisoners of war (POWs) back home, so in 1972 they started bombing Hanoi to force the North to the negotiation table. With China's help in pressuring the North, North Vietnam and the US signed a treaty in Paris, ending the Vietnam War on January 27, 1973. This was the 1973 Paris Peace Accords, but it was without any input from the South. After this agreement, the 1973 Nobel Peace Prize was awarded to the US Secretary of State, Henry Kissinger, and the chief North Vietnam negotiator, Lê Đức Thọ. The latter refused to receive the prize.

I felt sad for the country, the South and the North. The Americans had landed their army ground troops on Vietnam's land without asking. Now, they abandoned the war regardless of its ally's wishes, without considering the long-term effects.

The Americans just changed their focus: Now they wanted to align strategically and economically with China. America's interests had changed, and this shift in policy would be neither the first nor the last. Meanwhile, Việt Cộng and the North celebrated the Accords as a "liberation" of South Vietnam from American imperialism. They proudly claimed that the Vietnamese could defeat any superpower and, unthinkingly, brushed off any sign that showed otherwise.

In the fall of 1972, I was back for the final year of high school, but with a different class of students. The school had broken up my old classmates and shuffled us around—both to prevent future rallies and because there was a lack of students due to military drafts. Without my close friends around, I felt isolated. The message was clear: Study hard and stay off the streets. However, that didn't keep us in.

This time the government army invited the university and senior high students to an event as an act of good public relations: a prisoner exchange at the Thạch Hãn River in Quảng Trị Province.

After the Paris Peace Accords, North Vietnam was supposed to provide the US with the names of the POWs held by its forces. These American POWs, including US aviator John McCain, returned through the Operation Homecoming program at the Gia Lâm Airport in Hanoi.

The exchange of Vietnamese prisoners from both sides took place at several locations across South Vietnam under the supervision of the ICCS. One of these was at the Thạch Hãn River in Quảng Trị Province. The SVA provided transportation for the students to go witness one of the events.

Instead of dressing in the school uniform of a white shirt and blue pants that day, I wore a long-sleeved army camouflage jacket I had bought at a flea market. After locking my bike in the school parking lot, I ran to the rendezvous point on Lê Lợi Boulevard. I approached a big open-top army truck filled with students, but I didn't see any of my classmates.

"Hey, over here," a female voice called out from the parked army truck. It was Hoa, and she was in the twelfth grade at Đồng Khánh, an all-girls high school. Đồng Khánh and Quốc Học stood side by side along Lê Lợi Boulevard, on the bank of the Perfume River. Between them was a small street with a row of red phoenix trees on each side. When we looked out the classroom windows from the boys' school, we could see the girls with long black hair, wearing their white *áo dài*, under those bright red blooms. Even though many romantic stories emerged from this beautiful scenario, my friendship with Hoa had nothing to do with that. Her mother was the owner of a maternity clinic and the person who had awarded the buffalo boys their first soccer ball—the ball that I had shot a hundred times.

"Climb up here! Quick!" She reached down and pulled me into the high truck.

"Thank you, Hoa," I said. "I couldn't find my group."

"Oh! It's nothing," said Hoa. "They just left. This is the last truck."

She made space next to her for me to sit down. Twenty girls, whom I guessed were from the same high school, stared at me—the only boy on the truck. They scanned me up and down, spoke softly and then chuckled gleefully. For me—someone who was so shy—it was excruciating. That was the worst experience with girls that I ever had. I felt my face grow hot. I kept nervously changing the position of my arms, from laying them on my thighs to putting them in front of my chest. Nothing worked. I questioned myself. *Why don't I just stare back at them? Is this a chance to look at each of them? Who's the beauty queen? The cutest? Why don't I have the confidence to stare right back and be a judge?* But those forty eyes were too much for me.

At nine o'clock sharp, the truck started to roll. It turned right on Lê Lợi Boulevard, crossed the Perfume River, passed the Imperial Citadel and headed north on Route 1. Outside the city limits, we began to sing.

The countryside was so peaceful that it seemed impossible for a war to occur there. A blue sky enveloped the green rice fields, and boys with conical hats waved from the backs of water buffaloes. Those images were not what I had expected; that section of the road had been the scene of daily sharpshooting.

After nearly an hour of driving, we were on La Rue Sans Joie (or "The Street Without Joy"), named by the French during the Indochina War. Route 1 passed through an area where sand dune after sand dune reached as far as the eyes could see. Việt Minh had used the dunes as hideouts for shooting the colonialists' passing vehicles. Once we had passed those mounds, we reached the Boulevard of Terror (*đại lộ Kinh Hoàng*). The name commemorated the killing of thousands of refugees on the road south of Quảng Trị during the Easter Offensive in 1972, a year prior. Some of those survivors were the ones who had reached Huế and were sheltered at my school.

The students stopped singing as we passed through this fifteen-kilometre stretch of road. We all sat in silence. We thought of those victims, whoever they were—the people who had gotten caught in the crossfire.

The Easter Offensive had destroyed the Quảng Trị Citadel. The roads were empty, like a ghost town with collapsed buildings, except for a few skinny dogs with haunted eyes. Even with the noise from the engine, the dogs wouldn't run away; they kept looking at the noisy truck.

The students passed through the citadel to reach the Thạch Hãn River, the temporary boundary separating North and South Vietnam. The Geneva Accords in 1954 had established the 17th parallel as the border. Still, Việt Cộng pushed the line thirty kilometres south, to the Thạch Hãn River, during the 1972 Easter Offensive.

The truck dropped off the witnesses on the southern bank of the river, a short distance from Quảng Trị Citadel. The waterway was shallow and narrow, just over a block wide. I could see a flag on the opposite bank belonging to the National Liberation Front of South Vietnam: a yellow star on a red and light blue background.

A group of SVA soldiers stood near the riverbank. Hoa walked quickly in that direction, as if she already knew who they were. I followed her.

"Hi, Thanh," she addressed one of the soldiers, an officer of the South Vietnamese Navy who was a few years older than us.

"Hoa dear, you're here," the officer answered, as though he'd expected her.

She introduced me to Thanh, her fiancé, a Navy officer.

Thanh directed us to the river edge anchoring several small wooden boats. A South Vietnamese government flag, with three red stripes on a yellow background, was attached next to the motor at the back of each canoe.

"We will take the prisoners to the other side in these vessels," the second lieutenant explained.

"Can I go with them?" I asked.

"No, you can't," Thanh said. "It's not for students, but you can if you're a news correspondent." He looked at my old army camouflage jacket, which journalists also liked to wear.

Hoa glanced at me, smiling.

That's how I boarded one of the boats.

Each vessel picked up six or seven Northern prisoners dressed only in brown shorts. They had removed all other clothes before departing, to show they needed nothing from the South. They left everything behind. Two of the seven prisoners who would be uploaded to our boat were having difficulty moving. One had lost his right leg while the other had lost his left, and they depended on their comrades to move. Thanh told me they were injured somewhere around here during the Summer of Fire over a year ago. Their comrades had left them to die on the battlefield. Still, the South Vietnam Army picked them up and then airlifted them to a hospital in Hué for emergency surgery. After a few months of recovery, they were sent to prison before being released: a return from the dead. They boarded the parked boat and I acted as a ferryman. I used a paddle to help guide the canoe. It reminded me of a children's game I had played back home when I was a child on the canal. This was just another game, but a man's game.

On one of those trips with the released prisoners, my boat got stuck on a sandbar in the middle of the river. The load of seven people on board was heavy. I jumped into the water and tried to push the vessel. We finally freed it, but one of my sandals was stuck in the quicksand. I was unable to retrieve my footwear and went home barefoot, wondering where I would get the money to buy new sandals for my school uniform.

My old sandals remained on the river bottom, a lost souvenir at a historic event.

## CHAPTER 21

# Goodbye, Huế

I n June 1973, I passed the second round of the high school examination. That was important, because it qualified me for admission to a
university.

Passing with top marks might even get me one of the rare scholarships for higher education overseas. Unfortunately, the passing grades
for students at my high school that year could not compare with the
rest of the country, because of civil unrest and fighting in Huế. Only
one student in the whole city had qualified for a scholarship that year,
and that student was not me. My dream to go abroad to study engineering evaporated.

That dream had first started back in 1969 when I met Neil
Armstrong in Huế at the Bob Hope USO show. I hadn't heard of Bob
Hope, but Neil Armstrong was my idol. Every student knew who
Armstrong was at the time. I had dreamed of being like him someday—as an engineer or a scientist—to work on something new. "That's
one small step for man, a giant leap for mankind," Armstrong had said
in July 1969 when he stepped off the *Lunar Module Eagle* and onto the
moon's surface. That had happened just five months before he was at
Camp Eagle. I couldn't help but think about how the landscape of the

area around Camp Eagle was not that different from the lunar landscape: no trees, and full of bomb craters.

Before leaving Vietnam, Armstrong gave a talk at the main opera house in Huế. As a member of the American Cultural Center Library, I got an invitation to attend his speech.

I looked up at my idol standing on the podium and tried to listen, but I could only pick up a few English words. I do remember Armstrong mentioned "God" a lot.

After the talk, Armstrong stood outside the opera house door to greet the fans. He was tall and charismatic. He shook my hand and gave me an autographed picture. I said I admired him and wished to become an engineer like him. In that instant, I had identified my dream. I didn't know whether the astronaut understood my broken English, but he smiled at me—as though he agreed that I would be a good engineer—and then turned to greet the next boy.

At least Mr. Armstrong agreed, and that was enough for me.

But now, that dream of going abroad to study engineering was very slim. I had come up with a new plan, though: I would go to Saigon in a bid to go overseas. Saigon was the only place I would be able to expand my horizons. My mother tried to help pull together funds for my trip by raising a pig. However, it died in the crossfire during an armed clash between VC and US soldiers one night, and I was devastated about it.

Then one day, at a coffee shop, I overheard two young girls discussing their upcoming church trip to another city, Đà Lạt. The highland town was about three hundred kilometres from Saigon; it was already three-quarters of the way! I approached the girls and asked about the pilgrimage. They looked at me hesitantly as if I were flirting with or making fun of them. After the girls realized I was sincere, they told me a local Baptist church organized a free ten-day Bible camp at the Đà Lạt Convention Centre. The catch was that those wishing to register for the trip had to attend some Bible classes to prepare for the excursion. So instead of celebrating my graduation, I spent a few days in the class, reading the Bible for the first time and pretending to be Baptist.

I wanted to have a companion for my trip, so I told my childhood friend Lam (the one who had gotten shot during a student rally). Lam liked the idea and agreed to join me as we embarked on an unknown future.

When I told my mom about leaving, it was surprising news to her. She thought I had already abandoned the idea ever since the pig died.

"Why don't you stay," she asked, "and complete your schooling here?"

"I want to be an engineer," I told her. "But Huế doesn't have an engineering school. If I go to Saigon, I have a chance."

"But you will need money." She looked at me, and I saw the sadness in her eyes.

"I have a free lift. You don't need to worry. Then I'll get a tutoring job, as I have done for the last three years."

I didn't tell her that I wanted to run away from Huế and Dạ Lê, as far as possible, to escape the fighting. The war was hanging in the sky, blowing in the wind, snaking along the river and hiding under the rice fields. I didn't tell her that it was everywhere—from the armed helicopters that people run away from, to the Agent Orange in the air that they breathe in, to the flood of toxic water that they live with, to the rice-field land mines that people try to avoid.

I wanted to be somewhere else—anywhere else—just as long as it was out of here. I kept my ultimate dream of going overseas to myself.

---

At daybreak, the pilgrimage group boarded a bus at the Baptist church and headed south on Route 1 toward Đà Lạt. As it turned the corner at Ngoẹo Giằng Xay, a Y-shaped junction, I realized that I was going to leave everything I knew behind. My life was like that elbow bend, and I wondered what would be at the other end. A long list of memories passed through my mind. Every inch of this section of road had imprinted marks on my heart and soul. This is the hazardous junction that I would bike through twice every school day. Each time, I had to stay vigilant to avoid being run over by US Army trucks.

After ten minutes of driving, the bus passed by Dạ Lê village market. It was empty at the time; no one except the cleaning person was out at that early hour. I waved at him. I didn't know whether the man recognized me, but he nodded. The market was the most public place in the village. If you wanted everybody in Dạ Lê to know something, you told someone at the market. Here was where many underground agents from both sides worked. *Look at the contents of the food basket. Look at whom they talk to.* Many bad things had happened here, too. A land mine had exploded a week after the 1968 Tết Offensive, killing my two young cousins. On my way to school over the years, I had seen more than one dead body lying at the base of that big banyan tree in front of the market. The bodies were typically left in a public place to deter people like me from joining Việt Cộng. The dead face of Big Cat with his one remaining open eye will never be erased from my memory. I thought of my mother; she would be coming here this evening to pick up her goods for the next day's sales trip.

The last thing I saw of Dạ Lê was a pile of rubble: the remainders of my elementary school and my first refugee camp.

I waved goodbye to the market, my village, my family and my friends. It would be a long time before I would return. But I promised I would come back someday—at any cost.

---

Around eight o'clock that morning, the bus arrived at the entrance to the Hải Vân (Sea Cloud) Pass. It had a single lane, so we had to wait for the oncoming traffic to get through first. A passenger train was approaching the longest tunnel in Vietnam—even in Southeast Asia. It's over six kilometres long and passes under the Annamite mountain range.

As it curved along the Lăng Cô Lagoon, the train looked like a giant snake sliding through the lush green of the hillside. Some passenger cars were concealed under trees, but others glowed in the morning sun, with still water below, casting a mirror image on the lagoon's surface.

The next waiting point was at the top, at five hundred metres altitude. The pass was craggy and dangerous. One side dropped into the abyss of the East Sea while the other rose steeply up the Trường Sơn Mountains. My stomach lurched with each hairpin turn. This twenty-kilometre stretch produced more accidents and deaths than the whole road from Huế to Đà Nẵng. From looking at the number of small shrines dotting the way—all built in remembrance of those lost—you could tell how treacherous it was. Not only that, but VC sharpshooters sometimes aimed at vehicles on the pass. The road signs were riddled with bullet holes. In the most dangerous sections, it was not unusual to see a warning in the form of a real human skull wearing a tattered conical hat on top of a bamboo pole. Those humorous but demeaning signs were put up there by American soldiers. For the Vietnamese, it is taboo to play with a human skull.

As the bus climbed, the pilgrims all squeezed their armrests and held their breath. At the top of the pass, we had a chance to get out to straighten our legs and breathe in the fresh air. It was a significant relief. The views were usually hidden behind clouds at that elevation, but the sky was clear and blue on that day. We could see the white beaches of Lăng Cô and the dark blue ribbon of the East Sea in the distance, where many seabirds were swooping and diving.

The bus stopped briefly in Đà Nẵng to pick up ten more boys and girls. One of the girls smiled charmingly at me when she was boarding. I thought she was an acquaintance, so I looked back. No, I hadn't seen her before.

Night had fallen when the group arrived in the city of Nha Trang, and I didn't have a chance to see its famous white sandy beaches. Some people called it the Miami Beach of Asia. We stayed at a Baptist facility that night. The distance between Huế and Nha Trang was about five hundred kilometers, but it took over twelve hours to drive. VCs had blown up most of the bridges on the main route in the last few years, and the Saigon government had yet to repair them. To bypass the collapsed roads, drivers had to make many detours and cross makeshift bridges, which slowed down the trip and tortured us with motion sickness all day.

We left Route 1 behind early the following day to climb a narrow paved road heading west toward Phan Rang and the central highlands. The countryside was primarily red, dry and silent; no animals or birds could survive in this environment. Only dragon fruit trees could grow in this arid soil. Now and then, ancient Cham towers appeared in the distance. I didn't know whether these made me feel the stillness of solitude or the sadness of a lost civilization. Many Cham people still lived in this area and formed one of the Muslim communities in Vietnam.

As the bus approached the highlands, I saw an ugly sign of two white pipelines from afar, like a couple of giant snakes crawling side by side up the green hillsides. Those tubes belonged to the Đa Nhim Hydroelectric Power Station, which was constructed in 1959 with reparations from Japan for its occupation of Vietnam during World War II. Under Japanese control, a famine occurred in northern Vietnam. From October 1944 to May 1945, several hundred thousand people starved to death. The older generation still told stories about hearing the clip-clopping of oxcarts that picked up the dead each morning from the streets of Hanoi.

After passing the plant, I got my first glimpse of Đà Lạt Valley off in the distance. Like turning the pages of a book, the landscape had changed before my eyes. No more dry land and ancient towers, but green everywhere. This could have been somewhere else—no longer in Vietnam but someplace in Europe, a scenic and peaceful place—that I had read and dreamed about. The air around us was fresh and the steep slopes were dressed in a thick green carpet. The valley was dotted with white waterfalls, like silk scarves hanging from a mystic sky. That green carpet was mostly made of chayote vines, and people called the area *thung lũng tình yêu* (the valley of love). Đà Lạt was also known as a city of flowers. It had European-style architecture and used to be a popular getaway for wealthy French people during the colonial era.

Lam and I shared a dorm room at the Đà Lạt Convention Centre. During French colonialism, this place had been the Đà Lạt School of the Christian and Missionary Alliance, or the Villa Alliance. The Villa Alliance purchased the facility in 1928 to develop a school for the children of missionaries whose parents served in French Indochina. In 1972, a year prior to our arrival, the Alliance had converted the school into a convention centre.

This facility reminded me of Cercle Sportif, a recreational facility for the intellectuals and wealthy elites in Huế. Even though I had never been there, I passed it twice daily on my way to school. Outside, I could see a swimming pool, a tennis court in front of the yard and a semi-circular balcony overlooking the romantic Perfume River behind the facility. I wished I could visit it one day.

Now I stayed at the Villa Alliance. It also had a large gym, a tennis court, a ball field and a dining hall. Yes, a large restaurant: something new to me. There had been no such thing in either my junior or senior school. I was experiencing the type of food that I only saw in some magazines, like an omelette with bread and butter for breakfast each morning. (They were less tasty than I had imagined.) I also took advantage of the athletic facilities.

One of the girls who had smiled at me from Đà Nẵng, Han, followed me wherever I went. To the mess hall. To the gym. To the tennis court. Every time I met her, I felt the sin growing in me like a cancer cell. Maybe she sensed my false intentions and wanted to convert me. She kept asking me Bible questions and telling me to read the Bible and pray more often. She even followed me into my room and insisted that I write in her scrapbook. I would be the first to compose anything in it, she had announced. Lam told her he'd be glad to inscribe the opening, but she refused. She wanted me and would be willing to wait. She would have been disappointed had she known my real plan.

After a week at the camp, Lam and I decided to leave; we went to see the pastor in charge of the Huế delegation. We wanted to go to Saigon as soon as possible, so we informed him we were taking an entrance examination for our engineering studies at the Phú Thọ Institute of Technology. I showed him the exam notice. With no questions asked, the pastor took us to the Đà Lạt bus station, bought us two bus tickets to Saigon and wished us good luck. He even offered us money for a return ticket to Huế. Lam and I thanked him, but we refused the latter because we had no plan to return anytime soon.

## CHAPTER 22

# Saigon, 1973

After a week in Saigon, police raided the house where Lam and I were staying and arrested Lam. They sent him back to Huế because he didn't have the proper papers—neither a travel permit issued by the local authority for a civilian nor an on-leave document for a soldier. I didn't have them either, but in a stroke of luck, I had been able to escape the raid.

We had been staying with Lam's relative Cường, who was also from Dạ Lê and a government army veteran. He had lost an eye in the war and now wore a one-eyed mask day and night. He lived with his wife and two small kids in a tiny house next to a nightclub on public land.

When the police knocked on the door that night, I opened it.

"Yes?" I asked.

"A house search," one of the two police officers in white uniforms said.

The house had no actual hallway, just a small entry where I slept in an army cot each night. The collapsible bed blocked their way when I opened the door and stood face-to-face with the police.

"Clear the doorway!" another police officer shouted.

While I was folding the cot, Cường came to the door. "What's going on?" he asked. Police could suppress a civilian but not a veteran during wartime.

"Police," I said and then carried the cot outside.

Once outside, I left the house. Loud music and laughter rang from the nightclub next door, and the smells of cheap perfume, alcohol and cigar smoke filled the air. I walked briskly, getting as far away from the bar as possible.

The police had raided the house because of that club—they'd hoped to make some money if they could catch someone frequenting the place without proper papers. They took Lam's ID, saying that he needed a travel permit from the authorities in Huế authorizing him to leave the city. Lam and I were aware of these papers, but never bothered to get them. The police told him that they would send his ID home, and he would get it in Huế in a week. Everyone knew if Lam paid them cash on the spot, his papers would be returned immediately. Of course, he had no money and accepted his fate of returning to Huế. *Is the government just trying to get rid of Lam, a continuous troublemaker?*

Saigon was a relatively peaceful place compared to Huế. The war was not visible, except for some anti-war rallies on the streets, occasional grenade-throwing incidents in public areas and nightclubs full of carefree soldiers and American GIs. People learned about fighting from the radio, television, newspapers and rumours. The war was here to stay and took place somewhere else, far away from Saigon's "indulgent" city life. If you were not from the war zones, you wouldn't even know where they were on a map.

The next day, I went back to Cường's house to collect my belongings—two pairs of clothes, some underwear and my school papers. Without a place to go, I looked around for Mai, a girl I had recently met, and saw no trace of her. She was older than me by a year or two and worked in the nightclub next door. I'd been attracted to her ever since I first saw her. We liked to talk to each other. But lately, she'd been avoiding me.

Mai had approached me a few days after my arrival in Saigon and offered me a pack of cigarettes. She must have seen me picking up cigarette butts outside the nightclub. I politely refused at first, but then accepted her offer because I needed it: I hadn't had a cigarette for several days. She started bringing me food from the nightclub, too. But I no longer needed her charity. I showed her my membership card for the Nam Viet Journalists Association, which I had just received. I had contacted the association after seeing a notice in the paper advising its unemployed members to use the card for free meals. Although I was not a professional journalist, I had written stories for one of Saigon's newspapers, *Trắng Đen*. I gave my pen name and the name of the newspaper to the association office; I became a new member. With the card, I was entitled to have one free hot meal each day at the members' clubhouse.

Mai and I had talked about our families. She came from a poor family of seven kids in Cần Thơ, on the southwestern outskirts of Saigon. I had heard a lot about that beautiful city. Canh, a soldier friend of my dad's who used to come to our house, was from Cần Thơ. He told me about the beautiful girls there—the most beautiful girls in the country. The Mekong River flowed through the city, and it was ten times bigger than the Perfume River. People called it Cửu Long, or "Nine Dragons." The river consisted of nine estuaries that all flowed into the East Sea. All were initiated from the highlands in Tibet and then sailed through China, Myanmar, Lao, Thailand, Cambodia and South Vietnam. Those estuaries created a transportation network around the delta region south of Saigon, which consisted of several ferry terminals and well-known floating markets.

There were many floating villages in or near Huế. I even visited one on the Tam Giang Lagoon, but I had not yet been to a floating market. The former was formed by several fishing families living on small boats. During the day, they fished anywhere in the lagoon. At night, they anchored their vessels together to protect each other and practise traditional village values. They built a shrine for the village deity to provide an abundance of fish for the lagoon and to protect them during the typhoon season each year.

I wished to see a floating market, and Mai promised to take me to her village to see one. She told me all about the hundreds of shops, and fruits I'd never seen before: durian, jackfruit, papaya, mangosteen. Then suddenly, she started to avoid me. My landlord's wife confronted her and accused her of enticing me, as I would find out much later. I never saw her again.

---

My landlord's wife feared I would quit school if I became too involved with a girl. She understood that Lam and I were in Saigon to attend an engineering school, but she didn't know I had failed the entry exam. After so much travel, I had been too exhausted to perform well. To avoid being drafted, I had to settle for an entry-level class at the University of Saigon. I was disappointed: I could have taken a class like this in Huế, and I would not have needed to come here.

After leaving Cường's house, I met Hen, a hometown acquaintance from Dạ Lê who had a wife back home. He had left everything in the village to live the life of a homeless person in Saigon. Hen occupied a makeshift room and let me sleep there, too. With him, I had a place to sleep. Night after night, I slept with a broken dream and tried to seek a way out of that abyss of disappointment. During the day, I would attend my class, go for lunch at the social eating house, and then wander the city streets until I was tired. I would go home at night with an empty stomach. The Saigon weather was hotter and more humid than the norm. My body was like rice noodles boiling, too soft to do anything. I felt myself sink ...

---

After staying at Hen's place for a few months, O Trang, a distant aunt, asked me to tutor her two preteen sons. I had never really met her because she had left the village when I was still an infant. She owned a few stores in the centre of Saigon by the Bến Thành Market. Her house was a haven for military draft evasion, and you could count the "who's who" in Saigon's current regime among her friends. Mr. Lương, chairman of the Lower House part of the government, borrowed her black limousine with a chauffeur when he attended a formal function. She let me stay at her house to teach her kids, who were in fourth and fifth grade at Lasan Taberd next to Saigon Notre-Dame Cathedral. I received no pay, but room and board was covered. I had a meal each evening with her workers at the back of the bakery—the lower level of the building accommodated her well-known French bakery, Le Croissant. I was glad that everything was working out nicely.

O Trang and her two kids lived upstairs. She was the wife of a late well-known bakery owner and had a teenage daughter attending a private school in Đà Lạt.

She became more paranoid after the first week I was there. My aunt had nightmares about robbers invading her home. She asked me to sleep outside her bedroom door, armed with a golf club. I was often woken up in the middle of the night looking for intruders. At first, I believed her, but I stopped hunting for imaginary robbers after several false alarms. Even with these nighttime duties, my reward was the same—free boarding and a meal with her bakery workers.

Before I came to stay at O Trang's house, I had already registered for admission at the University of Saigon in the Faculty of Science for Mathematics, Physics and Chemistry (MPC). My class had at least a thousand students. Not even the largest lecture hall at the university had enough seats for us. I was usually late and ended up standing at the back. From there, I was unable to hear or see anything. Some students around me preferred to leave, saying it was no use standing there. They would rather spend time in the coffee shop outside the hall, talking to one another or teasing girls instead.

One morning, nobody was in the mood to tease anybody.

"Did you hear about Communist China attacking us?" a male voice said.

I turned around. Four guys were sitting at the table behind me.

"Two days ago," a student wearing a white shirt said, "Communist China invaded our Paracel Islands in the East Sea, slaughtered seventy-four sailors and occupied the islands." This battle of the Paracel Islands was lopsided, since South Vietnam was weakening due to the withdrawal of the US. We were in the last days of the war with North Vietnam.

"Fuck the Communists." A student in a green jacket stood up. "I think Communist China has had bad intentions all along; they help the North so they can influence Vietnam."

A long-haired student chimed in. "Something more is at play here. I think China wants to take over the East Sea. They claimed the South China Sea as their own because the name has China in it."

I was mesmerized by the conversation. It had been less than a year since the signing of the Paris Peace Accords between the US and North Vietnam. I asked, "Did the North do anything?"

The student in the white shirt looked at me. "Because of this so-called peace accord," he said, "the American and North Vietnamese forces stand by and watch, as if the invasion had nothing to do with them."

"There is a rally against the Chinese invasion today in the city," someone announced.

"Let's join in," the student in a green jacket said.

With the students in the coffee shop, I joined a march on Saigon's streets that day to protest the Chinese aggression. They held banners with statements like "The Paracel Islands belong to Vietnam" or "Our people are determined to stand behind the SVA." Over ten thousand students filled the streets in huge throngs; it was the most crowded rally I had ever attended, and it was my first and last political protest in Saigon.

## CHAPTER 23

# Overseas Scholarship

At the end of my first year at the University of Saigon, I noticed a small announcement on its bulletin board. The king of Iran, Mohammad Reza Shah, had offered three scholarships to Vietnamese college students to study in Iran toward a degree in petroleum engineering. Those scholarships were the Shah's gift to commemorate a new friendship between Iran and South Vietnam. I couldn't believe my eyes. University scholarship. Overseas study. Engineering degree. Best of all, I had a chance to get out of Vietnam, away from the war. I had to get one of those scholarships. I put all my energy into investigating that announcement.

Did I know anything about Iran or petroleum? Nada. Where's Iran? I didn't care. I just wanted to run away from the war.

I could recall some history. Besides Iran replacing Canada in the ICCS, people from the Persian Empire had come and lived in Vietnam as merchants since ancient times. One of those was Khương Tăng Hội's father. Khương Tăng Hội (Kang Senghui) grew up in Vietnam around the third century. He is regarded as the first Vietnamese patriarch of Zen Buddhism in Vietnam. Other than that, I had read only one book remotely related to the country: *One Thousand and One Nights*. These stories, like "Aladdin's Lamp" and "Ali Baba and the Forty Thieves," were about the Persian Empire. I enjoyed reading those stories, but I didn't learn anything about Iran's role in the petroleum industry. Vietnam had recently discovered oil off its coast—a big thing for Vietnam. I wondered whether this oil discovery had instigated China's ambitions to own the East Sea and claim its natural resources.

I went to the government office of oil and gas on Nguyễn Bỉnh Khiêm Street to learn about Rose 9—Vietnam's first oil well, drilled by Mobil Oil on the coast of Vũng Tàu. I met Lê Phi Sơn, a chemical engineer who recently repatriated from the US.

"I heard about the scholarships," Sơn said when I introduced myself to him in his office. "The country needs more petroleum engineers, and we don't have any right now."

Sơn invited me to accompany him on a boat tour to the well site from Vũng Tàu. From afar, Sơn proudly pointed toward the Rose 9 well. He stood on the gunwale with his giant tie, too big for his petite frame, flapping in the wind as he held onto the curved front glass of the boat with his left hand. Behind him, a flame from the oil platform appeared on the horizon. As the boat approached the drilling platform, he told me that a test was underway at the well's site to learn more about the formation pressure, fluid type and size of the oil pool.

That first glimpse of an oil well heightened my interest in the oil and gas industries, and my desire to someday help my country.

I applied and got one of the scholarships. The other two successful candidates were also students in my same faculty of science. I was excited when I read the acceptance letter. But it also reminded me that the scholarship would not include any travel expenses; it was the responsibility of the candidates to bear the cost. These conditions might not be a problem for the other two candidates, but they were for me. Where and how could I get the money?

I sent a letter to my father to tell him the good news: I was getting a scholarship to go overseas. I also mentioned the remaining two hurdles and hoped he could help, especially with the paperwork to pass the background check. This was a challenge for any poor student, especially from a war zone.

A month later, I received a letter from my father.

The family was so excited and proud of me, Dad wrote—not only the family but the whole hamlet. The village school hoped that more students would follow suit. The shoeless peasants were also proud that one of their members would study overseas. He assured me that I didn't need to worry about the airfare: The head of the family clan had agreed to organize a meeting to raise funds for me. The best news was that the local authority had cleared my background check, and he expected I would pass the security check.

The following month, I received more good news from the family. The clan head had collected some money to help me buy the ticket. My mother had also sold a few gold chains that she got on loan from the neighbours. In total, I received about one hundred dollars when converted into US currency. It was a large sum of money—more than my family had ever had—but it was only a quarter of the price of a one-way ticket from Saigon to Tehran. I was disappointed, but fully aware of my relatives' poverty. Toward the end of 1974, the war had become more intense; the rice paddies in the village lowland and the cassava fields in the highlands were full of land mines and unexploded artillery shells. People avoided those places altogether; nobody wanted to get killed or lose a limb. My relatives and the villagers didn't have enough food to eat, let alone money to give me charity.

---

It was a little more than a month before Christmas 1974. The winter semester had already started without me, over three months ago. I still needed to come up with the four hundred dollars I needed for a one-way airfare. The other two candidates were ready to go on short notice, but I was not. We had not left the country yet. Not because of me, but because of bureaucracy: We still needed to receive our passports. And to buy an air ticket, we needed a passport. To receive a passport, we needed a scholarship decree. We needed to know who to ask to receive a scholarship decree, and I didn't know who that would be. All I knew for sure was that I needed money to fly to Iran.

"What's wrong with you?" The accountant at the bakery, Thu, jolted me out of my reverie. I lifted a birthday cake from the display case and crushed the icing, accidentally sliding it against the glass. Some of the decorations were now lopsided.

"Sorry, miss. My mistake," I said to the customer. "Please wait a few minutes while we fix it." She frowned and then nodded. I thanked her with heartfelt appreciation.

I brought the cake to the back of the store. Lucky me—the best cake decorator was in and available. I had picked up some cake decorating skills at the bakery. Still, apart from my handwriting, my artistic skills were not on par with those of the professionals. Furthermore, I couldn't concentrate. My body was here, but my mind was somewhere else.

Serving customers was not my job; I just liked to spend some of my free time at the store. The supervisor, accountant, chauffeur and bakers were my friends; I could talk to them when needed. Now and then, they gave me some coffee money. Coffee and cigarettes were the two most essential items; most young Vietnamese couldn't live without them at the time.

After delivering the cake to the waiting customer, I sat next to the accountant's desk in the back of the store. "I should be more careful," I said.

"Have you talked to Madame yet?" Thu asked.

At the store, we all called O Trang "Madame."

"Yes, I have," I said.

"Then, what did she say?"

"She said I should let her know the departure time, so she can buy me a suit before I go."

Thu leaned forward and pressed his palms together. "Did you mention you may not be going because you have no ticket?"

"I mentioned it, but she didn't say anything," I said. "Maybe she didn't hear me."

"Why don't you ask her for a loan?"

I looked up the stairway that led to Madame's living quarters. She had come down and left the store a few hours earlier. "Maybe I should," I said, then shook my head. "Oh, no. I don't think so."

"Why not?"

"I overheard her telling a friend that she never loans money to relatives or friends," I said. "Lending to them is like saying goodbye to the money, she said."

While we were talking, Be, short for Robert, came in clutching a newspaper under his right arm. Be was Madame's chauffeur and had just brought her back to the bakery. She was speaking to one of the customers in the fabric store she owned next door, operated by her sister.

The chauffeur showed me the front-page news with a photo of the student rally.

"Is this you?" Be asked me. "It looks like you, with the hippie hair and eyeglasses."

I took the paper from the chauffeur and scrutinized the picture. "No, it's not me." But I kept looking at the photo. One student at the front, facing the riot police, did look like me. But I was too busy for this stuff.

"Let me see," Thu jumped in.

I handed the newspaper to the accountant.

"Oh, my God," Thu said while looking at me, worried. "If the police see this photo, you won't need to worry about the ticket anymore."

Be lent me the paper. I took it to my room and studied the black-and-white photo of the rally. The picture might have been taken several months prior, during the student march against the Chinese invasion of the Paracel Islands. No, it was a different one. The person in the photo was not me. The small red headline in the right corner of the bottom page caught my eye instead. In German, it said "Brot für die Welt," or "Bread for the World," to help the poor in Asia. I was poor and needed help, didn't I? So I wrote a letter to the charity agency.

About two weeks later, I received a reply, which I've included here verbatim (their English was not perfect):

Brot für die Welt

7 Stuttgart 1

Stafflenbergstrasse 76

November 25, 1974

Dear Mr. Duong,

We have received your letter of November 9, 1974, in which you asked us whether it is possible to help you. We understand that you are a student at Saigon University, Faculty of Science, planning to go to Iran for further studies.

Unfortunately, it is not possible for us to assist a person directly but only within a programme. However, in order to help you a bit further I would advise you to contact Mr. Ninh, the director of Asian Christian Service (42 Ngo Thoi Niem, Saigon) with whom we cooperate since years. Perhaps he can find a way to help you.

With kind regards,
Wolfgang Schmidt
Asia-Deck

With the letter from Brot für die Welt in hand, I went to the address to meet Mr. Ninh, its director. The Asian Christian Service (ACS) told me to return on Monday at three in the afternoon.

At that appointment, Mr. Ninh informed me that the organization had called a meeting. It agreed to assign a fund of nearly four hundred US dollars to buy a one-way air ticket from Saigon to Tehran for me to study petroleum engineering, starting this school year. To receive the fund, I had to come back once I had gotten the scholarship decree. Then, I would sign a commitment letter to confirm that I wouldn't accept any other help for this travel expense. The ACS would not be responsible for other expenditures during my overseas study. I agreed to all the conditions and promised to return.

I hopped on the old bike I had left at the gate. I had borrowed it from a classmate, and it used to make some clicking noises with every spin, but now it suddenly rode smoothly. Those annoying sounds had disappeared and my body hummed with joy.

"I'll give you back to your old boss," I said to the bike. "Anyway, thanks a lot."

The return trip seemed much shorter.

A few days later, I was walking through the bakery toward the stairs, and the accountant looked up as I passed his desk.

"You have a letter," Thu said.

The accountant picked up a white envelope from the basket before him and gave it to me. I received it with shaking hands. The return address was the Vietnamese Embassy in Tehran. That was what I had been waiting for: "go-ahead" instructions to complete all the required procedures. I opened the letter.

"What does it say?" Thu smiled, expecting good news.

"I don't believe it! I don't believe it!" I kept repeating to myself.

"The scholarships have been postponed until the next school year." The letter was in English, so I translated it for the accountant. "We've already missed the first semester, so the school thinks we won't be able to catch up. They want us to start next September."

I paced back and forth from the desk to the stairway.

"So, you'll go next year," Thu said.

"But my draft waiver will expire in June, and by then, I'll already be in the army." I crumpled the letter and threw it in the garbage can next to the accountant's desk. I was crushed.

Getting out of Vietnam was so close—I could almost hold it in my hands. But before I could grasp it, the plan disintegrated between my fingers. It was like tearing up a lottery ticket that then hit the jackpot. Could I put the pieces together again? I believed I could. But how? I didn't know. *Keep thinking*, I told myself.

I left the house and kept walking and walking, oblivious to time. I didn't know where I was going. Just walking and thinking. *There should be a way to overcome this.*

I didn't know how long I had walked. The night had fallen over Saigon. Tonight was my turn as a guard for the People's Self-Defence Forces in the neighbourhood. Like every male student at the university with an educational draft deferment, I had to report for duty two nights a week; otherwise, my waiver would be revoked. I went to the militia office for Bến Thành Ward and picked up a small amount of ammunition and a rifle. It was a Garand M1, the same type of gun that had been used to fire at me for an hour on the paddy field. I held the gun, hoping I wouldn't have to shoot anyone. The rifle had been a surplus from the US forces in World War II and then the Korean War, and now it was a leftover from the SVA. I had learned how to use it in high school as part of the compulsory military training, but except for target practice, I'd never fired a single shot.

As usual, my post that night was at the Quách Thị Trang Roundabout, named after the fifteen-year-old student shot in the square during a demonstration in August 1963 against the Diệm regime. With a rifle in hand, I sat under the base of the Quách Thị Trang Monument. The square was a well-known landmark in Saigon and was always full of people.

*Beep beep.* Car after car kept honking their horns to get the pedestrians out of the way. But many drivers honked for no reason: They were just competing for the most unpleasant sounds. Some of my friends had told me they somehow missed those sounds while away from Saigon, but I knew I wouldn't. I looked up at Trang's young, charming face at Quách Thị Trang Roundabout and the innocent statue above me. Following her gaze, I faced the Bến Thành Market. Many commercial ads were displayed at the top of its front wall, and the advertisement for Hynos toothpaste couldn't be missed. When I looked up, a giant billboard showing the head of a dark-skinned guy with big white, bright teeth was smiling at me. It reminded me of how I had used a piece of dried areca nut and sea salt to clean my teeth every day back in Dạ Lê.

On my first day here, I had been impressed by the busy and crowded market, which looked like a beehive. Everybody seemed to be in a hurry. They walked very fast and ignored the other people around them as if all Saigonese were being chased by an invisible force. Now, all the shops were closed, but people still walked in and out.

Behind the statue, several young girls in heavy makeup and skimpy outfits stood under the lampposts. They displayed their bodies and waved at the passing vehicles each night. Some honked or whistled back. I wondered how Trang would have felt about them night after night. She might have shared my feelings about it: We were all just the victims of war. And my duty tonight was to protect the young girls and keep a safe working environment.

On my left, headline after headline of electronic news was reflected on the dark wall. Some headlines were about Christmas shopping, as it would soon be December. But the most important one was about the fierce fighting in Huế and its surrounding areas.

If I couldn't go abroad now, it probably meant it would never happen.

Then I had a thought. Why didn't I write a letter to the Vietnamese ambassador in Tehran to ask for his intervention? I started composing the letter in my head.

Yes. I should tell him how hard I tried to find the money for airfare. I should explain that missing the first semester would not affect my studies since I'd already completed my first year of science courses.

Back in my room, I wrote the letter.

Three weeks later, I received a response from the Vietnamese embassy in Tehran. The letter was dated Christmas Day, 1974. Did the ambassador write it on his day off? Was there a Christmas Day in Tehran?

The Republic of Viet Nam

Ministry of Foreign Affairs

The Embassy

Teheran

Teheran, December 25, 1974

To: Duong Ngoc Anh

Saigon

RE: Scholarship from the National Iranian Oil Company (NIOC).

After receiving your letter dated 12/03/1974, requesting my intervention based on your situation mentioned in the letter, I contacted the office of the National Iranian Oil Company (NIOC) at Teheran.

The result, as of today, is that NIOC has sent a telegraph to inform us of a special exception: you are to receive the scholarship this school year instead of next year, as was previously stated. The Embassy has urgently telegraphed the Ministry of Foreign Affairs to inform the Ministry of Education to let you leave the country to start class as soon as possible.

I also request that you contact the Ministry of Education immediately for completion of all necessary procedures.

Best Regards,

Ambassador

Luong Nhi Ky

So, I'd be going overseas to study within a month after all.

Two days before I boarded an Air France plane to Tehran, Madame had taken me to a clothes shop and bought me a ready-made suit. She kept telling the store owner, her acquaintance, that her nephew had just received a scholarship to study overseas. With a rushed send-off, she didn't have time for a custom-made suit. I wondered whether her friends knew I was going to Iran, not France or America. If they did, they might think my aunt sent me there as a punishment.

## CHAPTER 24

# Iran, 1975

I was out of the war zone.

In the late evening on January 21, 1975, Air France Flight 197 landed at the Mehrabad International Airport in Tehran after a snowstorm. A layer of white—falling from the sky, sticking to the trees and coating the ground—had greeted my arrival. My first experience with snow.

Outside the airport with only a light suit on, I felt the coldness—like cold water flowing through my body—as the snow fell around me. The smell was fresh. The snowflakes glinted in the white lights of the terminal; they gave me a sense of weightlessness, relaxation and ease. I had a strange feeling that I had been here before. *Am I dreaming? No, this is real.* To make sure, I reached out to catch the snowflakes, but they melted in the palm of my hand. My worries disappeared and I felt much lighter, like the snow around me. I touched some snow piles on the pavement. It was smooth and not as cold as the ice that we used to make snow cones back home in Saigon. I must have read about a place like this and imagined it so vividly that I thought I'd experienced snow before. New, cold, exciting, fresh, amazing, peaceful—those were my first impressions of Iran.

The previous afternoon, Thiếu Dao, a classmate from my high school in Huế, and three other friends had come to the Tân Sơn Nhứt International Airport (now Tân Sơn Nhất) in Saigon to send me off. It was sudden; within a month, I had to go. That was it. Nobody from my family was there. I left Vietnam without saying goodbye to any of them. The village was in the fighting zone about nine hundred kilometres from the airport, making contact impossible. I already missed my family as I was boarding the plane. I just looked up at the northern sky, waved goodbye and promised to return in a few years.

"Taxi?"

The driver jolted me out of my daydream. I climbed in and gave him the address of the Vietnamese embassy, where I was instructed to stay. During the taxi ride, I kept quiet or smiled back at the driver when he spoke in what I assumed was Farsi. I couldn't understand a word. Here and there, he also asked me questions in English, and I could pick up a few words.

Even under a layer of snow, Tehran looked more modern than Saigon. Beautiful buildings. Clean roads. And more cars and far fewer bicycles on the streets.

The driver dropped me off in front of a small villa, a yellow-ochre French colonial building with a high wall. It reminded me of the government buildings in Saigon. The wrought-iron gate was locked, and the building was dark. I was a few hours late because of the snowstorm. There were many questions in my mind. I came without any instructions except the embassy address. *Has the embassy closed for the day? Is anyone there to greet me? Where will I spend the night? How can I get another taxi? I am alone in this new city, knowing no one beside the ambassador.* The cold seeped through my thin suit. I rechecked the directions, but the numbers on the gate looked like squiggly tadpoles with an upside-down V, a reverse number 7, and some dots.

The snow kept falling. It no longer seemed pleasing—like a shroud that buried me deep into my loneliness.

Below the indecipherable letters was a brass plate. I brushed off the snow and saw the Ambassade de République du VietNam sign and a gate bell. I pressed the button.

After a few minutes, a light inside the building came on.

"Hi, are you a new student?" a short Asian woman in her early thirties asked in Vietnamese as she peered through the gate. She had a southern Vietnamese accent.

"Yes, I am. I'm late." I was filled with relief.

"Please, come in," the lady said. "Aren't you cold?" She opened the gate just enough for me to pass through. She explained that she had just arrived from Saigon a week prior and had not yet found a place to stay. She was the ambassador's new assistant.

The embassy had closed for the day, but it served as a temporary guesthouse.

---

The following morning, I opened the window for fresh air. Beautiful scenery I had never seen before appeared in front of me. A small ray of the morning sun twinkled through the garden, full of white crystalline trees. It was even more striking than the scene at the airport. Everything was so clean and quiet, and I wanted to go outside and touch those ice crystals. No war, nor terror. The conflicts in Vietnam had dragged on and on for over two decades, since long before I could remember. I hoped I would leave all that behind. Even though I was sad for my family, at the same time, a new phase of my life had begun.

That evening, the ambassador, Lương Nhị Kỳ, and his wife, Jeanne, invited his new assistant and me to dine at their residence. Kỳ was in his late forties or early fifties and had a receding hairline. He was shorter and much stouter than his wife. Jeanne was in her late thirties, as glamorous as a movie star. She reminded me of Farah Pahlavi, then the empress of Iran, whose picture I had seen in a magazine. The ambassador's wife was Vietnamese but grew up in Paris as a French citizen. Kỳ told me that he had received a PhD in political science in the US and was an expert on Vietnamese–Chinese relations.

Kỳ had been the first South Vietnamese ambassador to Iran ever since Iran became the fourth member of the ICCS, in June 1974. The ICCS consisted of military and civilian personnel from two communist nations, Hungary and Poland, and two non-communist nations, Canada and Indonesia. After some protests regarding treaty violations, Canada withdrew and Iran replaced Canada as a non-communist nation.

Kỳ had had a challenging time in his new role. For the first six months, he had no aide. He did everything himself, including typing letters and sending cables. One of the first things he did was to ask the government of Iran and its king, Mohammad Reza Shah Pahlavi, to train South Vietnamese students in the field of oil and gas. Because of various bureaucratic delays, I was the only scholarship student who had come for undergraduate study in the oil city of Abadan, on the Persian Gulf. Two others might come the following summer.

## CHAPTER 25

# Fall of Saigon

After one day in Tehran, I left the capital to travel to my new college, located in the Persian Gulf. Toward the end of a twelve-hour bus ride, I got my first glimpse of Abadan, Iran's oil capital. Once an ancient civilization and mystical city, Abadan was now dominated by dun-coloured buildings, the skyline obscured with tall towers and flares—the Abadan refinery. I could taste the oil in the air as the bus approached the city limits.

I arrived at the Abadan Institute of Technology (AIT), which is now the Petroleum University of Technology. A senior student, Errol, greeted me at the gate. Errol, who was from Jakarta, Indonesia, would be my roommate for the next few years. It was Friday—a weekend in the Persian calendar—and the school was closed. Errol took me to the foreign student dormitory. All its guest students came from Algeria, Turkey, Pakistan and Indonesia—the countries that belong to the Organisation of Islamic Cooperation (OIC), with its head office in Tehran. The OIC is an international organization founded in 1969. It has fifty-seven members, primarily Muslim states, and Vietnam has never been one of them. I was the first Vietnamese or non-Muslim student at the residence, and as it turned out, I would also be the last. By default, everyone at the institute assumed I was a Muslim. On the afternoon of the date I arrived, a group of students began to pray in the dormitory hallway. They conversed mainly in English. I stood there by myself and did not know how to react. I felt like an outsider and realized I was different for the first time. It was a feeling that I would not be able to get rid of; it kept following me. One of the students wondered why I did not pray. When I said I wasn't a Muslim, the student wrinkled his nose and grimaced at me, like looking at a stranger. He could not believe that I, a non-believer, could function normally.

The dormitory was inside the college perimeter, surrounded by a tall wall. It was intended to isolate foreign students from the outside world. From the window of my room, I could see a small lawn with a brick wall. Not a soul. But I felt relaxed—no more noise or people around. No bombs. No explosions.

Even though I had made it to Iran, my heart and mind remained in Vietnam. When I left the country, intense fighting had been underway in Huế and its surrounding area. Now, Huế was on the brink of falling to Việt Cộng. I kept thinking of my family in the village.

I went to class on Saturday—a school day in Iran. It was the day after my arrival, and I was surprised that all the students dressed in Western clothes, including the only female student, the last girl admitted to AIT. No one at the institute wore a chador. Most of the teachers were visiting professors from the Petroleum Engineering Department at the University of Southern California, and instruction was in English. I had a lot of things to catch up on. New country. New customs. New language. New school. New teachers. New friends. Everything was brand new to me.

But something else had happened that I didn't expect. After a month at AIT, my ambassador in Tehran informed me that the institution might send me back to Vietnam if my marks didn't improve soon.

I had started in the second semester without any desire to learn. My mind was full of everything that was going on back home. My hometown had been cut off, and the collapse of the South Vietnamese government was near. I couldn't concentrate, and I was having trouble with my studies. The school policy was to send any student who was failing the first year back to their home country. I had already missed the first semester, and they didn't expect me to pass the second. If they were correct, the college would send me home—at my own expense. Now I understood why the scholarships hadn't included travel costs in the handout.

Dr. Ahmadi, my chemistry professor, called me to the front of the class one morning to write chemical reaction equations on the blackboard. The professor said it was a review of the previous semester that I had missed.

"Mr. Duong," said Dr. Ahmadi, leaning back in his desk chair, "show me a reaction of aqueous acetic acid added to solid sodium carbonate."

*What symbols? What formulas? Yes, I studied those reactions three semesters prior, at the University of Saigon. How can I remember an equation from that long ago?* I tried to scribble something on the board.

"Wrong, wrong, wrong," Dr. Ahmadi said. "The symbols of the reactants are correct, but the equation is all wrong. Go back to your seat."

I went back to my seat and pretended to be unflappable.

Dr. Ahmadi called me up to the blackboard in every class he taught. If I could not solve the problem, he asked Masood to do it for me. Masood was the brightest student in the class. I was humiliated, and felt this was Dr. Ahmadi's way of saying, "Those foreign students don't know a thing. We pay their expenses, so they come for fun, not to study."

Some of my classmates sympathized with me and brought their notes from last semester. They told me what to review and which chapter I should read before attending class. That should get me back on track.

One day, Sara, the dean's assistant, approached me as I passed her office.

"*Salaam*," she greeted me, smiling. Sara always wore a black skirt with a long-sleeved blouse, and she was one of only two female administrative staffers. That was the first time I really looked at her face. She was about twenty, with slightly dark skin, sandy hair and blue eyes. I hadn't noticed she was that beautiful and friendly.

"*Salaam alaykum*," I said.

"Your books have arrived. Can you come to my office to pick them up?"

I had ordered some textbooks and was waiting to read the upcoming chapter ahead of each class. I nodded and followed her.

After that day, Sara liked to talk to me whenever she had a chance. She asked me about my family's well-being back home and my progress with my studies. Her smile and concern made my day brighter—otherwise, my mood felt like the sky on a cloudy day.

---

Receiving any news or a letter from my family was something I wished for every day—a wish and form of hope that I needed for survival. Day after day, I went to the college's post office thinking a letter was waiting for me. Two months after arriving at AIT, I received my return letter: a red mark on the envelope I'd addressed. "Temporarily disconnected."

With the letter in hand, I looked out the window. Far into the desert on the left, a single bird flew aimlessly in the grey sky. Like a bird, I felt lonely. I wanted to fly away. No boundary. No separation. No displacement. I was starting to daydream again, picturing myself somewhere else.

*I want to be back in Dạ Lê, sitting with my siblings around the open fire in our front yard, sharing a bowl of white rice full of boiling cassava, waiting for Mạ to return from work with some sweet treats. I want to be in the paddy at the back of my house, to feel the gentle wind from the rice plants on my face each summer. I want to breathe the fresh air under the blue sky as the sun rises, to play a soccer game with the buffalo boys on an open field. I want, I want ... Everything is out of my reach.*

———————

I borrowed Errol's radio to listen to the news. Depending on the station, the reports said Huế had been either cut off or liberated from the rest of South Vietnam. Hundreds of thousands of refugees jammed Route 1 and headed to Đà Nẵng. I worried about the safety of my family. *Are they staying behind in the village, or are they on their way to Đà Nẵng? Will there be another Boulevard of Terror like the Easter Offensive in 1972?* The news of collapsed bridges on Route 1 between Huế and Đà Nẵng had forced thousands of refugees and military vehicles to turn back. Instead of going home, many refugees turned to the sea. They swarmed the Thuận An estuary east of the village and thousands of people drowned.

Unable to concentrate on my studies, I stayed up late each night listening to the radio—all the news broadcasts. By late March, the South Vietnamese government had lost control of the central provinces and of SVA Corps I and II. Corps I had been stationed in Dạ Lê at the former Camp Eagle. President Nguyễn Văn Thiệu ordered General Ngô Quang Trưởng to withdraw the troops of Corps I and gradually abandoned Huế and Đà Nẵng. Because of cutbacks on US support to his government, the president lacked the power to continue defending these two major cities. On March 29, 1975, North Vietnamese troops had complete control of Huế and Đà Nẵng. Thus, Dạ Lê had been cut off from the South. I hadn't had any news from my family, and I didn't know where to ask for help or how to track them down. Shortwave radio was my only source of information, so I sat by it day and night. The reception was poor; I heard a half-sentence and then lost the rest to static. It was frustrating, but I couldn't live without it. I switched from station to station, searching for an update on what was happening in Vietnam.

President Thiệu resigned on April 21, putting an end to his "Four No's" policy: no negotiations with the Communists, no communist political party, no coalition government and no surrender of territory to Việt Cộng. In his resignation remarks, he harshly criticized the Americans, first for forcing South Vietnam to accede to the Paris Peace Accords, then for failing to support South Vietnam afterward, and, lastly, for asking South Vietnam "to do an impossible thing, like filling up the oceans with stones." Vice President Trần Văn Hương took over the presidency. A week later, on April 28, Hương resigned and was succeeded by Big Minh. The regime was in a state of utter collapse. On the morning of April 30, Dương Văn Minh announced unconditional surrender. It was the end of the South Vietnamese government. The fall of Saigon!

I felt frightened, exhilarated and ambivalent all at the same time. I was happy that there would be no more fighting or killing among my people, but on the other hand, I feared what would happen under Communist rule. *Will Vietnam become another North Korea? Will the state be under Communist Chinese protection?* But the biggest worry was the safety of my family, and I had no news about them.

When I realized that I wouldn't be able to return to Vietnam to see them again, I was shattered. From that moment, I became stateless and familyless.

## CHAPTER 26

# News from Home

After Saigon fell to the Communists, I got the news that the Vietnamese embassy in Tehran had closed and the ambassador, Lương Nhị Kỳ, had left Iran. Like Kỳ, who was the first and the last ambassador of the South Vietnamese government to Iran, I was the first and the last student sent to the country by that now-defunct government. Kỳ had gone to a safe place in the US or France, but I remained in Iran, wondering how long it would take to get out—and whether I ever would.

I started questioning my single-minded determination to leave Vietnam to pursue higher education. I was going to achieve my goal of becoming an engineer. *But what good is that if I never see the faces of my family members again?* I felt sick at heart.

I became withdrawn and kept the sadness and worry to myself.

In one of my most despondent moments, my classmate Abdi came to my room with a radio cassette player in his right hand and a tape in his left.

"I think I have got Vietnamese music for you," Abdi said with a grin, as if no other gift could beat that.

"If you don't mind," I said, "I'd like to sit here alone for a while."

Abdi left the room without saying anything.

Then I thought maybe that had been rude, so I ran after him. "Sorry," I said, "what do you have for me?"

Abdi inserted the tape into the cassette deck and then pushed "play." He was right. I felt instantly better as soon as I heard the classic Vietnamese song "Sài Gòn Đẹp Lắm," or "Beautiful Saigon." The cassette was a collection of Southeast Asian songs recorded in Hong Kong, and "Sài Gòn Đẹp Lắm" must have been selected as a typically Vietnamese song. Abdi had found the cassette in the nearby city of Ahvaz; he saw "Saigon" in the title and thought of me.

Along with some family and childhood photos, this tape became one of the few possessions that could transport me back to the land of beauty I came from.

Some of my other Iranian classmates took turns comforting me and offered their sympathy. They took me to movies, invited me to their parties, gave me notes on the lessons I had missed and got me laughing at their jokes. They shared their handwritten notes from last semester and advised me which chapters to review before class. They used every trick to keep me busy and stop me from dwelling on my family and other problems back home.

———

The college did not send me home after all. There was no home to send me to, but that was not the reason I got to stay: I stayed because I finally passed the second semester, thanks to the help from my classmates.

I joined my classmates for a summer work placement. Every summer, the students at AIT had to apply for a three-month internship with various oil companies in Iran. In my first internship, I was excited to get a position with the Abadan Refinery, built in 1912 by the Anglo-Persian Oil Company (what would later become the British Petroleum

Company, or BP). For most of the twentieth century, it was the largest refinery globally, with a maximum daily input of 680,000 barrels of crude oil.

I could withstand the desert heat—even though some days the temperature almost reached fifty degrees Celsius—but the noise and the stench of the refinery were unbearable. The continuous roar of so many running engines was so loud that I couldn't hear what my supervisor said, even though we stood side by side on the platform. Everyone had to wear earplugs whenever we stepped outside the control room. But the noise was still there, and its repercussions followed me home, along with the smell—the noise lodged in my head and the smell was carried home on my oily clothes. And each night, the worries about my family that I had kept under control all day at work would consume me. I felt like my head might burst into a flame, burning me up at any moment.

I woke up at night soaked in sweat. It was the same feelings of anxiety I'd had during the Tết Offensive seven years earlier.

At the end of my first work internship, in September 1975, I received a letter from my father. I could tell where it came from by looking at the envelope made of cheap packing paper. I tried to open it, but my hands were shaking—I was too excited. After calming myself down, I separated the letter from its stubborn envelope. It was four handwritten pages long.

My dad informed me that I had a new baby brother, Cu-Út, and my grandma had passed away a week after his birth. Thus, my mom, after nine pregnancies, had one girl and eight boys. Cu-Út is the last, and I am the first, twenty-two years his senior.

Our family was enduring the same fate as everyone else in the village. Dad had been sent to a re-education camp for a few days because he had been a sergeant in the former SVA, while some of my classmates, its former officers, were not that lucky. One of my cousins, Giao, had committed suicide by handgun a few days before he was supposed to report to a re-education camp. Dad also mentioned that Mom had been silent and didn't eat much for a month after she learned that Anh Hai had died in a gun battle somewhere in Quế Sơn. But the worst was O Lan: I learned that Anh Hai and O Lan had gotten married and had two small children, but ever since his death, she would aimlessly wander around the village, and the village kids made fun of her.

The new government had also disclosed that Chị Mau died shortly before the war ended, somewhere in the jungles of central Vietnam, leaving no trace of her remains.

When the North and Việt Cộng cut off Huế from the rest of the country in the first week of March 1975, our whole neighbourhood, Xóm Bến, including Mom and my siblings, fled to Đà Nẵng, the letter said. They left without Dad, who had to stay at his post in Huế, so all of this was what my mother had told him. The family travelled on an SVA truck to Đà Nẵng, over a hundred kilometres south on the other side of the Hải Vân Pass, not knowing that Đà Nẵng would fall, like Huế, by the time they arrived.

The exodus began when O Manh's eldest son, Bao, returned to the village with an empty army truck. Bao, an SVA transport corps driver, had completed his military supply mission to the battlefront and returned to his base in Đà Nẵng. When he drove through the village, he decided to bring his family—his elderly father and two younger siblings—south with him. Bao didn't want them to share the same fate as his mother and youngest sister, who had died during one of the bombings in the Tết Offensive.

What he had not expected was that the entire neighbourhood also wished to evacuate from the war zone. They didn't want to experience another Tết Offensive. Over a hundred people—from my two-week-old brother to Bao's uncle, who was over seventy, along with their chickens and pigs—all squeezed into the open-top army truck and headed for Đà Nẵng. Like all trucks and buses on the run, it carried more than double its capacity. The hamlet became a death zone.

Route 1, outside of Huế, was jammed with people moving south on foot, bikes and motorcycles, just like the displacement from Quảng Trị Province to Huế in the summer of 1972. They moved in a group with no regard for vehicles. Drivers ignored their requests for help and kept honking to get through. The refugees transported babies and necessities—clothes, rice and poultry—using bamboo shoulder poles. Anything they could not carry was scattered on the road, along with dead animals. Here and there, the sick and elderly lay on the roadside next to vehicles that had run out of gas.

At the top of the Hải Vân Pass, thick fog prevented the trucks from going farther. They spent the night there. As the darkness deepened, the frost covered everything on the mountaintop. The air turned cold and damp and wet. Adults were sitting while their kids were sleeping nearby. They lay everywhere—on the road and in the open trucks—snuggling for body heat. Some had blankets, but others did not. My mom tried to warm the youngest member, Cu-Út, by massaging his body regularly.

The next day, they reached Đà Nẵng. The family stayed at my uncle's house. If people didn't have relatives, a makeshift refugee camp was waiting for them.

Ten days later, Route 1 from Huế was disconnected, and my father was alone in Huế.

By late March, Đà Nẵng was also under the North's control. Both Huế and Đà Nẵng were now cut off from the rest of the South.

After Saigon fell on April 30, 1975, people from the neighbourhood could return home. All the families, including ours, were reunited.

## CHAPTER 27

# Stateless Student

My classmates thought I would be lonely and depressed during the school breaks, such as Nowruz, the Persian New Year, which was celebrated the first day of spring, around March 21. Over the years, one after another, they invited me to visit their families and hometowns. Iran is a racially diverse country, from the Arabs in the south to the Aryans (or Indo-Iranians) in the north, with other smaller minority groups—including Armenians, Assyrians and Jews—in between. Their language varies, but most speak Farsi. My friends came from cities all over Iran: Tehran, Shiraz, Isfahan, Tabriz and Rasht. By accepting their offers, I had a chance to get to know the country and visit magnificent religious sites like Masjed-e Shah and Masjed-e Jameh and ancient places like Persepolis and Eram Garden.

One time, Abbas, another classmate, brought me along to his hometown of Rasht. Because Rasht had been known as the "Gate to Europe," most people I met there had a European appearance, with pale skin and blue eyes. It was not like the area around the campus, where the Arabs dominated. Through these observations and my Iranian classmates' appearances, I recognized that Iran had many ethnicities, not just Persian, as I had thought.

Like the village kids everywhere in Iran, the children of Rasht followed me around, calling, "Bruce Lee, Bruce Lee!" They treated me as though I was the first East Asian they ever saw in person. The kids asked me to demonstrate some martial arts as Bruce Lee did in the films. I showed them the moves I had learned from my childhood and integrated them with some of the actions from Bruce Lee movies I'd seen.

The Caspian Sea, which has been called a sea but actually contains freshwater, is the world's largest enclosed inland body of water by area. There are no sharks in the Caspian Sea, but the beluga sturgeon is the biggest freshwater fish. Caviar is processed from this wild sturgeon's roe. The first thing I wanted to do when I saw the Caspian Sea was to swim in it, and I had done the same thing in the Persian Gulf during my last internship. On the offshore platform, they'd posted a warning about sharks in the water, but it didn't hold me back from swimming. The oil workers told me sharks liked to frequent the production platform, where they could find an abundance of food discarded from the living quarters. The underwater welders used chemical repellent to keep the sharks away while they scuba-dived to repair the platform legs.

The city I loved most was Shiraz: the city of love and poetry. Shiraz is the burial place of two well-known Persian poets, Hafez and Saadi Shirazi. I quickly learned that Farsi was among the most beautiful languages I'd ever heard. Its phonetics were so pleasantly distinct when I first heard it. The city was also rich in history. Around seventy kilometres northeast of Shiraz lies Persepolis, founded in 518 BC. It used to be the ceremonial capital of the Achaemenid Empire (also known as the First Persian Empire). Shiraz also houses the historic Eram Garden.

As a Vietnamese person, Isfahan was more significant to me than other Iranian cities because it was the burial place of Father Alexandre de Rhodes, who developed the Vietnamese alphabet in 1621. This alphabet is widely used today as *Quốc ngữ*, the official national language of written Vietnamese (the same one that is used in this book). It uses Roman characters and accent symbols, or diacritics, to represent the Vietnamese speaking tones.

Once, I stayed in Isfahan for a week, but I could not find Alexandre de Rhodes' grave. Unlike the Persian poet tombs, which were tourist attractions, his grave must have been unmarked in some old church graveyard.

---

I worked on Kharg Island in the Persian Gulf during my last summer work term. At the heliport of the Pan Am Oil headquarters in Abadan, a helicopter was waiting to carry the students to the official site on the first day. A memory of my village, Dạ Lê, flashed into my mind: Someone in a similar chopper had once tried to kill me while I was riding on a small boat. I looked at the pilot. Later, I learned that the company had hired some Vietnam veterans to fly the aircraft carrying workers to the offshore platforms. I sat by the window, once the seat of the gunman, and looked for people below to see how I might have appeared to him. But we were already above the open water of the Persian Gulf. What I saw were white-capped waves and drops of seawater pulled up into the air by the force of the rotary blades. My memory evaporated—no rice field, just a delightful and peaceful scene: a rainbow that the morning sun and the water vapour from the sea had created.

"On your right, you can see the shoreline of Iraq," the pilot said through my headphones. "It's about a hundred kilometres long, and the shoreline up ahead belongs to Kuwait."

I just listened. It was too noisy to say anything.

"If a war is going to break out," the pilot continued, "I bet this is where the battle will be."

The Persian Gulf is sandwiched between Iran and other small Arab states—Kuwait, Bahrain, Qatar, United Arab Emirates and Oman. Although Iran covers half the shoreline, the name "Persian Gulf" is still in dispute by those Arab states who call it the "Arabian Gulf." Other terms, the "Islamic Gulf" or just the "Gulf," have also been proposed. It reminded me of the dispute over the sea in Southeast Asia. China calls it the South China Sea, while Vietnam calls it the East Sea and the Philippines calls it the Luzon Sea. I didn't think the name mattered that much, as long as the country claiming the name didn't act like it owned the sea, or bully the smaller ones. That was how conflict would start.

## CHAPTER 28

# Time to Leave

The Shah government treated all my classmates well; they got full scholarships while studying at AIT. And after four years, a job awaited them if they were not offered a scholarship for further graduate study at the University of Southern California or Stanford University. But, by the spring of 1978, the mood among my classmates had changed. They seemed to stop going to the city of Ahwaz and having late-night parties, and I had experienced the seeds of dissent among my schoolmates.

As a chronic procrastinator, I had delayed everything I could until the last minute of the final work term. Overloaded with coursework, I was studying furiously to graduate in June when three classmates came to my room. My door was always open to let in the cool air from the hallway, so they just walked in. Alireza, the shortest but the most intelligent guy of the three, had often come to the international student dormitory to play soccer or sometimes a game of bridge. I had hardly seen the other two, Shayan and Reza, except in the few classes we shared lately. At first, I didn't recognize Shayan, who had now grown thick facial hair. Reza, the tallest and thinnest, was the last to come in. He had no place left to sit, so he stood against the wall like a decorative Greek column.

"We have come to request a sketch of Hồ Chí Minh for our magazine," Alireza said. "We decided that the cover will feature a portrait of a revolutionary." He looked at me, smiling.

"Hồ Chí Minh as a revolutionary? On a cover?" I asked. The disclosure caught me by surprise. That was the first time I had heard about the group's magazine. The revelation shocked me, since the students at the college were mainly pro-Shah. That was not the only revelation: I now realized that Alireza was not a very religious student, but more of a Marxist-Leninist. Now, I understood why Alireza came to my dormitory more often than anyone else did. Was he spying on me?

"Yes," Alireza said. "We're publishing a private magazine and asking you for a sketch, since I saw your drawing of Mahatma Gandhi on your wall."

"When we think of revolutionaries, we think of Vietnam and Hồ Chí Minh," the bearded guy added.

That comment reminded me of the neighbourhood kids who used to mimic kung fu moves whenever they saw me, calling out "Bruce Lee." When I told them, "I'm from Vietnam," they smiled, turned their hands into guns and shouted, "Boom, Boom." Even children of kindergarten age had heard about the Vietnam War.

"I don't know about that," I said, shrugging my shoulders.

"It's because we don't like capitalists," Reza said.

"Why not?"

"The capitalists—the Americans and Japanese," Reza continued. "The Americans interfere too much in Iran's internal affairs while the Japanese try to saturate our economy with their products." He walked over to my desk. "Have you heard about Operation Ajax?"

"No, I haven't," I answered.

Reza put his hand on my right shoulder. "The CIA orchestrated Operation Ajax in 1953 to overthrow Mohammad Mossadegh," he said. "He was the most beloved prime minister of Iran and a symbol of anti-colonialism."

"The Americans did the same thing with the government of South Vietnam," I said, agreeing. "Coup d'état after coup d'état in the last decade."

"Do you know that the domino theory, Operation Ajax and the Vietnam War are all related?"

"I know that the Vietnam War was caused by that theory, but I don't know about that operation," I said.

"The Americans link this theory to two most vulnerable regions that they must protect, and you know where they are," Alireza said.

"Iran and Vietnam?"

"Yes," Alireza nodded.

"But what about the Japanese?" I asked.

Alireza opened his arms wide. "They're everywhere you look— Honda, Toyota, Canon, Sony. Japanese merchandise is filling our streets, stores and houses."

"They go everywhere and always have cameras hanging around their necks." Reza curved his hand in the shape of a camera, mimicking a Japanese tourist. "They take pictures of things and then find a way to improve them with made-in-Japan products—"

"That is good, isn't it?" I cut in. "Cheap, durable, and more efficient."

"But they've killed our homemade products," Alireza concluded. "So, what do you think? Can you draw us a portrait of Hồ Chí Minh?"

"As you have already heard, the Shah's government is going to kick me out of Iran soon. I don't have time to sketch for you. Can you use the sketch of Mahatma Gandhi instead? He is also a revolutionary and more famous than Hồ Chí Minh."

"Where is it?" Alireza scanned the walls.

"Oh, I—" I was going to say that I had taken it down because the

Pakistani students next door had complained. They told me privately that Gandhi was not their friend, and they would not come into my room if that sketch hung on the wall. It didn't bother me to remove it—sketching was just a hobby.

I opened the desk drawer, picked out the sketch and gave it to Alireza. He examined the portrait at arm's length and nodded.

That was the first time I noticed my classmates expressing anti-foreign sentiments and revolutionary ideologies.

———————————

By July 1978, my classmates were leaving one by one. I was the only one still living on the campus, and I had nobody around to talk to. I was still waiting for a job offer from the NIOC, my scholarship sponsor. In contrast, most of my classmates had gotten a job offer right after graduation. In mid-July 1978, I received a letter from the NIOC; its personnel department suggested that the oil company would offer me a job if I had Iranian citizenship. Some classmates who would also be its employees wanted me to be among their co-workers and encouraged me to do that. According to them, it was the only way, because an anti-foreigner campaign had recently gathered steam. Some people wanted to kick all non-native workers out of the country as soon as possible. My case was no exception. My scholarship stated that I should return to Vietnam—the one that no longer existed—once I completed my degree. That anti-foreigner drive was a byproduct of the movement against the Shah, who had been the king of Iran since his coronation in 1967.

Unlike the previous summers, when I'd had internships, I had nothing to do for the first time. The weather was unbearable, reaching over forty degrees Celsius on most days. At two in the afternoon, hardly anybody walked on the streets. People avoided the shimmering heat rising from the paved roads and the blowing sand from the dirt gardens. I locked myself in my room, only to go out in the early morning or late evening to escape the sound of the air-conditioner, which ran all day and night. To release stress, I took a quiet walk around the school in the morning and watched a Persian movie at the Rex Cinema after dinner.

About a month prior, I received two letters, one from the University of Southern California (USC) and the other from Dr. George Chilingarian, a petroleum professor there. I had applied for a graduate scholarship, as Dr. Chilingarian, a visiting professor at AIT, had encouraged me to do. At the time, Dr. Chilingarian was the Shahanshah Aryamehr Pahlavi Chair in Petroleum Engineering at USC. The Shahanshah Aryamehr Pahlavi funding, a part of the Pahlavi Foundation, was founded and headed by the Shah and sent Iranian students to American colleges and universities. One-third of my Iranian classmates received this funding to attend graduate school, mainly at USC and Stanford University in California. The USC letter offered a partial scholarship that covered only the tuition fee. The letter from Dr. Chilingarian advised me to accept USC's partial graduate study scholarship and work part-time for him.

The idea of going to America had created an inner conflict that kept me awake many nights. If I were going to America, I would never have a chance to see my family again. To see them one last time was my biggest wish, and it was also a promise I had made.

I missed my family and my country. Sometimes I would think I had overheard someone talking in my mother tongue, but then each time I stopped and listened, I couldn't find anyone. I couldn't trust my ears anymore. *Have I imagined that conversation? Is it all in my head, like an auditory hallucination?* I started to wonder if I'd lost my mind.

*Now is the time for me to leave. But where? Can I return home?* I knew it was my last chance to visit my family.

# PART 4

# *Home*

Dear Da-Lê,

I am writing this email to you without knowing where you
are, whether you are still at home in Canada, or travelling
overseas. You once told me you were visiting Malaysia but
were actually in Vietnam. It reminds me of the time period
after the fall of Saigon and later—in the late '70s and
early '80s. That was during the mass exodus of millions of
Vietnamese people to the West. Many lost contact with their
family members at home, and many more never made it to freedom.
They perished during boat journeys, buried at the bottom of
the Pacific Ocean, or while fleeing through the jungles of
Southeast Asia. No one knows precisely how many were lost.
The survivors are mostly known as the "boat people," and they
are mainly from the South, including your mom, who fled as
a teenager.

    During this turbulent time of mass exodus, I went back
home. I made a gamble: to return. As you know, my first

gambling lesson cost your grandparents just one hundred đồng—
and a flogging for me, as punishment. But the price I would pay
for this gamble might be much higher than that—it could have
taken my freedom. Looking back, I am glad I took that chance.
Not only did I learn a life lesson, but after my return trip,
I fully understood why millions of people were risking their
lives to escape Vietnam by any means. The divisions within
the country after the war hadn't stopped, and conditions had
gone from bad to worse. The division between the North and the
South is actually still there today, and the gap between the
rich and the poor is growing each day.

You mentioned that you met Vietnamese people in Malaysia,
working in vulnerable conditions with minimum-wage jobs.
First, many Vietnamese left as war refugees after the fall
of Saigon. Even after reunification, many continued to leave
in the late '80s as boat people. The fact that even today,
many still risk their lives to be smuggled out of the country,
reflects the challenging conditions Vietnam continues to face.

Da-Lê, when you told me you were going to Malaysia for a
business trip, I told you to inform the Canadian consulate
when you arrived. I did not mean the consulate in Kuala
Lumpur, but Saigon, where you were actually going to. I knew
all along but kept quiet, as if I didn't know. You wanted
to explore and learn about Vietnam, its people, its heritage
and its traditions. I didn't want your mom to get upset. She
occasionally had nightmares about being "boat people" and
about her life after the war.

You know what you are doing, and I trust you. I did many
things forty years prior without telling your grandparents.

Once they found out, I said, "Ba, Mạ, you don't need to worry. I know what I'm doing." That was also what you have told us today.

I am glad you are planning to travel all over the country. Doing so gives you a chance to know the land of your roots. You will learn the differences in accents, complexions and personalities in each region. Visiting is the best way to connect to the roots of heritage, family, culture, food and language. Yes, you might talk to Grandma; she has already told you about what I am going to say to you. But that was her view—mine might be different.

As you may notice, Vietnam's economy has improved since it adopted economic reform, or *đổi mới*, in 1986 and the US lifted its trade embargo against Vietnam. However, Vietnam is still under Communist control with an authoritarian regime, and that is something you should know before you leave Canada. There are some sensitive topics, such as discussing politics and human rights, or criticizing its leadership or ruling party. You can talk to the young people in Vietnam about anything, except those topics. Like you, the young people there were born after the war. Most don't know much about that conflict. Some believe that the leadership—the ruling party— represents the nation, and anyone against it is against the fatherland. For some of them, there is no difference between the ruling party and the fatherland. They forget that we call our fatherland Đất Nước Việt Nam, or Đất Nước for short. *Đất* means soil, and *nước* means water. I don't know the reason why we call it Đất Nước in the first place, but as you are in Vietnam, you can see that the majority of Vietnamese live on the soil near the sea. There, wet rice and fish are abundant and have become Vietnam's primary food consumption. So, our fatherland is where we were born, and it existed long before any rulers on the land.

When talking about Đất Nước, I should explain these two words, *đồng bào*, a little more: That's what we call the people who live on the land.

You will soon recognize that everyone in Vietnam is *đồng bào*. We call each other that as if we are family members. I know that in the past, you had gotten frustrated over how to address my Vietnamese friends when they came to see us. You can use *you* and *me* in Canada, but you can't do that in Vietnam. The way you should address them is either Uncle, Aunt, Brother, or Sister, depending on their age, even though they are not related to you. That is why Vietnamese also use *đồng bào* for compatriots or fellow citizens, but it's more than that: *đồng* means "the same," and *bào* means "womb." It means that all Vietnamese people all come from the same womb. These words may come from the traditional legend of Princess Au Co, who gave birth to a hundred eggs, from which a hundred children were born to form the country of Vietnam. Fifty of them followed the mother to the highlands, while the father took the remainder to the sea. That was our first division. We are the same, but we do not always agree with each other.


Da-Lê, as you have said, you were surprised when you went with your O Hạnh to the Dạ Lê market; most people there recognized who you were, a child of a used-to-be-young boy who had left the village long ago. You resemble my younger sister, which made you wonder what would have become of you if I had stayed in Vietnam, and never came to Canada.

For the older generations, it is hard to see the head of a family leaving his ancestor's land; he is the nucleus of the clan, and his siblings live around him. As a child, I had learned some of my future responsibilities; I followed the adults when they cleaned and repaired our ancestors' graves each year, and my duty at the time was to learn and remember each location.

You told me your grandma, who was in her nineties, had taken you with her to visit some graves of our ancestors. I am glad you did that, even though that old custom is no longer strongly reinforced. During and after wartime, people had to move somewhere to survive; the village culture and family bonds became weaker, and the traditions came second to living your own life. I left the village. But my responsibilities remain, and those have now been redistributed equally among my younger cousins and siblings, including Hạnh, staying on the ancestors' land. You said everyone you met there was either your cousin or your nephew. There were so many—you were unable to count them all. So, if I didn't run away, you would be one of them. You would be a hard-working, family-oriented village girl.

Now you know why your grandparents had wished to return to Vietnam after living in Canada for some time. I sponsored them to Canada in 1996 under the family reunification class, so they could live near us. Even if they were happy to be here with us, they were still miserable, missing the more crowded family life of Dạ Lê. The ancestor worship and the relationship to their land were also big things for them. They want to spend the rest of their lives in Dạ Lê and wish to die and be buried on their soil. This is why they moved back in 2018.

Love, Ba

## CHAPTER 29

# Moscow, 1978

As promised, I went home to visit my family after several years
away. This was what I wished to do. I had just left Iran without informing anyone back home, not even my parents. Some of my
Iranian classmates advised me not to do this—they had heard that many
Vietnamese were fleeing the country en masse. People were sailing the
ocean in small boats in all directions to seek freedom. The survivors
became refugees in makeshift camps all over Southeast Asia. The gamble I was willing to make would take me in the opposite direction of
that exodus. Returning was a risk, and I wondered if it would change
the course of my life.

I contacted the embassy of the Socialist Republic of Vietnam in
Moscow, which also looked after the Vietnamese nationals in Iran. That
embassy agreed to issue me a travel document to return to Vietnam.

By the last week of July 1978, I had received the papers to go to
Moscow. Without delay, I took a bus from Abadan to Tehran and
boarded a train to the capital of what was then the USSR. Leaving Iran
without a visa for re-entry meant I might not be allowed to return.
*Goodbye, Iran.*

The train ran along the coast of the Caspian Sea through the famous oil city of Baku, in what is now Azerbaijan. It passed through the oil fields, which had been, at one point, the largest in the world. Oil derricks sprouted up everywhere along the tracks. The area looked like a junkyard jungle: skeletons of old pump jacks, discarded derricks and abandoned wellheads. Several small ponds with brackish water were connected by long canals to discharge water into Baku Bay.

After a few days on a train, I arrived in Moscow and was impressed with its metro system, the first one I had ever seen. It looked like a spider web of lines and connections crawling underground. In contrast to the streets above, which had very little traffic and few pedestrians, the metro was full of people who moved in an orderly fashion, like ants in a supercolony. I felt smaller and smaller among the tunnels and subway cars until I turned myself into an ant integrated into the crowd.

I was on the way to my hostel, where a few hundred Vietnamese students from communist countries all over Eastern Europe were convening. Like me, they had completed their studies overseas and were on their way back to Vietnam. I shared a room with five boys and two girls returning from Romania. We became friends and went everywhere as a group of eight. At the dining hall, they presented their ID cards for free food. I didn't have mine, so I showed my new passport that I had just gotten from the embassy to one of the hall staff. With a surprised look on the man's face, he asked me to move forward to an empty line while the rest of my group remained at the end of a long line. For the last three years, I had tried to blend in, and now I was still different from the rest. *Why?* I wondered. *Is that because everyone else here is from the North, while I am the only one from the South?*

There wasn't much food to select from. I put out my tray. A girl gave me a couple of slices of dark rye bread, *chyorniy khleb*, and a scoop of stir-fried vegetables. After getting a glass of soda, I stood to the side with a food tray and waited for my group to catch up. After several years of being dispatched to far-flung universities, the students who jammed the mess hall were happy to see one another. I felt as if I were already in Vietnam, but I was still uneasy about the VIP treatment when the man had seen my passport. I picked up a small piece of bread and chewed it.

"Anh, remind me again: Are you a student in Iran?" Trường, one of our group of eight, asked after we seated ourselves at an empty table.

"Yes," I said, wondering why he had asked.

"The dining hall staff thinks you're a diplomat because of the colour of your passport—eggplant," Trường said.

"Really?"

Trường was born in Thái Bình, a northern province west of Hanoi, and liked to tell jokes. Everyone in the group enjoyed telling jokes. Their subjects were Nicolae Ceaușescu of Romania, his wife, Elena, and the people living in communist countries. They also made fun of other famous leaders at the time, like Leonid Ilyich Brezhnev and Josip Broz Tito. This was their last chance to get the communist jokes out of their systems before they returned to Vietnam, where they might not be allowed. They had many to dispose of—everything they saw could be a tale. Trường looked at the long cafeteria line and asked, "Have you heard the story about Ceaușescu and his wife?"

"No, I have not," I said.

Trường said, "When they were looking down at their country from a helicopter, Eleana told her husband, 'Look at the long rivers.'

"'No, those are roads,' Ceaușescu said, disagreeing.

"'No, sir and madame. Those are queues!' the pilot said."

Another time, when we passed a grocery store, Trường said, "A young man came home from work early and found his wife in bed with another man. The husband told his wife angrily, 'Are you crazy? Why are you fooling around while the store is selling butter?'"

Our group toured many places in Moscow, but the two I remembered most, besides the Moscow Metro, were Red Square and Lenin's Mausoleum. The latter was also called Lenin's Tomb, located in Red Square in the centre of Moscow. When we saw a picture of Lenin hanging on the wall in the mausoleum, Trường had another story for his new friend.

Since the students were returning home after several years of studying overseas, buying gifts to bring home was a big thing in their minds. I followed them gift-hunting, but couldn't afford to buy anything. There were four most popular items selected: bicycles, sewing machines, wristwatches and radio receivers. Cameras and irons were also in demand. Those commodities were abundant in the West but rare in communist countries. Blue jeans and US currency could also be had through one of the African students. (Nobody knew how they got them.) Even if I could afford these items, I wouldn't have wanted to buy any: They looked rougher, heavier and uglier than anything I had seen back home in South Vietnam. Trường told me that he had to get his basic necessities, like toothpaste and toothbrushes, from the Vietnamese embassy in Bucharest during his time there. Was he joking with me? It was hard to tell after he had told me so many tales.

Students who bought bicycles or sewing machines would use the railway to travel to Hanoi through Peking (now we call it Beijing). I would have liked to visit China by train, but I didn't have a week to spare.

## CHAPTER 30

# Hanoi, 1978

My new friends and I had landed at Nội Bài International Airport, thirty kilometres north of Hanoi. It was opened early that year to replace Gia Lâm Airport, which had been bombed repeatedly and was severely damaged during the Vietnam War. Following the Paris Peace Accords in 1973, it became the site of Operation Homecoming: the return of American POWs from North Vietnam. Some were the B-52 pilots captured during their bombing missions in the North.

The new international airport was more like a regional air base. As I stepped down the stairs from the plane, the first person I saw was an old lady squatting on a bench next to the tarmac, her posture like a farmer in a wet rice field. It reminded me of Dạ Lê.

After collecting my luggage inside a flat-roofed building, I had no problem passing through the immigration gate, except I had to leave some banned stuff behind. In my case, it was the cassette tape of "Beautiful Saigon" that Abdi had given me and some film negatives from photos I had taken in Moscow. I did not care what the immigration officer confiscated as long as I still had my passport, and cash to get out of Vietnam when needed. The officer told me the government would return the seized items in a week. I gave him Madame's address in Saigon—the old one I knew—just in case of return. Except it was no longer Saigon, but Hồ Chí Minh City. The name had changed two years earlier, with the reunification of Vietnam on July 2, 1976.

A bus took the returned students and me from the airport to Hanoi. The former capital of North Vietnam was now the capital of reunited Vietnam. Surprisingly, the Long Biên Bridge crossing over the Red River had survived the bomber attacks. Still, it looked dilapidated and needed a fresh coat of paint. A familiar scene appeared on the sidewalk of the bridge. An old lady was transporting goods on her right shoulder using a bamboo carrying pole, just like my mother had several years back. The differences were that the lady wore a brown cloth headband and a long-sleeved shirt rather than a conical hat and black *áo dài*. The bus dropped us off at the terminal next to Đồng Xuân Market. My friends asked me how long I would be staying in Hanoi. "Just a few days," I said, to visit the city and book a flight to Huế.

Vu, one of the returning students, handed me a piece of paper. "Here's my address—Hàng Bài Street, near Hoàn Kiếm Lake," he said. "From my house, you could walk anywhere you want in Hanoi."

Quang and Tam, who also lived in Hanoi, invited me to stay at their houses. I promised to spend a night each if I were still in town. I was moved by their hospitality.

"Is there a travel agency around here?" I asked Vu. "I need to book a flight."

Vu gave me directions to the nearest agency and offered to take my luggage to his house so I would not have to carry it around.

---

After I had booked a flight to Huế, I went for a sightseeing tour on foot. Although I was seeing Hanoi for the first time, the street names and old colonial buildings felt familiar. I knew the landmarks by heart and felt like I was coming home: Hanoi was the ancient capital of Vietnam, and thus it had a long history that I had learned about in school. The city had also become the background for many popular Vietnamese novels.

The city before my eyes looked exactly like the pictures I'd seen in books, but much older and poorer. Bicycles jammed the narrow streets, and electrical lines criss-crossed the city sky. People were everywhere: On the streets. On the sidewalks. In the alleys. Most men still donned army clothes and especially those army-green safari hats (*mũ cối*), even though the war was long gone. I had a feeling that those clothes were all they had.

*Creak, creak.* An old tram from the colonial era—likely built in the late nineteenth century—rumbled slowly through the narrow streets. I could walk much faster than the tram. It seemed like time had been frozen in Hanoi for the last twenty years. The war had stopped time from moving over the city. Only one landmark was new—Hồ Chí Minh's Mausoleum in Ba Đình Square.

That evening, I went to Vu's house. I could not ignore the loud and steady sounds of street megaphones attached to utility poles. They felt like a giant osprey nest over my head, with many tangled black cables. They were everywhere on Hanoi's streets. Those loudspeakers broadcasted steadily, whether people below listened or not. They bombarded us with the communist ideologies, the heroism of its workers, the military draft and patriotic songs. No, I hadn't heard wrong—there was a military draft for the new coming war.

Under an authoritarian regime, propaganda was amplified or reinforced by repetition. It started in the early morning and continued until late at night. The host's voice was passionate—he was a proud patriot. I wondered why people had not gotten headaches or tired of those talks.

These loudspeakers had been an integral part of life during wartime for the advocacy of mass mobilization, frontline updates and crucial air warnings about bombing raids from American aircraft. People relied on them to escape to their shelters. They also used them for news, the only source that the Communist government would allow its people to hear during the war. The practice remained in place even in 1978, after the war had long gone—denouncing "the enemy of the people" and praising the great leadership role of the Communist Party. The voices on the loudspeaker reminded citizens to be thankful for everything they had. It sounded artificial, like complimenting a landowner for renting the land to farmers. This made me uneasy, but I didn't know how others felt. I had no doubt that this would suppress freedom of expression since they had nothing to compare it with. They were living in an echo chamber where no alternative arguments existed. It continued until people were tricked into believing the misinformation the megaphones were spreading.

This reminded me of a conversation I'd had with Lang in Moscow. When we were alone, Lang, wearing a pair of thick eyeglasses, whispered into my right ear, asking whether I knew anything about the guillotine. I asked him what it was. He said the South Vietnam government had moved that machine around the country to behead its dissidents. He said he felt sorry and angry, and he wished he could grow up faster and fight to liberate the South Vietnamese people from the Americans and from Diệm's regime. I told Long I hadn't heard anything about that. If there was such a machine, they must have hidden somewhere. The South used to have a relatively free press and surely would have reported on it.

The new ruler believed that most people associated with the previous South Vietnam government were "traitors"—that's why millions of them had been sent to re-education camps all over the country.

When I arrived at Vu's house, he was bowing in front of a family altar located in the middle of the house. On it was a picture of a man who I assumed was his father, a writer. His work was still available in the South. (Vu had told me about his family when we were in Moscow.) His father had passed away in 1960 when he was five years old. I had read many books by Northern writers when I was in grade school in the South. This was not the case in the North, where writers and poets from the South were banned, and their books were confiscated and burned.

Vu's mother looked older than her age, and Vu was her only son. Right away, one of his elder sisters took me to Hồ Hoàn Kiếm ward's administration office to register for my *hộ khẩu*—a record required by law in Vietnam—for a two-night stay at their house. At the registration, no questions were asked.

On the way back to the house, some barefoot kids huddled in the street, talking about "fighting the red Chinese." They went quiet as we passed by.

"What were they talking about?" I asked.

"China will soon teach Vietnam a lesson," Vu's sister said.

Like China, the new government in Hanoi had also taught its people in the South a lesson. Over a million military officers, government workers and supporters of the former South Vietnam government had been imprisoned in "re-education" camps. It was the same technique employed by the People's Republic of China during the Cultural Revolution or at the gulags under the Soviet Union.

"How will China teach us a lesson?" I asked.

"They'll invade Vietnam," Vu's sister said.

"Do you think we will have another war?"

"Yes, I do," she said. "We all do, and we've prepared for it."

The Vietnam War ended on April 30, 1975. North and South had been reunified. So, no more fighting. Vietnamese people wished to live in peace and begin developing the country. But the war had not truly ended yet. Under the Khmer Rouge, Cambodia had started waging war against Vietnam the prior year. That confrontation had nothing to do with the two countries. Vietnam and its neighbour, Cambodia, were just two pawns in a conflict between the communist superpowers—the Soviet Union and China. China had backed the Khmer Rouge of Pol Pot, who also started a campaign of genocide against both his people and the Vietnamese. At the same time, the Soviet Union supplied arms to Vietnam to counter Pol Pot's aggression. Thus, the old Indochina territory again became a surrogate battleground, this time between the Soviet Union and China, fighting for supremacy in the communist world order.

If the Chinese invaded Vietnam, that would be the fourth permanent United Nations Security Council member invading the country with their troops in modern times. First, the British occupation force landed at Saigon in 1945 to receive the surrender of Japanese soldiers after the Second World War. While the British were there, they allowed the French to return and reassert their authority back in Vietnam. This initiated the First Indochina War between the communist-dominated nationalist movement (Việt Minh) and the French colonial forces. And then, the American Marines landed in Đà Nẵng in 1965 to begin the Second Indochina War, also known as the Vietnam War. The Soviet Union, the fifth permanent member, had backed Vietnam during those periods. No country had this unfortunate fate with these five most powerful nations, and I felt it was not just by chance. Vietnam was in the wrong place at the wrong time.

Around six a.m. the following day, I awoke to the noise of those street speakers again. A few seconds afterward, the sound of a baby crying from the neighbouring apartment started to harmonize with the broadcasts. The people seemed to get used to the noises, but not the baby and me. It woke us up. We were too new to that alarm.

Later in the day, I was having a beer with Vu at the Hòa Bình Hotel on Lý Thường Kiệt Street. (You needed a passport to buy alcohol at hotels at the time.)

"The police want to work—*làm việc*—with you," Vu told me with a concerned look. The police wanting to "work with you" was a serious message in a country under authoritarian rule. Nobody wants to hear that.

"Why? What did I do?" I anxiously asked.

"I don't know," Vu said. "They came to the house and asked for you to come see them tomorrow morning. Here is the address." Vu handed me a piece of paper.

I had planned to stay with other friends in Hanoi but changed my mind after hearing this. I checked into the hotel that evening, so the host families would not have any problems.

———

The next day, I walked to the appointed office and was sent into a room where two middle-aged men were waiting. They each stood up and shook hands with me, introducing themselves as the officers from the Vietnam Oil and Gas Ministry; they needed to ask me some questions.

"What did you study in Iran?" the tall manager sitting on my right asked.

"I studied exploring, drilling and producing oil and gas."

"Have you graduated?"

I looked at him. "Not yet." I did not want to tell them that I had graduated, might be stuck here and had nowhere to go. I had no entry visa to Iran or any other country. "I'll have a degree in petroleum engineering once I get back to school next month," I lied.

Both wrote something in their notebooks.

"Tell me, what did you do besides study?" the overweight interviewer on my left asked.

I told them about working two summers at Abadan Refinery and one summer on the drilling and production platforms in the Persian Gulf. "Abadan Refinery is the largest oil refinery in the world," I said. "I hope Vietnam will have one soon."

"Will you stay and help Vietnam, then?"

"Well, as my document states," I said, "I am here to visit my family and must be out of Vietnam at the end of the month."

They urged me to stay and help the country. In the meantime, the government was trying to accommodate me as much as possible.

"After you leave this office, go to the Foreign Ministry and ask for Mr. Lập," one of the interviewers said. "He'll give you an introduction letter, so you have no problem with the local authorities. You need it—believe me." He wrote down the address and gave it to me.

## CHAPTER 31

# Dạ Lê, 1978

Two days later, I flew to Huế and landed at the Phú Bài Airport.

It had been five years since I left Dạ Lê for Đà Lạt on the Baptist pilgrimage, and many significant events had taken place in the country over that time. Still, the village landscape hadn't changed much, except it looked poorer and gloomier. That was my first impression from the window of the bus that took me back to Dạ Lê.

The familiar landmarks—church, đình, market and pagoda—were still there. The paddy was the same as when I left, but there was no sign of water buffalo boys playing in the distance or kites flying in the sky. Many farmers were working in groups, but I heard no singing or laughing. It felt like a spirit world—the silence of departed souls, just quietly working, like living ghosts.

The village market was almost deserted. Unlike the image implanted in my mind of a bustling place alive with yelling and laughter, there was now only a smattering of people looking at the scarce merchandise. A long line of people waited outside a shop on the other side of the market, standing quietly like shadows of their former selves. I remembered the joke about Ceaușescu and his wife, Elena, when they had mistaken the long snaking queues for rivers and roads. The jokes had become a reality. An uneasy feeling spread from my gut.

"They must have been waiting all morning," a young woman said to an older lady next to her. Both were sitting in front of me.

Her friend agreed. "I saw the same line when I passed it at dawn."

"What are they waiting for?" I chimed in.

The younger woman looked at me quizzically as if she wondered what planet I had come from. Once she saw my luggage, she smiled.

"Don't you know?"

"No, madame," I said.

"Are you from Hanoi?"

I didn't want to disclose my long story, so I nodded.

"You have the Huế accent like us," the younger woman said, "and I thought you were making fun of us." She looked out the window and said sadly, "They are waiting to receive a rice ration."

"Rice?" I blurted out.

"Yes, sir. The quota for each adult had been reduced to six kilograms of rice a month."

I calculated in my head. "With that quota, each person will get less than a half bowl of cooked rice a day. How can you live on that?"

"We can't," the older woman said. "We live mainly on *bo bo*."

"What's *bo bo*?"

The younger one looked at me again with wide eyes, as if everybody in Vietnam knew what this was, so why was this young man asking such a stupid question? Probably to them, I looked like a Communist agent sent from Hanoi to spy on its people. They looked at me: Well fed. Well dressed. Not like the people on the bus. Then they stopped talking to me.

*Bo bo* is sorghum, a type of foreign grain, like rye or a black cereal. It was mainly used for animal fodder in other countries like India and the Soviet Union. I couldn't believe that people from a rice-exporting nation like Vietnam had to wait in line all day long for a rice ration that was insufficient to live on.

By the time that conversation terminated in the silent treatment, I had already missed my stop. I got off at the crossroads in the next village and walked several blocks back to my childhood home. At the village boundary, I saw the familiar Buddhist temple. One of the temple's front gate columns had been damaged during the war. Its debris was still littered on the ground. The ruins brought flashbacks from the Tết Offensive. War was not a nightmare I could wake up from; it was right next to me. I could touch and feel the artillery craters and the pickaxe marks on the asphalt. I closed my eyes. I was so emotional as I walked. It felt like all the organs in my body had stopped working.

I had not told my family I was coming home. I hadn't told anyone in the village I knew about my plan to return. If I had, my parents would have discouraged me from coming back, wondering why on earth I would move in the opposite direction of the mass outflow.

When I turned the corner leading to my house, an oxcart stacked with dry rice stalks about ten feet high blocked my way. The cart was pulled not by an ox or water buffalo, but by an old man in a tattered conical hat, with the help of two skinny little boys. They were struggling to push the wagon out of a pothole in the middle of the trail. I put down my luggage and rolled up my sleeves to lend a hand. One of the kids moved aside to make room for me.

"One, two, three ... one, two, three."

After a few minutes, we pushed the oxcart over the pothole. As I picked up my luggage and passed the cart, the man looked at me from under the rim of his tattered hat. I looked back at him and felt tears coming down my cheeks—I was looking at my dad at last.

"Ba!" I shouted for joy and sadness at the same time.

Dad looked startled and asked, "*Con tôi*—my son?"

His body started shaking. I went over and held his right hand, which was rough and cold. I kissed it and felt tears on my hand. Was it his tears or mine? I didn't care, because it was all the same: happy tears.

"Yes, I'm back," I said.

The old man suddenly abandoned the cart—letting it tilt to one side—to get hold of me while the kids ran into me and held me tightly. It reminded me of when Mom and my siblings clung to my body after I'd escaped the shooting incident in the rice paddy.

"How is Mạ?"

"She is alright. She'll be so happy to see you," Dad said. "She prays for you every night."

He was thinner, darker and looked like an old man, even though he hadn't yet reached the age of forty-five.

"Why didn't you tell us you were coming home?"

"I didn't know for sure that I could come back," I said.

"It's not the right time to come home, you know," Dad complained.

"Yes, I know," I said, "but I'm here to see you and the family, and then I'll leave the country again in a week."

My father didn't seem to believe me. "By boat?"

That was the means people were using to leave the country at the time.

"No, by airplane."

"Can you do that?" he asked with wide eyes.

"Sure, I can, Ba. You don't need to worry."

Dad left the oxcart behind and walked me home, even though he kept looking back at the cart. I could tell he was worried someone might steal it. The boys ran home ahead of us, then one returned and stayed by the side of the oxcart.

Down the road, under the bamboo tree shade, Mom ran toward us, trailed by a line of my younger siblings, like a mother duck crossing the street with her ducklings. My body felt lighter than air and my heart beat faster. I dropped the luggage and ran toward her, my angel. She was just a block away, but that short distance seemed too long to me.

At last, I held her in my arms. She was so small and so light that I lifted her easily. She was crying.

"*Con*, you are here," Mom said. "I thought we would never see you again."

---

My parents' house was still lit by an oil lamp. No tap water, no electricity. The same for the village. The daily water supply for the family was stored in a large jar filled up from a well. When night fell, there was no light in the hamlet.

I looked up at the sky: It seemed brighter, with more stars than I remembered. That was when Thai walked through our front door. The last time we'd met was when he caught me trying to escape the hamlet to Huế in the 1968 Tết Offensive. Thai and I looked each other over from head to toe. Thai was much heavier, and he no longer carried an AK-47 on his right shoulder. Instead, a multi-coloured pen was tucked in the upper pocket of his white shirt. I wondered whether he had learned to write.

After we had settled down on the front table, my sister brought us tea. I invited him to share a pack of cigarettes, just Tam Đảo ones made in Hanoi. He looked at me, unblinking and clearly displeased with my offering, and picked them up. I told myself, *Sorry, Thai. I don't have French wine or American cigarettes for our reunion.*

Ten years had passed, and I was not actually thrilled to see him. I would have rather reunited with Old Dog, the buffalo boy leader. From Thai, I learned that Old Dog had died on a battlefield a few months before the war ended. He had enlisted with the SVA shortly after I left the village.

"Are you kidding me?" I said.

"No, I'm not. Old Dog didn't let anyone know he enlisted."

That was why I hadn't heard about him since the Tết Offensive. I thought he had left the village for the jungle, as my other friends had. Thai said that because Old Dog was underage at the time, he'd had to add another year or two to his age to enlist. I wondered what had led him to make that decision.

Thai had remained in the village and became a big boss—a local kingpin—with a new name, Bạt, supervising a few thousand workers building a vast irrigation project. It was an attempt to prevent seawater from going further upstream of the Perfume River during the dry season. The project, South Perfume River Irrigation, was to dig a six-kilometre-long canal diverting the upstream water of the river into the Lợi Nông Canal. This new shortcut canal would reduce the flooding each year and prevent the saltwater from going further upstream.

The project employed many thousand free labourers from neighbouring villages, including Dạ Lê. The workers were young men or women, including students and teachers, who had to bring their own food to work. The techniques used were the same as when the Lợi Nông Canal was first created a few hundred years ago. They dug the dirt by hand and carried it in bamboo baskets. I don't know what the working atmosphere was like in the time of kings. But as Bạt described it, it was extraordinary under the new authorities. They worked while listening to many epic songs from the loudspeakers. Around them was a forest of red flags with big yellow stars and colourful banners that claimed people could do impossible things, such as "Squeeze the soil into the water, change it to rain," or "Dig mountains and fill the sea." The villagers laboured under the harshest conditions—a lack of food, not enough warm clothes to wear and no place to sleep. Somehow they forgot their hunger, the cold and the lack of sleep, and kept working. The authorities must have known that if they kept repeating these slogans and songs day after day, the villagers would come to believe that everything was good and that they were living their dreams—and not being exploited.

After three years of hard work, a big celebration had been planned for the project's completion. But a short time later, the new canal was abandoned—after all that, it did not work as it was supposed to, preventing the seawater from going further upstream. In fact, it was worse than before.

———

The villagers had also recently welcomed some people returning from the North. One person, Chú Nam, who I ran into on the village road, had caught me by surprise. I had known him since childhood—he had lived on the trail leading to our house. Although he was returning from the North, he was not one of those *di tập kết* people. He had disappeared during the 1968 Tết Offensive with two other men who had left their hideout in Huế to go home and turn themselves in. These people were believed to have been killed and buried in the mass graves of the Huế Massacre. But not Chú Nam—as it turned out.

"Oh! *Chào* Chú!" I said, meaning "Hello, Uncle."

"*Chào* Con!"

I asked him about the other men.

"I don't know. We were separated on the second day," he said, sadly. "I was lucky to survive."

That was all he told me. He didn't want to talk about his ordeal, but he wanted to hear my story instead.

All other returnees were *đi tập kết* people like Lam's father. They had left the hamlet when Lam and I were only a year old, so we didn't know any of them. Some even brought back a wife and kids. Their mentality was also very different from the locals. They thought the villagers, who had lived under an oppressive regime for so long, would wave the red flags to welcome them home as their liberators, that everyone should thank Uncle Hồ and the Party. But when they returned to Dạ Lê after the war ended in 1975, they saw desolation: sad faces and ruins all around them. They had assumed the villagers must be impoverished, so they had brought bags of rice and some dried food as gifts for the family members they had not been in contact with for over twenty years. They were surprised to see that the villagers were poor, but there was plenty of rice everywhere. The extreme poverty and real famine became a reality three years later under the new government: The villagers were now starving.

One thing I noticed on my first day back was that the village looked much cleaner than the one I knew. In the old days, there were so many big piles of buffalo dung on the trail, and now you could not find one. They just disappeared. One of the *đi tập kết* people had asked any kid he saw playing nearby to collect them to use as fertilizer. He just practiced what he had learned from the North. "Don't waste black gold," he said. The village kids all tried to hide whenever they saw him, because they didn't like picking up buffalo poop. When he heard about my return from overseas, he told me I should express my gratitude to Uncle Hồ and the Communist Party for allowing me to return to a free and independent country. I just nodded my head.

## CHAPTER 32

# Subsidy Period

It took me only a few days at home to fully comprehend the hardships of the "subsidy period," or *thời bao cấp*, and the country's planned economy. It was obvious from my family's new routines and how little they ate.

Lanh was in the army, stationed in the North, and I couldn't see him during my visit. Vinh was eleven but still looked like a toddler. He had a big head with curly hair that I recognized immediately, even though he didn't know who I was. I met Cu-Út, my youngest brother, for the first time—he was only three years old. Each day, my dad had to pull the cart, and he had no time to rest even though his son had just returned from overseas. My mom tried to prepare a meal for me—just rice, without mixing any other stuff in. But that didn't fool me. My young siblings looked so happy and surprised to have such a meal, while the older kids and my parents ate so little, it was as if they were fasting. How could they work with a hungry stomach? They must have eaten something, perhaps *bo bo* or dried cassava, when I was not present? They didn't want me to see.

My family had been impoverished during wartime, but they were much more impoverished under *thời bao cấp*, even though they now worked much harder. Food and other necessities were scarce and only bought or exchanged using government handouts. Food stamps and rice booklets were issued based on cooperative work, family background and class ranking. The central government controlled everything.

Many villagers used to be farmers, but now there were no more private rice lands. Under the centrally planned economic system, the central state made all production and distribution decisions. All farmers, like worker bees, worked on one of its collective farms; they produced food to feed everyone and fought against any outsiders, but in the end, they were starving.

My parents worked in the hamlet's rice cooperative, which assigned the family to look after one of its water buffaloes. These farm animals were important livestock for the wet rice farmers. Like horses, buffalo were raised not for meat but for labour—horses for riding and water buffaloes for plowing the rice fields and pulling the heavy cart.

But someone had stolen the beast a few months ago. My family had been so depressed and devastated ever since. After work, my dad went to various underground slaughterhouses and barns in neighbouring villages beyond Dạ Lê to try to identify the lost beast. It just vanished without a trace. Now my dad had to work hard, pulling the cart himself, to pay back a debt: the cost of one water buffalo. That was too much when one day's pay was just a kilogram of rough rice—not even white rice. We would not have been that miserable if the family had owned the animal. But it belonged to the cooperative, and its members were accusing my family of selling it for meat. Killing any livestock without a licence was illegal, and killing one that was not yours was a felony. (The villagers were supposed to get an application approved before killing any domestic livestock.) But the government could not prevent many animals from disappearing, because people were so hungry and desperate.

The food ration for each member was based on the points awarded for their daily work in the cooperative. Each family received food stamps and a rice receipt booklet. The latter was the most valuable possession people had. Nothing—except maybe a death in the family—would make them more sorrowful than the loss of that booklet.

---

Our family of ten couldn't survive on the rice quota alone, so my mom mixed *bo bo* in with the rice. However, they couldn't eat that type of grain every day because it's too hard on the stomach; they sometimes ate dry slices of cassava root to avoid starvation.

Eating cassava root and sweet potato instead of rice was nothing new. My aunt, O Lâu, used to cultivate them in her *nương rẫy*, which was a milpa—like a clearing or garden plot—re-established in the dry-land section of the hamlet. But under the planned economy, her *nương rẫy* became part of the collective farmland. I met O Lâu at her house, partially financed by the new government. After all, she was one of the heroic Vietnamese mothers—a "Mother of a Revolutionary Heroine." She was smoking a small handmade cigar, but somehow, she still managed to shout at me when I met her at the door.

"*Tổ cha mi!* Now you show up. How many years later?"

"*Tổ cha mi*" is an affectionately offensive swear phrase that, loosely translated, curses all your ancestors before you. She would use it to show her love to me when I was younger. I was used to it, just like I got used to the tobacco smell whenever I walked into her house. Her dimly lit kitchen was full of dry tobacco leaves she had harvested from her land and hung from the ceiling for over a year. When she needed a smoke, she picked a dry leaf from the ceiling and used it to roll her cigar instead of cigarette paper.

I approached her with open arms.

251

"*Chào* O. Are you healthy?" I said.

She didn't answer, but hugged me and cried and cried while she looked into my face—like she was making sure I was a real person. Six years ago, as a teenager, I had disappeared completely from her life. And so had her daughter, Chị Mau.

"*Con Mau chết rồi, con ơi.* My Mau died, my dear," she finally said, after she threw her cigar out into the front yard. That was her ashtray.

Tears kept coming, flowing down my cheeks and dropping on her grey hair. She said she didn't need that title of respect as one of the *những bà mẹ Việt Nam anh hùng*, or heroic Vietnamese mothers, but wished to have her *nương rẫy* back instead. She was willing to trade the title and the financial support from the government for it, so she could keep working on her land, instead of having nothing to do and constantly thinking of her daughter.

Besides O Lâu, I also noticed other silent protesters among the villagers, like Ty, my old classmate whose father used to own a rice mill. After the reunification, the mill belonged to the village's rice cooperative. When I went to the plant to visit Ty, I saw him listening to the music coming from a tape player, but I hardly heard it because of the sound of the mill. I asked him how he could listen to the music in such conditions. He said he deeply missed the sound of the banned music but was afraid that passersby would hear it and report it to the new government. (All illegal music was supposed to be surrendered for burning or destruction.) I sat down on a tattered chair and tried to listen. It was a beautiful song with nostalgic lyrics about a pilot flying over Tam Giang Lagoon—a short distance from the village—and reminiscing about his recent weekends in Saigon. I didn't understand why the government had to destroy these tapes. It made me think about my tape of "Beautiful Saigon."

Any family associated with the previous South Vietnam government got the worst ranking for family background. Because my father was a former SVA soldier—a sergeant with the *ngụy quân*, or government puppet army—my siblings had all been labelled as having a "puppet family" background, or *gia đình ngụy*. The new government considered the previous one a puppet government of foreign powers, especially the US. My younger brothers all faced a bleak future. It was unlikely that they would pass the university entrance exam. Even if they graduated from university, no decent job would await them. An easy way out was to join the army, as my oldest sibling, Lanh, and several of my cousins did, and they were training to fight against the Khmer Rouge or even a Chinese invasion. There was no shortage of possible wars for them.

This heavy discrimination contradicted how the previous South Vietnam government had classified different families, which had been based more on talent and merit rather than family background. There was no such discrimination against *đi tập kết* people's children, like Lam, as far as I knew. He was born when his father left the South for the North, like my dad did after I was born. Since he was the only son of his family, he was exempt from having to join the army. Unlike me, he could study without the constant worry of being drafted. After the fall of Saigon in 1975, one of my cousins, Dzu, made it into medical school, but the new government kicked him out because of his family background. His dream to become a physician was over. He came to visit me at the house to bid farewell. As he was leaving, he whispered, "See you in America soon." He meant that he was planning to join the masses of people voyaging to Hong Kong by boat, with hopes of eventually reuniting with me in America.

Because of the food shortage, the central government encouraged the villagers to move south, where the land was uncultivated, to form what was called a new economic zone (this was part of the New Economic Zones program, or NEZ). It was the same tactic that Vietnam had used for many hundreds of years to advance the South. Several of my cousins had left the village with their families to join the movement. Some of them became the new settlers in the South. Others were buying time by selling their belongings to black-market contraband smugglers until nothing was left to sell.

For those with nothing to sell, a crazy notion became popular: trash digging. They would scrounge around and dig up the underground rubbish dumps around the old Camp Eagle site that the Americans had abandoned six years earlier. It was all garbage and unused supplies from when the camp closed in early 1972. Instead of bringing supplies back to the US, the soldiers dug holes and buried everything on the spot.

There were two types of dumps: burned and unburned. The burn sites were less attractive but still valuable. Many kinds of stuff could be found there, such as scrap metal. People had no idea then that they might later suffer from burn-pit exposure and get asthma, rhinitis, sinusitis or even cancer. Some items such as plastics, rubber, chemical mixtures and medical waste produced dangerous toxic smoke when burned.

In the unburned sites, people found many things to reuse: beer cans, wine bottles, cigarettes, plastic spoons, newspapers and magazines. If you were lucky, you might find a box of canned food. Their contents still tasted good even if the expiration date had long passed. Items such as an aircraft battery, armour, an old tire or a retractable shovel were also valuable.

Finding these unmarked dumps was not an easy task. People dug anywhere around the perimeters of the old camp. Some very unlucky folks had hit an undetected land mine that the Americans had forgotten to remove when they left. Some just lost a limb, but others died as a result.

The land mines were not only around the perimeter of the old camp but also everywhere in the village: In the gardens, in the ravines and in the canals. There were many stories of people who had died when a land mine exploded. The farmers collected and defused them and then sold them as scrap metal. Sometimes, village kids were just curious about a new thing or would use it as a toy.

This was not the first time Vietnamese people did not get enough food. During the French colonization period, they were always hungry. But it wasn't as severe as the 1945 famine in northern Vietnam in French Indochina, when the country was still under Japanese occupation at the end of World War II. Half a million Vietnamese had starved to death; their corpses were thrown onto piles. And the most recent famine was the siege during the 1968 Tết Offensive. It was like living through it again but with an unforeseeable timeline or endpoint. Nobody knew how long the "subsidy period" would last. If it didn't end soon, Vietnam might become the second North Korea.

---

Before leaving Huế, I visited my old high school, Quốc Học. Walking on Lê Lợi Boulevard alongside the Perfume River, I was steeped in memories of my school days—except the heat was more intolerable than I could remember. The red flowers of the royal poinciana trees were reflected on the windless surface of the river. In the branches above, cicadas flapped their wings in a shrill drone. They were making fun of me. The hotter I got, the louder they got. It was almost forty degrees Celsius. Even though I had just returned from a desert country, I had to stop in the shade of every tree along the road. A *xích lô* (a bicycle rickshaw) appeared out of nowhere.

"Need a ride?" a man asked.

Like my dad, the rickshaw man was old and petite, so skinny I could have easily carried him in my arms.

*How could I let him pedal me in this heat?* I whispered to myself.

"You don't look like a guy from around here."

"Why do you say that?" I asked.

"You have lighter skin, and the way you dress," the man said. "Are you back from Saigon?"

That was not the first time people picked me out from the locals. The children in Hanoi called me *người Sài gòn*, or a Saigonese. It was rare for a native Vietnamese person to visit Hanoi or Huế from overseas at the time, so they called anyone who was well dressed *người Sài gòn*.

I told the man that I was a student at Saigon University.

"Do you know Dr. Chu Phạm Ngọc Sơn?"

"Dr. Sơn teaches physical chemistry. You know him?" I asked, curious.

"He got his PhD at the University of Michigan, while mine was in engineering at MIT. We both left the US the same year," the man said sadly. "After the war, I lost my job here at the university because of my background."

This was becoming a familiar story. One of my former teachers here in Huế had been put into a re-education camp for two years. After the new government released him, he had no job.

The rickshaw man started pedalling hard and left me behind. I wondered if I might be one of his former students. He probably didn't want me to ask any more questions. He reminded me of Thai.

The times had changed. Now it was *hồng hơn chuyên*, or "red over talent," as the intellectual elites and the communist countryside yokels were forced to exchange jobs. *What will this country be like in the future?* I wondered.

## CHAPTER 33

# Hồ Chí Minh City, 1978

After two weeks in Dạ Lê, I boarded the "Reunification Express," which connected Hanoi to Saigon, about a thousand kilometres away to the south. I hoped this would not be the last time I said goodbye to Dạ Lê.

When I arrived at seven a.m., the Huế station was already lively. People moved in all directions. Some held hands. Some carried bags. Some were sitting on the floor beside their luggage. Once the train opened its door, the passengers boarded simultaneously. They were too quick for me: When I got in, the cabin was already overloaded, and its floor was full of goods. There was no space to walk through. After several young boys climbed up on the train roof for the fresh air, I took their seats with my bags balanced on my knees. I knew that if I got distracted, my luggage would disappear in a second.

Once I had settled in my seat, I looked out the window. Except for train whistles every now and then, the station was quiet, unlike the first time my mother had taken Hạnh, Tuấn and me by train to visit my father. This was when he had been hospitalized in Đà Nẵng. I was about nine at the time. We boarded the train in the early afternoon and occupied two window benches. Hạnh and I both stood up and looked out.

Vendors of all ages, from preschoolers to old people, thronged the station. They sold local seafood products and Huế's cake specialties, along with the common exotic fruits—jackfruits, mango, banana and guava. The food smelled so good. I was hungry and wanted to eat anything that I could get my hands on. Hạnh lay on the train floor, crying and kicking at Mạ's legs. The more my sister cried, the redder her cheeks became. Tuấn looked at his sister and started crying too. I usually hated their screaming, but that time was different, because I wanted my siblings to shout louder so that Mạ would buy something for us.

The vendors knew what I wanted; they slipped the food through the train's open window under my nose and into my hands. Mom said no; I had to give it back. Even with my siblings' crying, she refused to buy anything and told us we had plenty of food. Mạ had cooked sticky rice and salted sesame seeds the night before, enough for our trip. After half an hour of craving and crying, we survived the ordeal with a handful of sticky rice.

Now, those vendors were long gone, and those delicious foods I remembered from my childhood were available only on the black market.

---

The train reached Tháp Chàm and stood still for a few hours. The air was so intense and hot inside the compartment; it smelled like a mixture of dried sweat and urine, and the humidity made my body feel like a wet noodle in a bowl. I had been on the train for two days. I tried to open my eyes wider, but I couldn't ...

I woke up when my train came to a sudden stop at Saigon station.

I came home alone, and I left Dạ Lê alone. Most of my classmates and cousins who used to be SVA officers were still in re-education camps all over the country. My visits to see their families had a lasting effect on me, because we were about the same age. I kept thinking about their fates as compared to mine. I knew that the camps were about more than just reform: Re-education, in this case, meant *học tập cải tạo*, an attempt to make over a sinful or incomplete individual. So, the mandate was about making over or re-creating a person. After three years of re-education, they still could not become complete citizens and earn their freedom.

There were also so many systems and so much bureaucracy that had become part of life for the prisoners' families, too. With all the hard labour and a lack of food, the prisoners required *thăm nuôi*—visiting and feeding—as support, especially during this subsidy period. Organizing these visitations each time was not a simple task. The prisoners' families had to obtain visit permission from the bureaucracy. Not only did they have to travel a long distance, but the hardest task was to collect enough food supplies from the black market.

Brown sugar and milk powder were valued the most. The visitors also brought condensed milk, arrowroot powder, dry bread, dried sweet potato, dried shrimp, sugar, dried fish, canned food, roasted peanuts, candy, medicine, tobacco, soap and toothpaste. To gather all those things, the visitors would have had to collect them daily for several months, which cost a fortune when food and other necessities were scarce. During the subsidy period, these items were difficult to buy, either with money or food stamps.

While in Huế, I heard so many sad stories that I didn't know whether all of this was real life, or a bad dream. I often heard my friends say, "See you in America" when we departed.

---

Saigon had become Hồ Chí Minh City. Most of its streets also had new names—common names that one would have used for the characters if you wrote a novel about farmers in the rice paddies, or workers in the factories. Most streets were named after the Việt Cộng martyrs who, I was told, had died during the recent war. I felt out of place, as if some-one had occupied my home and moved all the furniture around. A place I should know, but didn't.

At the Bến Thành Market, at least, a familiar face welcomed me back to Saigon—Quách Thị Trang, the student killed at this square fif-teen years earlier. Her monument was still standing in the same spot where I had been stationed with a rifle in hand as a guard, two nights a week. That square used to be the busiest place in the city that never slept—but not that day. It looked like it was under the spell of a late afternoon nap: quiet with very few people on the road.

I passed by the street-side restaurant next to the market and wit-nessed a scene that broke my heart. Two kids were fighting for the remaining rice and chicken on the used plate a customer had left. I walked away, since I was afraid to do and or say anything, as my family had warned me. I was also too surprised and saddened to react—I could not believe what was happening in my beloved city on my first day back. I wondered whether this resulted from the war, the centrally planned eco-nomic system, the current US economic embargo on Vietnam, or all three.

Five minutes later, I was home.

"It's you!" That was how Madame greeted me when I walked through the front door of the old bakery. She sounded upset.

"*Chào* O. Hello, Auntie."

"*Chào* Con," she answered and then hugged me.

"Aren't you happy to see me?"

"No," Madame said. "I didn't think you were stupid enough to come home." Her voice sounded a little shaky.

Madame held my hand and pulled me deep inside the house. She looked around to make sure no one was listening or watching.

"I'm living here illegally," she said. "My kids and I were sent to the New Economic Zone near the Mekong Delta. We bought our way home without my *hộ khẩu* papers." She looked at me. "This house is no longer mine," she continued. "I'm just a guest—or a prisoner—in my own home." She pulled me closer. She said someone with a northern accent came by and asked her about me a few months ago. The guy informed her I would be coming home soon. She thought the man wanted to give her a hard time. People knew about her return from the NEZ, so she was easy prey. She usually paid a bribe to make them go away.

She looked at me with a frown. "What the hell are you doing coming home?"

"I've come to visit you for a few days," I said, "and then I'll leave."

"Are you sure you can get out of the country again?" she said, doubtful.

I had heard this chorus many times before, but her tone, this time, hit me deeper than ever. "I'm sure, Madame," I answered. "You don't need to worry about me. I found the way in and I can find a way out." I was tired of convincing people that I could leave the country, and nobody believed me, which made me doubt myself.

*I can get out, can't I?*

Unlike my cousins and uncles back in the village who volunteered to go, Madame and others like her—wealthy urban merchants in Saigon—were displaced unwillingly to the NEZ to make room for the influx of people from the North, who were the winners, and essentially the new authorities. I could not imagine how Madame had survived this hardship, when everyone had to work with their own hands to build their houses, cultivate their new land and grow their food.

As the law required, I must register my own *hộ khẩu* at the Bến Thành Ward's administration office, which is where I used to go to receive a gun for my night guard duties. A man in his late forties was sitting at the table, taking apart his handgun. "Can I help you?" he asked in a distinctive southern accent.

"I've come to register my *hộ khẩu*," I said.

The man looked up at me, smiling. "For how long?"

"Three nights," I said softly.

"Please, fill out this application." He handed me a form. "After it's completed, leave it here and come back in a week."

I was trying to understand why they needed a week or more to approve a request to stay three nights. By the time of approval, I would be long gone.

"But I'm only staying a few nights," I said.

The man stopped smiling and changed his tone. His face twisted into a scowl. "That's your problem," he said gruffly.

I showed him my travel document issued in Moscow and the introduction letter from the Foreign Ministry Office in Hanoi, to no avail. I remembered Mr. Lập's words, "You need it. Believe me." He was only half right. The administrator said it was the Thiệu regime that had sent me overseas, not the revolutionary government, so I'd be treated like anyone else—runaway Vietnamese. I had no problem registering in Hanoi, but this was Hồ Chí Minh City, not Hanoi.

Back at Madame's home, I told her about the incident.

"Did you bribe him or give him any money?" she asked.

"No, I didn't."

"You should have given him five or ten US dollars instead," she said.

"Why US dollars, but not Vietnam *đồng*?"

"A US dollar is always a dollar," she said, "whereas the *đồng* can be replaced by another type of *đồng* at any moment." She explained that the new government frequently changed the currency. Each time, it limited how many old *đồng* a household could exchange for new bills. The new government kept the extra for now; otherwise, the remaining old *đồng* was worthless. Madame curved her thumb and index finger to form an O shape. "The second exchange was a few months back, and it's still fresh in people's minds. The rumour is that a third is coming."

Madame saw a slightly puzzled expression on my face, so she offered a specific example. "Five months after the fall of Saigon, people in the South received one Southern 'liberation' *đồng* for five hundred *đồng* from the previous South Vietnam government. In this exchange, each family could have a maximum of two hundred new *đồng*, and I lost most of my cash. Then a few months ago, we got one new 'reunification' *đồng* for every 'liberation' *đồng*. We get poorer after each exchange." These limited but consecutive exchanges might have been the new regime's first seeds of corruption, unwittingly sowed.

*What will this country be like in the future?* I wondered again.

After talking to Madame, I went to a travel agency to secure the earliest flight back to Tehran. The Air France office was where I had purchased a one-way ticket to Tehran over three years earlier. Again, I bought a one-way airfare, not knowing where I would end up and whether I would ever return. The agent booked me the ticket after examining my papers issued in Moscow, even though I did not have a visa. No questions were asked. I wondered if the type of my passport had made the booking easier.

The next morning, just my third day back in Saigon, I hurriedly said goodbye to Madame.

She whispered, "See you in America."

I realized that a reunified Vietnam was only in name. There was still a gap between the Northerners and the Southerners in real life, like an imbalanced scale.

I boarded Air France Flight 197 out of Vietnam the next day, even though I didn't know where my next home would be. I held no entry visa to any country, including Iran, but I still hoped someone, somewhere would open its doors to me.

## CHAPTER 34

# Iranian Revolution

When I returned to Abadan in late August 1978, thousands of people filled the streets, denouncing the Shah and shouting "*Marg bar Shah, marg bar Shah!*" ("Death to the Shah, death to the Shah!"). The protest was led by mostly women wearing black clothes and head scarves.

The front page of the local newspapers featured pictures of victims' families, outraged at the Shah. Four hundred people watching a movie called *Gavaznha* ("The Deer") had been trapped in a movie theatre and burned alive. Had war and terror kept following me from Huế to everywhere I went? I couldn't believe this had happened at the Rex Cinema, the very same cinema where I had spent time less than a month ago, when I had nothing to do while waiting for my travel documents. I might have been one of those victims if I hadn't taken the gamble of going back to visiting my family.

My classmates had all left the dormitory complex except one, Amir, who worked as a lab instructor at the college. He advised me to stay on campus. Some of the professors and instructors at AIT had yet to return to Iran from the US. Would they be willing to return?

I ran into Sara a day after I was back. Her dress had changed; she wore a hijab without a smile. Sara seemed to avoid me, unlike before I left the country, when she'd asked me to see her as soon as I returned to Iran.

My flight from Hồ Chí Minh City had landed in Tehran the day prior. As expected, the Iranian immigration officers at the Mehrabad International Airport did not allow me to re-enter Iran. I didn't have an entry visa.

"Why do you want to go to Abadan?" the officer asked.

"I'm a student at AIT," I said.

"You better not go back there," the officer said. "There was a big fire at Rex Cinema in Abadan last week."

"A big fire?" I asked, surprised by the news.

"Yes, a few hundred people died," he said.

My mind just turned blank; I didn't know how to react. After a minute of silence, I said, "I am sorry to hear that. But I must receive my degree and pick up my stuff there." I showed the officer the documents from my college, including a letter from the institution informing me that I would get my degree in August. For some reason, AIT had not officially received my diploma certificate from Quốc Học High School. So I had left the college without my actual degree, except for a card from the Shah addressed to my name, expressing his congratulations to the AIT graduating students. At first, I was disappointed when I didn't have an actual paper copy of my degree. But with some thinking, I was able to use the mishap to my advantage: It was a good reason not only to get out of Vietnam, but also to return to Iran. My plan had worked so far, and now I was facing the last hurdle.

The immigration officer examined the papers and then looked at me. He told me to wait while he walked away with my documents and my passport. I waited and waited. It seemed all the passengers except me had left the terminal. Half an hour later, the officer returned.

"We'll give you a seventy-two-hour entry to complete your work," the officer said, and handed me my passport and papers. Two days to travel, and one day to do what I would need to do in Abadan. All the stress accumulated in my head during the last thirty minutes of anxious waiting disappeared. I wanted to yell or let out a sigh of relief to release the tension, but I just smiled and said "thank you" instead.

Back in my dorm room, I listened to the radio. The Pahlavi government reported that it was Islamic militants who had set fire to the Rex Cinema. Meanwhile, the Islamic militants blamed the Shah and his intelligence service, SAVAK. It was the same old story—no one was responsible for the deaths of innocent people. Memories of the Huế Massacre in 1968 flooded my mind.

Years later, one of my Iranian classmates later told me that the theatre fire was a trigger point for the Iranian Revolution. There was a parallel similarity in the mass killings. The shock of the 1968 Tết Offensive, with mass graves, was what began to turn American public opinion against America's involvement in the Vietnam War. That led to the 1972 withdrawal of its forces, the 1973 Paris Peace Accords, and finally, the fall of Saigon in 1975. *Has this ruthlessness, without regard for humanity and no compassion, become normalized?*

The seventy-two-hour period had passed, and I hadn't gone anywhere. I became a stateless fugitive in a foreign land.

## CHAPTER 35

# Tehran, 1978

Iwas back in Tehran. When I arrived, a classmate, Abdi, picked me up at the bus terminal and drove me to his house in one of Tehran's suburbs. Like many of my Iranian former classmates, he now had a full-time job. Abdi worked in a small chemical office nearby and was hardly ever at home. Not only did I live there for free, but I also had a massive residence to myself. The house was stuffed with all the food I needed. It helped. I had spent all my savings on the trip to Vietnam, and my monthly allowance from the NIOC had been cut off since last June. I had developed a bad habit over the years of associating with my Iranian classmates: I took advantage of their hospitality. I'd grown accustomed to free expenses on any trip I was invited to.

But after a week, I wanted to escape the looks from his neighbours each time I left or arrived at the house. I didn't like the way they looked at me. This was not the first time I had stayed at a friend's house in Tehran. Reza, another classmate, had brought me to Tehran during his family visit after our first year. I stayed with his family for a week. Not only was his family happy to host me, but his neighbours were friendly, and their kids followed me anywhere I went, asking me to play with them. The Iranians held the top mark for hospitality globally, I had learned. But things were different now, and I could tell the difference from their looks toward me—their hospitality had shifted to suspicion.

So I moved to Amir Kabir Hotel, which was a budget-friendly hostel. Located in the old Tehran centre, it was convenient for making contacts and finding good leads for my next move. My roommate at the hostel was Mohammed, a refugee from Ethiopia, who ran away from the Marxist-Leninist regime of Mengistu Haile Mariam. Mohammed's hair was like tall wild grass, and he had a long Afro pick hiding in his back pocket, which he used to comb his curly hair every half an hour. But he always laughed at *my* hair: "You have a bird's nest on your head," he would say when he first saw me in the morning. As a displaced teenager, he had passed through many refugee camps in North Africa. Through United Nations High Commissioner for Refugees (UNHCR) intervention, Mohammed ended up in Tehran. The agency paid for his living expenses at the hostel while he was waiting to settle in the United States. His case had gone nowhere for the last two years. Even with that short time in Tehran, he spoke Farsi fluently, unlike me—I only had some conversational, day-to-day Farsi. He spent much of his time going around the market and making friends with *bazaari*—the vendors.

After settling at the hostel, I applied to migrate to the US at the US embassy. I was equipped with a letter from the University of Southern California granting me a partial scholarship, and my expired passport from the now-defunct government. I said nothing about my recent travels to Vietnam.

The interview with the US immigrant visa unit went something like this:

"So, you are from Vietnam?" An immigration officer in his late forties or early fifties scanned my file, then studied my face.

"Yes, I am."

"When did you come to Iran?" He looked at my face some more.

"January 1975," I said. "Three months before the fall of Saigon."

"You aren't a refugee or one of those boat people?"

"No, I was a student at AIT."

His blue eyes stared at me. Then he asked, in a hopeful voice, "Did you contact the US embassy right after the fall of Saigon?"

"No, I didn't." I shook my head.

The officer sighed. "You should have. Had you contacted us when you still held a valid South Vietnam passport, we could have helped you." He paused and looked at me. "Some Vietnamese trapped in Iran after the fall of your government did that. And now, they're already settled in the United States."

"My embassy closed without informing me to contact your office for help," I said, which was not entirely true.

Even though the Vietnamese embassy did not tell me this, someone else did. But at the time, I believed that if I went to America, I would never have a chance to see my family again. So I had felt I had to find a way to meet them one last time, before doing anything else.

"We will send your file to Washington for reconsideration and let you know the result soon," he said, closing the folder.

After that interview, I dropped by the INS office every two weeks for any updates. I was stuck in this cheap hostel, Amir Kabir, for several months, and I needed money. Abdi had given me some cash to pay for the first few weeks, but now I started looking for work. Four years of engineering study did not help me much in my job search—but befriending Suzuki did.

When I had first arrived at the hostel, a Japanese cyclist, Suzuki, sat alone in the corner of the lounge. I recognized him right away from a newspaper story in the English language version of the *Kayhan*, the daily newspaper in Tehran. The cyclist had toured West Germany and Turkey and would continue through Iran, Pakistan and India. He worked as a portrait artist to fund the journey and gave talks and interviews to the local newspapers and TV stations.

Suzuki liked to keep to himself and got used to blowing hot breath into his palms and then rubbing his face. People who didn't know his background might look at his odd mannerisms and think he was a crazy person. He'd developed the habit of warming himself up on the road, and now he did it unconsciously as if he were in the middle of nowhere.

"I saw your picture in the paper along with your inspirational story," I said, extending my hand for a handshake.

"Please, sit." He motioned to an empty couch. "Are you Singaporean Chinese?"

"No, I'm Vietnamese."

"Oh. I like Vietnam." His face lit up a little. "I wish to cycle through Vietnam."

"You can't do that now," I responded.

He nodded in agreement. "What are you doing here?"

"I'm on my way to the US."

"What are you doing this afternoon?"

"Nothing." I shook my head.

"Do you want to go with me to a park? Any park that tourists like to visit will do." Suzuki smiled.

"Sure," I said.

I suggested the square of the Shahyad Tower (King's Memorial), built in honour of the Shah. That massive monument, forty-five metres (148 feet) tall, marked the gateway into Tehran. I'd first seen it three years earlier on my first visit with my classmates. They told me it was built with eight thousand blocks of white marble from Isfahan. When I walked through the gate for the first time, I was captivated; the tower was the tallest structure I had ever seen.

Several local sketch artists had already set up their shops in the square. Sitting on stools with their pencils and markers, they thrived by drawing funny portraits of tourists for a few hundred rials. Suzuki set up shop too, posting his picture from the *Kayhan* paper on a display board next to his bike. I soon learned that many Iranian visitors preferred having a Japanese artist draw their portraits for souvenirs. After a few days, he encouraged me to try, as he was overwhelmed with requests and he knew I needed work. I had told him I liked to sketch famous people in my free time.

The most challenging thing was to achieve a likeness in the fifteen or twenty minutes that a customer was sitting for a portrait. Suzuki explained how to recognize the unique facial features—wide nose, thin lips, droopy eyes, prominent chin, complicated hairstyle—and their proportions. He told me to highlight those characteristics to enhance the likeness.

After a week in Tehran, Suzuki left for Pakistan and India. I continued to work as a street portrait artist—the worst one. And as the anti-foreign sentiment intensified, I was hassled at work. Some young guys ran off with my display sketches.

"Eh! Japan, go home," someone shouted at me.

"Me? Not Japanese. Vietnamese," I responded.

They left me alone. I thought I was safe on the street. But I'd been mistaken for Japanese many times. A few years back, Iranians had treated me respectfully, but now, as the Islamic Revolution drew near, I felt more vulnerable when I was out on the street.

The propaganda wave that had taken over the streets of Tehran was not much different from being back home during the Vietnam War.

---

Two things that made me feel better living in Tehran were that I could still find some Vietnamese street food, and speak my native language whenever needed.

There were no Vietnamese restaurants in the capital, but some private and family-operated at-home eateries served monthly dine-in meals for a small number of single men from the South Korean diaspora. They gathered at the premises each evening after work, talking and drinking. Some served food that was hard to find anywhere in the city, like Western beers, wines and pork meat.

One of those owners was a Vietnamese widow who had remarried a Korean man. Like most Vietnamese women who were living in Tehran at the time, the owner's previous husband was a South Vietnamese soldier who had died in the war and left her with young kids. These women then married foreign workers or soldiers stationed in Vietnam before the fall of Saigon. After the South collapsed in April 1975, they evacuated with their new families to Iran or other countries, where their husbands' employers moved for new contracts. The eatery owner had three boys in their teens. Not only could her kids speak Vietnamese, but her new husband also conversed in the language well. I called him Uncle Min. Unlike other South Koreans in Tehran, who worked for contractors, he sold his own art to the shop owners at the Tehran Grand Bazaar. Day after day, he walked from shop to shop to show his art samples and convince the *bazaari* to order the goods. He could develop a black-and-white photo on the white base of a china plate— any image the shop owners supplied. Once he collected the orders, he went home and worked in his studio. He showed me how to mix some chemical compounds to produce a milky white liquid to cover the base of the plates. He stored them in the darkroom for drying.

Uncle Min used a photo negative or a film to develop the white-and-black image on the plate; he had yet to learn to create a colour photograph. I helped him touch it up with colour by hand if someone wanted one.

One day, Uncle Min asked me whether I could paint an oil portrait for some people in the bazaar. I told him I would try, even though I didn't know who I was going to paint, or for whom.

## CHAPTER 36

# Ayatollah Khomeini

On the first day of the winter of 1978, I walked to the Tehran Grand Bazaar. Its immensity made me feel small. The Grand Bazaar consisted of several mile-long corridors, each specializing in different goods, from carpets, gold, jewellery and perfume to clothes, underwear, herbs and spices. Besides the stores, the Grand Bazaar contained banks, mosques and guesthouses. It was like an underground city, with multi-storey buildings linked by domed ceilings at each intersection.

With Uncle Min's map drawn in my palm, I wove through the crowds, looking for Mr. Mehdi's carpet store. I kept asking for directions, getting lost and then asking again. Finally, I arrived at the large store, which had multiple storeys. From a distance, I could see Mehdi, who was as Uncle Min had described, standing with a couple in front of several rolls of carpets. I didn't hear what they were talking about, but I believed he was busy serving them.

Mehdi asked me to paint Ayatollah Khomeini, an Iranian Shi'a Muslim religious figure who had gradually become more popular day by day. A new rumour had swept the country lately: that his face had appeared on a full moon seen by millions of people. The picture of an older man with a long, grey beard and black turban popped up everywhere. Like Hồ Chí Minh, who had been glorified by schoolchildren, villagers and peasants in the early days of the Vietnam conflict, the new myth of the Ayatollah appearing on the moon attracted ordinary people, peasants and *bazaari* in Iran to the ideas and causes of the revolution. The Ayatollah had lived in exile in Iraq since 1964 and was not yet allowed to return to Iran. I had only seen his picture displayed on the streets during the rallies. I looked at Mehdi, hesitant to say anything; I didn't want to be in trouble with SAVAK.

"I'll pay you good money for it," the man said. He looked sincere, so I changed my mind; I needed money to live.

A week later, the weather was getting colder as winter approached, but the political climate was getting hotter. Whenever I walked somewhere, I chose my route carefully. The busier the road, the safer I felt.

It would take me half an hour to walk from the hostel to the Grand Bazaar. Covering Khomeini's painting with newspaper, I set out at around ten o'clock in the morning. On the way to the bazaar, I encountered a demonstration. "Long live Khomeini!" and "Death to the Shah!" thousands of people were chanting. Soldiers were aiming rifles at the crowd. I approached the soldiers, facing the rally. I was shaken; I was holding a picture of Ayatollah Khomeini under my right arm, the same one that some demonstrators held on placards above their heads. But I was standing on the wrong side; nobody around me had the Ayatollah's portrait. Back in Vietnam, I had been on the other side of those rifles. There, we were all young boys in student uniforms, but here I saw girls and women, some with hijabs or chadors, also standing at the front.

I followed some people on a detour around the rally. Eventually, I approached the Grand Bazaar from the north side through the main gate, Sabzeh Meydan.

A teahouse was near the entrance, with people inside drinking tea, smoking hookahs and making conversation. I'd been to many teahouses in Iran but had yet to acquire a taste for them. In Vietnam, people drank tea in a small cup, without sugar, preferably in a quiet and harmonious place. Drinking tea was for old people who sat and watched life pass by. Younger people like me preferred drinking coffee or beer, and smoking cigarettes. And the way the Iranians drank tea was different from the Vietnamese custom. Teahouses in Iran were meeting places, noisy and crowded, like the cafés in Vietnam. Iranians will tell you that they love to drink chai tea (but it's pronounced "cha-ee") and always drink it with sugar. One day I'd asked Abdi to teach me how to drink tea the Persian way.

"First, select a sugar cube," he said, "and place it between your front teeth. Like thizz—"

I picked a "quad"—a white sugar cube—from a cup placed on a silver tray in front of us and followed his instruction.

Abdi spat out the cube so he could talk. "Bite it down lightly," he said. "Now, bring the cup to your mouth and sip through the sugar cube."

The hot fluid sweetened as it passed through my lips.

Even though I was here last week, I entered at a different gate today and got lost. After struggling to find the way, I arrived at Mehdi's store. He liked the painting and asked me for two more for his neighbours. I agreed.

The Khomeini paintings sold like hotcakes. I thought every shop owner at the bazaar seemed to want an oil painting of Ayatollah Khomeini to hang in their store. With each delivery, I got more orders.

———

In mid-January 1979, the Shah fled Iran to Egypt, in exile. By February, Ayatollah Khomeini returned to the country from Paris.

Guests staying at the hostel—young backpackers, travelling students and out-of-job foreign workers—had increased each day, especially the latter. They came to Tehran from all over the country. My neighbours in the next room were two young men from Bangladesh and Sri Lanka. They had come to Iran looking for work, so they could send money home to feed their families. But for the last several months, they had been out of work. Foreigners were no longer welcomed after the revolution started. Before the political turmoil, jobs were everywhere for anyone who wanted work. Now, we sat around in the lobby with nothing to do and talked about politics. Some days they took me to the park to meet girls from the Philippines who worked as maids or babysitters. They had left their boyfriends or even their husbands and kids behind in the Philippines to work alone here. To reduce their isolation, they spent Fridays together in the park, talking with and supporting one another. But they, too, would be leaving soon because their employers—primarily doctors or university professors—were also in the process of going to America or Europe.

My roommate, Mohammed, spent more time at the hostel.

"Have you heard Khomeini returned to Iran after fourteen years in exile?" Mohammed asked me when he saw me cleaning my corner of the room, putting away all my painting stuff.

"Yes, I have. That is why I stopped painting," I answered while scrubbing some paint stains from the dirty tile floor.

"A good choice. It has become too dangerous for you to frequent the Grand Bazaar," Mohammed said.

"Not only the bazaar, but any public place."

The government troops and supporters of Shah Mohammad Reza Pahlavi faced angry crowds almost daily. The face-offs usually occurred outside public buildings, at the Shahyad Tower square, or in front of foreign embassies. Whenever a rally caught me off guard, I changed my route to avoid trouble.

"Why don't you apply for refugee status like me?" he asked.

"Do you really think I should?"

"I think you should. If you get the status, you don't need to work."

This is the same advice that the INS officer at the US consulate gave me the last time. Before leaving the office, he said I should go to the UNHCR to ask for help. The agency had resources and the legal obligation to help people in my situation.

"I'll think about what you said. Thanks, Mohammed," I said.

"But maybe not. If you do, do not cancel the application at the American embassy. That route is still the shortest, unlike mine. Years of waiting and waiting," he advised.

He stayed in the room all day long, but he knew many things happened in the world outside. One thing he did day in and day out was read—just endless reading. I wondered how and where he got all those English novels.

Before I decided what to do next, Ali, the hostel owner, convinced me to visit his friend Ahmad's studio, a block from the hostel. Ahmad needed an animation artist for his subcontract project to produce a children's animation film for a local television station. The shop was a small room on the ground level, furnished with only two tables and a couple of chairs. It was a start-up, and Ahmad had been the only employee until I joined him.

We worked on a four-minute animated short about a black chick among a half-dozen yellow chicks. The baby was bullied for being different; it was heartbreaking. I accepted the job because I could relate to the story: I was always the one who was different during the years here. No one looked like me. Everywhere I went, I stood out. I was tired of being different. I wished to be the same as everybody else around me—to belong to the group. The larger the group, the better. Like the black chick, my appearance always revealed me, even though I tried to blend in.

My job was to draw the frames of hatching eggs on a fixed background, which Ahmad had already prepared. Every second of animation for two characters required at least twenty-four frames. When a character was added to the scene, the number of frames doubled. It was a slow, tedious process. In the first week, I completed over a hundred frames, eight feet in length, or four seconds of the film. Ahmad drew faster, but we never passed the ten-second mark per week. Four minutes equalled two hundred and forty seconds. I didn't want to think how long it would take to finish all the frames. I wouldn't be here, anyway.

One morning, I arrived at the studio with a limp leg, a black eye, and an injured hand—my dominant right hand. The injury ended my two-month stint at the cartoon studio. Two young boys had struck me from behind as I walked home from the studio late the previous night, through a back alley. They beat me up badly. I wondered whether it was a predetermined act motivated by the anti-foreigner sentiments, or whether they had taken advantage of catching me in a dark and desolate place. Maybe they wanted to test my kung fu—to fight with Bruce Lee in real life.

Now unable to work, I finally filed an application for refugee status with the UNHCR office in Tehran. Because of the Islamic Revolution, the agency granted me refugee status within a week so that it could look for a third country that would accept me for relocation. The UN refugee agency gave me a monthly living allowance during the waiting period: I was no longer required to work for a living. I still went once a month to the US consulate office, too, hoping to get an answer from Washington.

## CHAPTER 37

# Hostage Crisis

A round noon on November 4, 1979, when I left my room and went down to the lobby, most of the hotel's guests were already there. I could see the worry on their faces. They were standing in groups, talking.

The hostel manager, Ali, informed me about the takeover.

"Have you heard the news?"

"News about what, Ali?"

"The US embassy has just been taken over by a group of students—your friends."

"What? What did you say?" I asked, surprised by the news.

"The militant students are holding all US embassy staff as hostages," he clarified. He was joking about them being my friends—I did not know these students.

"I'm planning to go to the INS office this afternoon," I said, devastated and disappointed.

"Lucky you. If you had been there this morning, you may already have become one of those hostages."

Mohammed, my roommate, was sitting in the corner by himself. I approached him.

"How are you, Mohammed?"

"Fuck those students!"

"I think they will release the hostages soon."

"Why do you think so?"

"Because they are diplomats, they should have diplomatic immunity by international law," I said.

"I don't think there are any laws with those guys."

"Let's wait and see," I told him.

"Even if they release the hostages, it doesn't help my case. All documents at the embassy have already been shredded or stolen. Almost three fucking years!" he said. "I have been locked up here for nothing."

"Don't worry. The Iranians cannot keep us here forever; the agency will move us somewhere," I said.

"I don't think so," Mohammed said, and looked at me. "How is your application status?"

"Haven't heard anything."

"So we're in the same boat: second-class refugees."

"I don't understand what you mean," I said.

"You will understand if you wait long enough, like me."

---

Those living at the hostel started to realize that the takeover of the US embassy wouldn't be over quickly. The number of foreign guests at the hostel dwindled each day. Some had left the country by air or bus, if they could afford the fare. Others, such as unemployed foreign workers or trapped visitors, were waiting for help from their embassies to get home. Like Mohammed and I, they just stayed and waited.

I spent most of my time at the hostel, too. My classmates had warned me to avoid deserted streets since, with my East Asian features, I stood out as a foreigner.

Mohammed became erratic. He kept talking late into the night about his dreams of the US, which I had heard a thousand times. I told Mohammed I would strangle him if he would not stop talking, but to no avail. Each morning, he sat by himself in a corner of our room, staring into space, and he would speak to the wall. I hoped I could get out of Iran soon.

As Mohammed had predicted, those students ignored all the protests from the American and diplomatic communities. It violated diplomatic immunity to arrest the diplomats and seize the diplomatic compounds. They kept holding the hostages and occupying compounds, since they had gotten a green light from Khomeini. According to news Mohammed heard on the radio, Khomeini had issued a statement supporting the takeover and said that the embassy had been an "American spy den in Tehran."

A rumour was going around at the hostel that the initial plan was to hold the embassy for only a short time. However, this changed after Khomeini had given his full support. The students were demanding the Americans return Shah Pahlavi to Iran for trial and execution.

By November 7, three days after the US embassy's takeover, the interim revolutionary government collapsed. Khomeini became the Supreme Leader and was officially known as the "Leader of the Revolution." Everyone at the hostel realized that the ordeal wouldn't be over soon, even though the militants had released thirteen hostages—mostly the women and the African Americans. Fifty-three American diplomats and citizens remained as hostages inside the compound.

In the first week of December 1979, the UNHCR informed me of a new interview, at the Canadian immigration office. This route—

Canada—would be my last hope. I desperately needed a visa to get to my new home, if there was to be one.

The Canadian embassy in the northern section of Tehran was about six kilometres from the hostel. To get there, I had to walk through parts of the city where protests were taking place daily. This area also housed two of Tehran's four universities: the University of Tehran and Tehran Polytechnic. Students from these universities formed the core of the Muslim Student Followers of the Imam's Line, the group that had sieged the US embassy a month earlier.

I left my room shortly after ten one morning. The weather was a little cold for mid-December, so I shoved my hands into my coat pockets. Amir Kabir Street was empty, without a single car on the road and no kids playing on the sidewalk. Just concrete and metal, leafless trees and a grey sky. I quickened my pace.

Ten minutes later, I ran into a big demonstration on Roosevelt Avenue. Raised fists. Angry faces. Black head scarves and chadors.

"*Marg bar Āmrikā, Allāhu 'Akbar, Khomeini Qa'ed!*" they shouted. It was the same slogans that I had heard night after night from my room. The chants of "Allāhu 'Akbar" pounded like drumsticks on my temple, and my heart thudded in time to the rhythm.

The crowd was impenetrable. I turned left on Shah Reza Street to bypass the rally and headed to Shahyad Tower square. But the route just led to another rally. With my coat collar pulled high and my head down, I kept making detours to avoid the crowds.

After two hours of walking, I made it to Darya-e-Noor Street, and the Canadian embassy. The narrow road was eerily empty of traffic and pedestrians. Feeling like a child walking alone through a graveyard, I approached the white building.

A sign on the wall outside the main gate directed me to the immigrant visa unit. I presented myself to the receptionist, saying I had an appointment with John Sheardown at one o'clock. It was a quarter to one. She told me to have a seat in the waiting room. To my surprise, it was empty. I'd expected a room full of people, as I'd experienced at the US immigration office a few months before. At least the wait would not be that long. I picked up a magazine on the coffee table but barely glanced at it. My mind was too busy anticipating the questions.

An hour passed. Nobody asked me to come in. I got up to remind the receptionist, but she was gone. The premises were so quiet that I could hear my breath. *Is something wrong?* I thought of the armed holdup of the American embassy last month. *Not again, please.*

Finally, the receptionist appeared and asked me to follow her. She directed me to an office. A tall man in his early fifties greeted me at the door with a friendly smile. He motioned for me to sit in one of the two chairs in front of his desk, on which lay a small red maple leaf flag and a gold nameplate—John V. Sheardown.

"So, you want to come to Canada," he said. "How did a young Vietnamese man like you get stuck here in the first place?"

Secretary Sheardown looked at his visitor with a distracted expression while I briefed him on my situation.

"Have you been to Canada?" he asked.

I shook my head. "No, sir."

"Do you have any relatives or know anyone living in Canada?"

"No. No one, sir."

Sheardown scanned my file. "In your application, you mentioned you want to live in Toronto. Why Toronto?"

"No special reason. It's the first city that comes to mind when I think of Canada."

The Secretary removed his reading glasses and leaned back in his chair. "The application says you have completed a BSc in petroleum engineering in Abadan."

"Yes, I did. Have you been there, sir?"

"No, I haven't," he said. "But I heard about the Rex Cinema fiasco."

Secretary Sheardown waited a few minutes and asked, "Do you know who the Canadian prime minister is?"

"A paper here showed a cartoon of a horse-riding cowboy, holding a gun in his hand," I remembered.

"Yes, that's him, Joe Clark," he said.

"Is he a real cowboy?"

"I don't think so," the Secretary said. "It's just that his hometown is outside of Calgary, where a large cowboy festival takes place every July. If you were to come, you might consider Calgary—it's the oil capital of Canada and a growing city." He looked at the file. "What are your current savings?"

"I have about six hundred US dollars."

"As a refugee," he said, "you may have trouble finding a job in your profession. If that is the case, what will you do?"

I hadn't anticipated that question.

"I'll work as a street portrait artist," I answered without thinking.

"Did you say portrait artist?" Sheardown was surprised.

"Yes, sir."

The Secretary gave me a paper pad and a pencil. "You can demonstrate your skills right now. Draw me."

"Now?"

"Yes, now."

I had made a big mistake. *Why didn't I say a job that couldn't be tested on the spot? I should have said "janitor" or "busboy."*

Secretary Sheardown sat patiently as I drew. After fifteen minutes, he said, "Show me what you have."

I handed him the drawing. It was the worst portrait I had ever sketched, and my chance of going to Canada depended on it.

"Not bad," he nodded, kindly. I thought he was being nice about it. He continued, saying, "The UNHCR will be in touch with you. Two things you should know if you're accepted: You will pay your airfare to Canada, and you must get a laissez-passer—a travel document—from the Islamic Republic of Iran."

## CHAPTER 38

# Canadian Caper

I was approaching the Islamic revolutionary guard in a green army jacket standing at the gate of the Interior Ministry of the Islamic Republic of Iran. The soldier carried an automatic rifle on his back. He looked at me as I showed him a note. After reading, the guard returned and then directed me to a booth on his right.

Inside, I faced another guard. I explained that the United Nations had sent me here to get my laissez-passer. He asked me to show an ID. I handed him my expired student card. After studying my face, the guard signalled me to follow him. We crossed the front yard, entered the main building and climbed two sets of stairs. On the third floor, we followed the hallway and passed several offices. At the last office, the guard knocked on the door. A man's voice beckoned us to come in. The guard introduced me to Farhad, a middle-aged man dressed in Western clothes with a pair of round eyeglasses perched on his nose. He looked like one of my college professors. Farhad invited me to sit in front of him, searched the files on the table and pulled out a paper.

"I have prepared a laissez-passer for you as the UNHCR requested. Please check it for any mistakes."

The document was written in three languages—French on the left, Farsi on the right and English on the fill-in. I could read neither of the first two. However, my picture was on it, and I could check my name, my dad's name and date of birth, and the handwritten notes in English recording my height, weight, hair colour, et cetera.

"I don't see any mistakes," I said, passing the document back to Farhad.

"Today is December 19. You must leave Iran by January 18. You have thirty days—that is all we can give."

"Thank you, sir."

"Good luck. Remember, you must leave within thirty days."

I nodded and said goodbye. I was still thinking about the deadline. *Thirty days is a lot of time, and I want to get out of here as soon as possible.* But I left the building happy and hopeful that I'd soon be in Canada to start a new phase of my life.

On my way back to the hostel, four teenage kids came out of nowhere and blocked my route. Before I could react, they all pounded me at once and then disappeared down a small alley. Unlike the previous incident, when I was alone in a back alley at night, this attack occurred in daylight on a busy street. Some pedestrians who witnessed the incident helped me stand up while two men ran after the boys.

"Are you okay?" a man asked.

"Do you need a ride?" another man asked.

"I'm okay." I pointed at a building about a hundred metres ahead. "My hostel is right there. I can walk."

The two men came huffing back. One of them said, "They were fast, and we couldn't get hold of any of them."

"Thanks for your help," I said.

"The propaganda against foreigners has influenced those kids. We're sorry for what's happened." The man sounded sincerely concerned.

"I understand, don't worry." I knew that I had once been just like those boys, capable of doing any crazy thing without a second thought. They were at the most dangerous age, especially if under some fanatical influences. Luckily, they didn't get a hold of any guns.

I limped back to the hostel.

---

On Christmas Eve, the manager of Amir Kabir Hotel, Ali, told me I had a letter as I passed the front desk. It was from the Canadian embassy. I opened it at Ali's desk.

Canadian Embassy

IMMIGRATION SERVICE

December 19, 1979

Mr. Anh N. Duong

C/O Amir Kabir Hotel

Amir Kabir Street, Tehran

Dear Mr. Duong, A.N.

I wish to inform that the Laissez-passer issued by the Iranian Government appears to meet Canadian Immigration requirements regarding travel documents.

Visa will be issued to you when you show us proof of transportation to Canada.

Yours truly,

J. V. Sheardown

First Secretary

"Did you get it?" Ali asked.

"Yes, I will go to Canada next month," I said proudly. I already felt that Canada was my new country, and thought about how sweet "Ca-na-da" sounded, and how beautiful the maple leaf flag was.

Ali approached me and put his hand on my left shoulder. "Congratulations. It's a nice country. What city will you live in?"

"Toronto."

"I was there several years ago," Ali said, "on my honeymoon in Niagara Falls."

"Niagara Falls?"

"Niagara Falls is one of the wonders of the world. It's just a ninety-minute drive from Toronto. You will love Toronto. It's a beautiful city, and its CN Tower is the tallest structure in the world."

After the Christmas holidays, I contacted the UNHCR to inform them that I was ready to leave Iran and needed my entry visa. My agent said she would notify me of the date and time. I also let Ali know I was waiting for an important phone call or mail from the UN.

The only thing I needed was proof of transportation to Canada. That wouldn't be a problem; I had saved the money, put it aside and never touched it—all thanks to Ayatollah Khomeini.

I waited for an appointment with the Canadian embassy. A few days, then a week. I called the UN, and the agent told me to wait some more. A week turned into two weeks. No phone calls. Three weeks, a month.

Thirty days passed, and my laissez-passer expired.

*What is going on? Has Canada closed its embassy?* I wondered. *If that were the case, the UNHCR would have let me know. Another embassy takeover?* I knew I would have heard about it on the news. I thought of other possibilities, but nothing made any sense whatsoever. I was in the dark—I could see nothing, and I heard nothing.

On January 29, 1980, news of the Canadian embassy's closure finally leaked out, and people at the hostel started talking. It had been a month and ten days since the embassy sent me the notice—forty days of uncertainty. Would this end my hopes of getting out of Iran?

"Will you still be able to go to Canada?" Ali asked.

"I don't know," I said. I couldn't think of anything else to say.

I felt I could touch it, my dream to go to Canada. The worst thing that could have happened to me had happened—again and again.

I was disappointed but not devastated. I had faced so many setbacks; this was just one more.

I was back to my daily routine, waiting for a phone call or a letter from the UNHCR telling me to go to the Australian, New Zealand or British embassy—whatever embassy would be fine. I preferred these options because English was my second language.

A week later, I did receive a letter from the UNHCR in Tehran. It was not going to be Britain's embassy, or Australia's, or New Zealand's, but the Embassy of Switzerland.

The letter directed me to the Swiss embassy to obtain a transit visa to Zürich. From Geneva, I would get my Canadian entry visa. The embassy hadn't forgotten me after all.

As I would find out later, John Sheardown and Ken Taylor, the Canadian ambassador, had devised a plan to smuggle six US diplomats out of Iran, known as the Canadian Caper. During my time associating with Secretary Sheardown, he had sheltered some of these very Americans at his residence. At the same time, the embassy had also started to close by shredding the classified documents, moving unclassified material to the New Zealand embassy, and sending the non-key staff members home at the time of my interview. The embassy of Switzerland sent me the letter three days after the smuggled Americans had safely arrived in the US.

Without further delay, I booked the first available Swissair flight
to Zürich. But many people wanted to get out of the country, and the
available airliners were limited. The earliest flight was two weeks later,
and that is when I finally said goodbye to Iran. Ali and Mohammed
were there to say farewell, and I took a taxi to the airport. Mohammed
told me he had heard nothing from the agency—he would have to wait
some more. But "See you in America soon" were Mohammed's last
words to me.

I haven't seen him since.

I arrived at the Mehrabad International Airport at 6:30 in the
morning for the 7:30 flight on Bahman 29, 1358, of the Persian calendar—
Monday, February 18, 1980. Even at that early hour, the waiting room
was full of people, but the air was heavy and silent. I could hear some
small whispers from an old lady standing at the end of the room. The
mood was quiet but tense. Several military guards wearing green army
jackets faced the passengers. As I entered the waiting room, a guard
clapped my left shoulder and said, "Passport."

I looked up at him. "I don't have any passport but an Iranian travel
document."

The guard looked at my document, then at my face, back at the
picture, and again at me. "Step aside, please," he said.

"Why?"

"You can't go."

Thoughts exploded in my head like crossfire in the night. *Have I
done something wrong? Are they going to arrest me? What if they don't let me out of
the country?*

The guard pressed his lips together and directed me to an empty
chair at a table facing an immigration officer. He gave the officer
my travel document, whispered something in his right ear, and then
walked away.

The officer looked at me. "What country are you from?"

"Vietnam."

A smile spread across his face. "I like Vietnam. Where are you going?"

"Zürich, Switzerland."

"Did you know your travel document expired a month ago?"

"Yes," I said. My voice was barely a whisper.

"Why did you let it expire?"

"I didn't let it expire. The UNHCR couldn't arrange for me to leave the country on time."

The officer raised his eyebrows. "Why didn't you ask for an extension?"

"An agent at the UNHCR told me it didn't have time for an extension and that I could get it at the airport." I lied. I was unable to get an answer from the agency at the time.

The immigration officer stamped and scribbled something on my Iranian travel document without further questions. He handed it over and let me go through. Once inside the boarding room, I felt like I was walking on clouds. I sat on a bench, thinking about this new journey. *Is this happening?* I looked around. The room was quiet, and everyone was looking out the window. A Swissair plane with "Aargau" written on its nose waited on the tarmac.

The same plane had smuggled six American diplomats out of Iran a few weeks earlier, and it would fly me out to Zürich.

I arrived at what is now Toronto Pearson International Airport in Ontario, Canada, on February 20, 1980, with eighty dollars in my pocket.

A new chapter of my life had begun. No more running. I was home.

# *Last Letter, Hope*

Calgary, Fall 2023
Dear Da-Lê,

At last, in February 1980, I had arrived at my destination—
Canada. This is also where you would be born, eight years later.

What John V. Sheardown, the First Secretary at the
Canadian Embassy in Tehran, told me during the interview was
half right. He was correct I should move west, but he was
wrong that I might not find a job in my profession. After
three months of working as a busboy in a Toronto bar, walking
several kilometres home in the early morning hours every
night in the frigid temperatures of the Canadian winter, I
moved to Calgary for an engineering job I found thanks to
Operation Lifeline and the placement office of the University
of Toronto. This job lasted thirty-five years until I retired
in 2015.

Da-Lê, you have asked me how I felt when I landed, at last, in
Canada after such arduous journeys. I was excited and looking

forward to my new chapter in life, but I still felt uneasy in my heart and was nervous about the past.

When I first came to Iran, it was a peaceful country, and it gradually turned into a troublesome place. After four years, over four hundred people were locked in and burned alive in a movie theatre in Abadan, where my college was. When I left the city in 1978, Abadan was under siege for a year, and a part of it was flattened out by bombing during the Iran-Iraq war (1980-1988). I felt I had brought the terror of Huế anywhere I went.

That recurring thought pattern has changed now. When I arrived in Canada, it was the most peaceful country in the world. And after forty years of living here, it's still more peaceful than ever. I have realized that I am not bringing the terror with me after all.

But terrible things are happening around the world. If you look around during these times of geopolitical crisis, conflicts are everywhere, from the Middle East to Eastern Europe. Most resemble the war I experienced. They range from suicide bombs to guerrilla tactics to human shields to urban warfare to continued bombardment. The biggest casualties are the civilians who get caught between the two. If I look at the live reports on television, it's like replaying my childhood. That is another reason I write this story: to serve as a reminder of how war can divide and damage people and communities, not only during wartime but also for generations after.

But we should not forget our hope for the future.

As I mentioned in one of the previous letters, most South Vietnamese ancestors had migrated from the North. First, the settlers of the Lord Nguyễn soldiers, then prisoners, and finally, the impoverished farmer families. We also remember the groups of settlers who had been exiled from China after each change in dynasty over the years. These settlers helped Lord Nguyễn open and develop the South.

You will notice differences in how North and South Vietnamese people live and think. The South is known to be more easygoing or liberal, while the North tends to be more rigid or conservative. While all across Vietnam we share some of the same ideals—such as a love for independence and equality—the ways in which we want to achieve these ideals are different. Whereas Northerners might put more value into leadership and power, Southerners would respect enterprise and a capitalist economy. Therefore, we must not only reconcile the North-South division but also acknowledge our differences in lifestyles and attitudes; otherwise, the conflicts will remain in each of us.

You said you had talked to people of different generations in Hanoi and Saigon, older and younger. The elders, who have been remarkably traumatized by the war on both sides but still think positively, have forgotten all the past. Some younger ones said they couldn't change what happened yesterday, so they look forward to the future, when Vietnam has more freedom and development. These are the people who give us hope.

Da-Lê, you're correct about the people giving us hope. That is why the people of Vietnam just received some encouraging news that most of us, including me, have been waiting for for almost fifty years: Vietnam will recognize the US as its dear friends, no longer its traditional foe. That reflects the people's hope; they welcomed the US president each time he visited the country. Thousands and thousands of Vietnamese filled the streets in Hanoi, and especially Saigon, to cheer on when all four previous US presidents, Clinton and Bush, Obama and Trump, passed through. It was friendly enough in 2016, when President Obama visited, that he ventured out to public places to try some Vietnamese street foods. A few decades ago, that would have been unthinkable.

It was a very different scene compared to what happened when the leaders of China and Russia visited, when the streets of the capital were mostly empty, with some unwilling schoolchildren made to stand there and wave red flags. The warm welcome for the American presidents in the 1990s and 2000s is how Vietnamese people show their sincerity now, and their hopes for the future, after having lived under the strong influences of China and Russia for so long, ever since the fall of Saigon.

If you ask Vietnamese people to choose a friend among the superpowers, I do not doubt that they would prefer to make friends with America over China or Russia. They see what South Korea has become, compared to its northern sibling. Vietnamese people have recognized that most countries, including China, want to make America a friend rather than an enemy.

On September 11, 2023, Vietnam hosted President Biden with the highest honour any foreign guest could get in Hanoi, with all four senior government leaders. The visit has transformed two countries from wartime foes into respected partners. The Vietnam War is officially closed, and hope is renewed. With this reconciliation, I hope the segregation and division among the Vietnamese, both inside Vietnam and throughout our diasporas worldwide, will be resolved soon. It comes a half-century late, but it's still better than never. We have only one way to go: the future, not the past.

I wish to say the same for the US and Iran relations, but they worsen with time. I still see rally after rally on TV, which resembles what I faced over four decades ago on Tehran's streets. I wonder if these young protesters are the daughters or granddaughters of those who helped bring down the Shah.

Da-Lê, the journey by boat to Hong Kong, or any country in Southeast Asia, was not easy, but this was the journey that brought many of us here. You told me you recently dropped by Uncle Dzu's house while on a business trip in San Jose. Now you know his backstory. He was the student that the new authorities kicked out of medical school after the fall of Saigon in 1975. A few months after meeting me in 1978—when he whispered to me, "See you in America soon"—he did indeed leave Dạ Lê for Hong Kong by boat. After a year in a refugee camp, he came to the US and got married there in 1981. I went to his wedding in California and brought O Trang—or Bà Trang to you—who owned the bakery where I had stayed before leaving for Iran in 1975. It was our first reunion since parting ways when I was last back to visit my family. Shortly after I left the country, she had gone by boat to Malaysia with her three children and resettled near Los Angeles, in Little Saigon. Uncle Dzu worked in tech and became a successful Silicon Valley businessman. Bà Trang spent over twenty years in North America, but when she was getting old, she returned to Vietnam like your grandparents did.

And my generation is getting old, too. Your mom and I keep going to the family doctor regularly. My physician asked me about smoking. I was proud to tell him I quit almost twenty years ago because of you. I still remember when you, as a teenager, asked me to go to your room for a talk. Once I was in, you closed your door and then made an earnest request that I must quit smoking—a habit I had for over thirty years at the time. I made the promise and am glad I did get rid of one of the past sediments deposited in me.

Finally, Da-Lê, I am happy to learn you have also tried to find your roots and to understand the historical conflicts for yourself. You did what you had wished to do: visit Vietnam and our ancestral homes, to connect with our culture. After each trip, when you return to Canada, you seem much happier. You have started using "Da-Lê" more and "Ashley" less when introducing yourself. You even call your film production company Da-Lê Films. I am glad you have found something you were looking for: the true you.

Love, Ba

# Vietnamese Glossary

## VIETNAMESE TERMS

**áo dài**: a long white traditional dress worn by Vietnamese women

**đi tập kết**: any person who left the South for the North in 1954

**đích tôn**: a first son of the family, where his father and grandfather are also the first sons

**đồng**: Vietnamese currency

**gia đình ngụy**: puppet family

**học tập cải tạo**: re-education

**kẻ thù nhân dân**: an enemy of the people

**lá vằng**: healing herbs of the forest

**nhà ái quốc**: a patriot

**ngụy quân**: puppet army, the South Vietnam Army (SVA)

**nội chiến**: a civil war

**thằng giả chết**: a death cheater or death pretender; someone who fakes their death to avoid capture

**Việt Cộng** or vc: Vietnamese Communists

**vùng xôi đậu**: sticky rice and beans, a nickname for a war zone

## A PRIMER FOR HOW TO ADDRESS PEOPLE

**Con**: son, daughter

**Ba, Má**: father, mother (Mạ is a local Huế dialect word for "mother")

**O**: a local Huế dialect term for Cô, an aunt or any young female of a typical aunt's age

**Cụ**: a local Huế dialect term for Cậu, a maternal uncle (or any young male at typical uncle age)

**Chú, Bác**: a paternal uncle (Chú for younger than your father, Bác for older than your father)

**Chị**: an older sister (or female the age of an older sister)

**Anh**: an older brother (or male the age of an older brother)

**Em**: a younger sibling (or person the age of a younger sibling)

# A Chronology of Events

**1953** I was born in the village of Dạ Lê in central Vietnam, under French Indochina.

**1954** Vietnam becomes two: North (communist) and South (non-communist).

**1963** The strategic hamlet fence around the village is constructed; Buddhist religious incident in Huế; Diệm regime collapses.

**1965** US Marines land in South Vietnam; Việt Cộng (VC) appear in our village; and after the first major battle, Dạ Lê becomes a village at war.

**1967** The US builds Camp Eagle in Dạ Lê.

**1968** Tết Offensive; Dạ Lê under VC control; I work as a VC labourer; I become a target of an armed ambush; escape to Huế.

**1972** Easter Offensive; the US closes Camp Eagle.

**1973** I arrive in Saigon for college; Paris Peace Accords signed for ending the Vietnam War; prisoner exchange; Iran replaces Canada as the fourth member of the International Commission of Control and Supervision.

**1974** I receive the Shah's scholarship to study in Abadan, Iran.

**1975** I arrive in Iran in January; Vietnam's South falls on April 30.

**1976** Vietnam reunification; I reconnect with my family through the mail.

**1978** Islamic Revolution starts; I return to Vietnam while millions of its people escape; I go back to Iran; the Rex Cinema fire kills hundreds in Abadan.

**1979** I apply in Tehran to migrate to the US; witness the Iranian Hostage Crisis at the American embassy in Tehran; interview for a refugee visa to Canada. The Canadian diplomat who interviewed me, John Sheardown, was at the same time organizing the "Canadian Caper," a covert operation to smuggle six US diplomats out of Iran.

**1980** I land in Canada at Toronto Pearson International Airport.

**1985** I marry my wife, Kim Anh, after meeting in Calgary, Alberta.

**1986** Our son, David Quoc Nguyen, is born, also in Calgary.

**1988** Ashley Da-Lê is born in Calgary.

# Acknowledgements

Writing this book has taken over seven years. The earliest versions of our family story grew bit by bit, from many short emails to my daughter, Da-Lê, into the current version: a full-length manuscript. I'm very grateful to the Banff Centre for Arts and Creativity for a ten-day Emerging Writers Intensive in 2017, where the seeds of this project were planted. Banff also welcomed Da-Lê for a two-week writing residency in 2022 focused on father–daughter collaborations. Thanks also to the Canada Council for the Arts for a 2021 writing grant to support our work.

I also thank Ellie Barton, Steve Sych and C. Pham for editing earlier drafts; Barbara Pulling for her manuscript evaluation and connecting me to Anna Comfort O'Keeffe, the publisher of Douglas and McIntyre; Ariel Brewster for editing the book; Diana Nguyen for cover illustration; Stephanie Fysh for proofreading and the rest of Anna's team at D&M.

This memoir wouldn't be possible without the following people: Diana Duong for double-checking my Vietnamese and Nilofar Shidmehr for her Iranian cultural consultancy; and Deb Rhodes, Sheila Reader, Vince Duong, Hung Phan, Kader Houssaine, Hai Nguyen,

T. Hoang and the late poet Nguyen Duc Batngan for their feedback. Thank you for giving me many valuable suggestions to make this story what it is today.

Besides thanking Ashley Da-Lê Duong, who was with me from the beginning to the end, I want to thank my mother, Nguyễn thị Bảy, who is in her nineties now but still recalls many stories from my childhood in Vietnam, and my father, Dương Văn Mừng, who passed away two years ago when my writing was just beginning to take the shape of a book.

The last words of this memoir are reserved for my wife, Kim Anh Dao, for putting up with me while I was writing this and for my son, David Quoc Nguyen Duong, for his encouragement.

# About the Author

**Anh Duong** was born in Thừa Thiên Huế, Vietnam, and lived there and in Saigon until the mid-1970s, when he moved to Iran. He arrived in Canada in 1980, and worked for decades as an engineer in the petroleum industry in Calgary and Houston, Texas. Embarking on a writing career, Duong participated in the Banff Centre for Arts and Creativity's Emerging Writers Intensive in 2017. He lives in Calgary.